Bears & Balls:
The Colbert Report A-Z
(An Unofficial Fan Guide)
Revised Edition

SHARILYN JOHNSON

REMY MAISEL

Third Beat Productions

Copyright © 2015 Sharilyn Johnson and Remy Maisel
Published by Third Beat Productions
All rights reserved.
No part of this book may be reproduced in whole or in part, or stored in a retrieval system, or transmitted in any form or by any means, electronic, mechanical, photocopying, recording, or otherwise, without written permission of the copyright holders and publisher.

ISBN: 978-0-9939422-2-8

Edited by Karen Backstein
Cover illustration and design by Kurt Firla

Photo credits:
Preface – © 2007 Sharilyn Johnson
Allison Silverman – The White House (Public Domain)
Operation Iraqi Stephen – US Army
Tapings – Official White House Photo by Lawrence Jackson (Public Domain)

Bears & Balls: The Colbert Report A-Z (An Unofficial Fan Guide) is not affiliated with, licensed by, or endorsed by Viacom Media Networks, Comedy Partners LLC, Comedy Central, Spartina Productions, Busboy Productions, or any parties associated with the creation or production of *The Colbert Report*.

Contents

Preface 1

In the Beginning… 4

Authors' Note 5

A 7
A Colbert Christmas: The Greatest Gift of All (2008) 7
Agaporomorphus Colberti (2009) 8
Air Colbert (2007) 8
All You Need To Know (2005-2006) 8
Allison Silverman (2005-2009) 9
Alpha Dog of the Week (2006-2014) 10
America Again: Re-becoming the Greatness We Never Weren't (2012) 11
AmeriCone Dream (2007-) 11
Andrew Young (2008) 12
Aptostichus Stephencolberti (2007) 13
Art Stephen Up Challenge (2010-2011) 13
Atone Phone (2006-2014) 14
Audience Guy Carl (2006) 14

B 15
Balls for Kidz (2006-2009) 15
Basketcase: Stephie's Knicks Hoop-de-Doo (2010) 15
Bats**t Serious (2013-2014) 16
Bears & Balls (2007-2014) 16
Better Know A District (2005-2014) 17
Big Gay Roundup (2011-2013) 20
Big White Chocolate (2007) 21
Bill O'Reilly (2005-2014) 21
Black Friend Alan (2005-2006) 22
Bleep Blorp the Robot (2010, 2014) 22
Blitzkrieg on Grinchitude (2006; 2010-2014) 23
Bobby the Stage Manager (2005-2009) 23
Bring 'em Back or Leave 'em Dead (2005-2006) 24
Brooks Brothers (2005-2014) 24
Buckley T. Ratchford (2010) 24
Bud Light Lime (2008-2014) 25

C 26
California (2014) 26
Called Out Board (2006) 26

Cameos (2005-2014) 27
Captain America (2007-2014) 27
Carell Corral (2010) 28
Catholicism (2005-2014).. 29
Character Breaks (2005-2014) 30
Charlene (2005-2014).. 31
Cheating Death (2007-2014) 32
Ching-Chong Ding-Dong / #CancelColbert (2005, 2014) 32
C.O.L.B.E.R.T. Treadmill (2009) 35
cOlbert's Book Club (2013-2014) 36
Colbert Bump (2006-2014) 37
Colbert Cruise (2006, 2014) 38
Colbert Galactic Initiative (2013)... 38
Colbert Info News Veranda (2013) 39
Colbert on the Ert (2007, 2010) 40
Colbert Platinum (& Colbert Aluminum) (2007-2014) 40
Colbert Report Special ReporT (2005-2014)... 41
Colbertnation.com (2005-) 42
Colboard.com (2006-2009) 42
Col-Bunker (2005)... 43
Cold War Update (2008-2014) 43
Cooking with Feminists (2006) 43
Craziest F#?king Thing I've Ever Heard (2006-2014)............................... 44
Credits (2005-2014)... 44

D.. 46

DaColbert Code (2005-2009) 46
Daft Punk (2013).. 46
Dartmouth (2005-2014)... 50
Das Booty (2008) 50
Dead to Me (2005-2007) 51
Delawert Report (2010) 51
Democralypse Now: The Delightful Dismemberment of the Democratic Hopescape (2008) 52
Difference Makers (2006-2014)... 52
DonorsChoose.org (2007-) 53
Doom Bunker (2009)... 53
Doris Kearns Goodwin (2006-2014) 54
Doritos (2007-2014) 54
Dressage (2012) 55
Duets (2006-2014) 56
Dungeons and Dragons (2006-2011) 58

E 59

Eagle's Nest (2005-2006) 59
Ear (2005-2014) 59

Edit Challenge (2007) 59
Eleanor Holmes Norton (2006, 2008-09, 2014) 60
Emmys (2006-2015) 61
Enemy Within (2008-2014) 61
Esteban Colbert (2009) 62
Esteban Colberto (2006-2014) 62

F 64
Fallback Position (2008-2014) 64
Fantasies Board (2007) 64
Filliam H. Muffman (2006-2014) 65
Finale (2014) 65
Flameside (2005-2013) 69
Formidable Opponent (2005-2014) 69
Formula 401 (2006-2014) 70
Four Horsemen of the A-Pop-Calypse (2006-2014) 71
Fract (2005-2006) 71
Frank the Roommate (2009) 71
Franklin F. Flagworth (2006-2014) 72
Future Stephen (2007, 2009, 2014) 72

G 74
Gipper (2005-2014) 74
Glenn (2011) 74
Global Edition (2008-2014) 74
God Machine (2007) 75
Gorlock (2008-2014) 75
Government Shutdown Wedding of the Century (2013) 75
Grammys (2009-2013) 76
Green Screen Challenge (2006) 76
Guests (2005-2014) 78

H 80
Ham Rove (2011-2012) 80
Hans Beinholtz (2010-2014) 80
HD (2010-2014) 81
High-Five (2013-2014) 81
HipHopKetball: A Jazzebration (2006) 81
Hobby Hovel (2010) 82
Hoo-Ha Lady Zone 5000 (2012) 82
House (2005-2011) 83
Hungarian Bridge (2006) 83
"I Called It!" (2005-2014) 85

I 84
I Am A Pole (And So Can You!) (2012) 84
I Am America (And So Can You!) (2007) 84

The In-Box (2005-07, 2013-14) 85
Indecision 2008 (2008) 86

J 88
Jay the Intern (2009-2014) 88
Jimmy (2005-2014) 89
Jimmy Fallon (2007-2014) 89
Jon Stewart (2005-2014) 90
Joy Machine 92
Judge, Jury & Executioner (2007-2012) 92

K 93
Ken Burns (2005, 2009-2012, 2014) 93
Killer (2005-2010) 93
Knut the Polar Bear (2007) 94

L 95
Lady Heroes (2012) 95
Laser Klan (2013-2014) 95
Le Colbert Report with Stephane Colbert (2010) 96
Leg wrestling (2009) 96
Lord of the Rings (2005-2014) 96
Lorna Colbert (1920-2013) 98
Lorraine (2005-2014) 98

M 99
March on Washington (2006-2013) 99
Maurice Sendak (2012) 99
Meg the Intern (2006-2008) 100
Meta-Free-Phor-All: Shall I Nail Thee to a Summer's Day? (2007) 100
meTunes (2008-2012) 101
Michael Stipe (2011-2012, 2014) 101
Microwave (2007-2014) 101
Monkey on the Lam (2007-2013) 102
Movies That Are Destroying America (2006-2013) 102
My Fair Colbert: Stephen Colbert's Crown Jewels (2011) 102
Mysteries of the Ancient Unknown (2010-2012) 103

N 104
Nailed 'Em (2008-2013) 104
NASA (2006-2014) 104
Neil deGrasse Tyson (2005-2014) 105
Nutz (2006) 106

O 107
On Notice Board (2005-2013) 107
Oopsie-Daisy Homophobe (2013) 107
Opening sequence (2005-2014) 107

Operation Iraqi Stephen (2009) 108

P 112
P.K. Winsome (2006-2014) 112
Patterson Springs, NC (2005-2010) 112
Peabody Awards (2008, 2014) 112
People Who Are Destroying America (2008-2013) 113
Pistachios (2014) 113
Portrait (2005-2014) 114
Presidential Run (2007) 114
Presidential Run (2012) 115
Prince Hawkcat (2014) 116
Pumpkin Patch (2010-2014) 116

R 117
@RealHumanPraise (2013) 117
Rain (2007) 117
Rally to Restore Sanity and/or Fear (2010) 118
Reddit (2009-2014) 119
Remix Challenge (2009) 121
Richard Branson (2007, 2011) 121
Rock & Awe: Countdown To Guitarmageddon (2006) 122
Russ Lieber (2005-2007) 124

S 125
Saginaw Spirit (2006-2007) 125
Shofar (2006-2014) 126
Shout Out (2006-2011, 2014) 126
Smile File (2013-2014) 127
South Pole Minute (2006) 127
Speedskating (2009-2010, 2014) 127
Spiderman (2008) 129
Sport Report (2005-2014) 129
Starbucks (2006-2014) 130
Stelephant Colbert (2009) 131
Stephanie Colburtle (2007) 131
Stephen & Melinda Gates Foundation (2006-2011) 132
Stephen Jr. (2006-2009) 132
Stephen Settles the Debate (2005-2008) 134
Stephen's Sound Advice (2006-2010) 134
StePhest Colbchella (2011-2013) 134
Steve Colbert (2010) 135
Studio 136
Super PAC (2011-2012) 137
Sweetness (2008-2014) 146

T 147
Table of Contents (2005-2014) 147
Tad the Building Manager (2005-2014) 147
Tall Women Lifting/Carrying Heavy Things 148
Tapings (2005-2014) 148
Tek Jansen (2006-2013) 150
Thought for Food (2010-2014) 150
ThreatDown (2005-2014) 150
Time-Traveling Brandy Thief (2010, 2014) 151
Tip of the Hat/Wag of the Finger (2005-2014) 152
Toss (2005-2014) 152
Truthiness (2005) 154
Tube Socks (2005-2012) 154
Twitter (2008-2014) 155
2011: A Rock Odyssey (2011) 156

U 157
Un-American News (2005-2012) 157
United Farm Workers of America (2010) 157

V 160
Vancouver Olympics (2010) 160
Vilsack Attack (2006-2010) 161

W 163
Was It Really That Bad? (2005-2008) 163
Watership Down (2005-2014) 163
Wax On & Wax Off at Madame Tussauds (2012) 163
What Number Is Stephen Thinking Of? (2005-2007) 164
Wheat Thins (2012) 165
White House Correspondents' Dinner (2006) 166
Who's Attacking Me Now? (2006-2014) 166
Who's Honoring Me Now? (2006-2013) 167
Who's Not Honoring Me Now? (2006-2013) 167
Who's Riding My Coattails Now? (2006-2011) 168
Wikipedia (2006, 2008, 2011-12) 168
Wilford Brimley Calls (2005-2006, 2009, 2012) 169
The Wørd (2005-2014) 169
WristStrong (2007-2014) 171
Writers Guild of America Strike (2007-2008) 172

Y 175
Yacht race (2011) 175
Yahweh or No Way (2009-2012) 175
Yellow Ribbon Fund (2008-2014) 175
Yet Another Day (2005) 176

Z	177
Z96 Morning Asylum with Stevie C and Dr. Dave (2009)	177
In the End…	179
Works Cited	181
Works Cited – The Colbert Report & The Daily Show with Jon Stewart	197
ACKNOWLEDGEMENTS	227
About the Authors	228

Preface

Bears & Balls was written with one goal: to heighten your enjoyment of *The Colbert Report*.

We combined the show's best moments and behind-the-scenes insights into more than 200 encyclopedic entries. On every page, we want you to say, "whoa, I totally forgot about that!" or, "whoa, I didn't know that!" (Though if you're reading this on public transit, we prefer you just *think* those things.)

This is a book for anyone who's been impressed by Stephen Colbert's skilled rhetoric, appreciative of how he fully embraced his character's idiocy, or awestruck by his staff's ability to make anything happen. But deciding what this book would be also meant deciding what it wouldn't be. Namely, a celebrity biography.

Therein lies the Catch-22: because knowing the difference between Stephen Colbert the comedian and Stephen Colbert the character made *The Colbert Report* so much more enjoyable to watch. (You do know it was a character, right? Good.)

So, who is Stephen Colbert? The most basic explanation is that Stephen Colbert is not "Stephen Colbert." They're different people, with different goals, and—arguably—only one of them is real. It's an important enough distinction that throughout this book, we use the shorthand of referring to the right-wing pundit character as "Stephen" and the mild-mannered man who created him as "Colbert."

That isn't to say that the two can be easily separated. Their personal histories differ, but only about half the time. Their politics are contrasting, but the real Colbert has wisely protected his audience from learning too much about his personal ideologies. Their mannerisms and tones of voice often signaled to us who we were watching outside the context of the *Report*, yet even then, he'd allow his two personas to overlap whenever it made sense.

But parsing this out any further is a futile exercise, and an unnecessary one. There's only one aspect of the real Colbert that adds value to the viewing experience: his decency.

Beneath what he characterized as a "well-intentioned, poorly-informed, high-status idiot" is a comedian whose love for his job, and his love of connecting with an audience, always shone through. And this isn't just starry-eyed fanspeak. Even the *Report*'s showrunners acknowledge the value of his true personality rising to the surface.

Stephen Colbert at the New Yorker Festival, 2008.

As former executive producer Allison Silverman explained, "the real Stephen is a genuinely kind person. Even when he plays this character, the audience still detects that Stephen's a good-hearted guy."

Executive producer and *Daily Show* host Jon Stewart concurs: "he's a good person, and that allows his character to be criminally, negligently ignorant," he said.

Colbert, in contrast to "Stephen," is modest. As he told Charlie Rose in 2006, "I don't know if I'm a decent person. But my intention is comedy. And I'm having a really good time when I do it. And I think the audience can see that."

We'll take it.

Indeed, fun was the key ingredient here. Colbert often refers to his show's production as the "joy machine," a process that would purely be a machine - a burden - if it wasn't approached with joy. He said his joy was the process of creating the show with his team, and his job as a performer was to show his audience what that joy looked like.

Likewise, it was our joy to watch the show for nine years. Now we get to share that joy with you, and we're happy to report that our process was joyful. It wasn't uncommon for us to spend hours combing through old episodes to find that one mention of that one thing that references that one *other* thing, and at the end of it wonder, "why does my jaw hurt? Oh, right…."

We expect this book to trigger your desire to similarly relive these moments in video form. At the end, you'll find an extensive listing of referenced clips from *The Colbert Report* and *The Daily Show with Jon Stewart*. We recommend viewing these through the official Comedy Central websites, and we've included active urls on the book's website (www.colbertfanguide.com/citations) so you can do so without the hours of searching. Of course, we can't stop you from voluntarily jumping down the rabbit hole once you're there.

And speaking of rabbit holes, one other thing we won't get into: heavy analysis. Much can be (and has been) written about the show's impact on culture and politics, but rest assured this is a book without a thesis statement. Ultimately, we're chronicling *The Colbert Report* because of the impact it had on us personally: it made us laugh really, *really* hard.

Sharilyn Johnson & Remy Maisel

In the Beginning...

As Stephen Colbert likes to point out, *The Colbert Report* is the only show that started as a promo for itself.

By 2003, Colbert was a veteran correspondent on *The Daily Show with Jon Stewart*. The show had successfully evolved from a parody of a local newscast into a sharp satire, and Colbert's confident, dense reporter persona was a favorite among viewers.

That's when *Daily Show* writers Chris Regan and Steve Bodow created the first of several fake promos for a non-existent show called *The Colbert Réport*. These bumpers (short segments that would air going into commercial breaks) were loud, splashy montages of Colbert as a bombastic, egotistical pundit shouting down his "guests" and stating his uninformed opinions as fact.

In September of 2004, Colbert, Stewart, and *Daily Show* executive producer Ben Karlin pitched that idea as a full series to Comedy Central. The following spring, it was made public: *The Colbert Report* (sans accent) would follow *The Daily Show* four nights a week. It premiered October 17, 2005.

Authors' Note

Throughout this book, the character of Stephen Colbert is always referred to as "Stephen," and "Colbert" refers to the real-life Stephen Colbert.

A

A Colbert Christmas: The Greatest Gift of All (2008)

Singing! Dancing! Celebrity cameos! They're all part of 2008's *A Colbert Christmas: The Greatest Gift of All*, inspired by the Andy Williams specials of yesteryear.

A ferocious bear is on the loose outside of Stephen's mountain cabin. Since Stephen is trapped inside, he can't get back to New York to tape his Christmas special. But one by one, big-name musical guests materialize: Toby Keith, Feist, John Legend, Willie Nelson, and even Jon Stewart perform holiday songs written by lyricist (and former *Daily Show* executive producer) David Javerbaum and composer Adam Schlesinger. Elvis Costello, Stephen's headliner for his big-budget Christmas special back in New York, checks in with Stephen by phone to let him know how rehearsals are going. (He reports that the Jonas Brothers perished after falling through the ice while rehearsing the skating number.) The bear ultimately gains access to Stephen's cabin, but Santa Claus (played by George Wendt) saves Stephen from the pending attack by slaying the bear and cutting him open, revealing a recently eaten Costello.

A Colbert Christmas was shot on the *Colbert Report* set during the fall of 2008, on a schedule that at times overlapped with the show's. Viewers noted that in the September 15, 2008 episode, Stephen interviewed his guest at his C-shaped desk instead of in his normal interview area. A giant American flag concealed that part of the studio, presumably hiding part of the elaborate Christmas special set.

Since the DVD release features two versions of the special—one with audience reaction and one without—many people assume the laughs came from a traditional laugh track. But live audiences screened the fully edited special at the *Colbert Report* studio, and their authentic reactions were recorded and used as a separate audio track.

The DVD release also includes an 18-minute Book Burning Yule Log, which incinerates copies of *Our Body, Our Selves*.

Agaporomorphus Colberti (2009)

What has six legs and is way cooler than a spider? That was the question on the front of a birthday card sent by scientists from Arizona State University and the University of New Mexico to Stephen, along with a framed print of a beetle. The researchers were responding to Stephen's call for "something cooler than a spider to be named after him," and although they couldn't get him the giant ant or laser lion he asked for, they were able to christen the Venezuelan diving beetle *Agaporomorphus colberti* in his honor.

Air Colbert (2007)

(See also: Richard Branson)

It's a bird! It's a plane! It's . . . a plane named Air Colbert! Flying high atop the list of things named after Stephen is the first plane in Virgin America's fleet. The plane is Virgin America Airbus A320 N621VA, with its name decaled on its nose. Virgin America is owned by British billionaire and business tycoon Sir Richard Branson. Branson told Stephen that he named the San Francisco area-based plane after Stephen in an attempt to win over conservatives. Stephen was offended to learn that the plane's name did not entitle him to pilot it. Air Colbert flew Virgin America's inaugural flight on August 8, 2007.

All You Need To Know (2005-2006)

Wish you could get the day's news, without it always being so darn detailed? Then Stephen's knack for "condensing large issues into small statements" gave you exactly what you needed. All You Need to Know was a short series of setups explaining a news story, with punchlines in the form of Stephen's summary of the story (directed either to viewers or at an individual). Samuel Alito appointed to the Supreme Court? All you needed to know: stock up on Trojans. Oil executives accused of price gouging? All you needed to know: how to siphon gas, as demonstrated by Stephen. Rumors of secret CIA prisons in

Europe? All you needed to know: nothing (it's classified). And that's all you need to know about All You Need to Know.

Allison Silverman (2005-2009)

One of the show's original head writers and later a co-executive producer, Allison Silverman is widely considered to be the second most-influential member of the *Report's* early creative team (after the man himself, naturally). She worked with Colbert previously as a writer at *The Daily Show*, and left a staff writing job at *Late Night with Conan O'Brien* to work for the *Report*, which at the time had only an eight-week commitment from Comedy Central. Colbert once said that Silverman is one of the only people who can identify when he secretly agrees with his character. (Silverman said that the two Stephens disagree "well into 80 percent of the time.")

Allison Silverman and Colbert tape a segment at the White House in 2009.

Silverman is the only staff member to be a subject of The Wørd, which closed out her final episode of the show on September 17, 2009. Stephen couldn't bear the thought of losing her, so to prevent an on-camera meltdown, he cited "false memories that will make me glad she's leaving." But one of his outlandish memories was actually true: he did lose a bet to her over whether the word "lutefisk" was funny. (During the 2007 segment in question, Colbert couldn't resist breaking character in the wake of the bombed joke to tell the audience he'd just lost $50.)

In addition to The Wørd, the closing credits for her final episode were altered to replace every name with "Allison Silverman."

After leaving the *Report*, Silverman went on to write and produce *The Office* and *Portlandia*.

Alpha Dog of the Week (2006-2014)

This biting segment honored the ballsiest people in the news cycle. Stephen singled out public figures who "swung their sacks" by publicly and unabashedly contradicting themselves, lying, or disregarding others, and showed the audience why they should be admired for their behavior, not humiliated the way the lamestream media would like them to be.

Stephen paid tribute to proud hypocrites like anti-gay crusader George Rekers, who was caught with a male prostitute; the pro-life Tennessee Representative Scott DesJarlais, who encouraged a patient he had an affair with to get an abortion; and the Virginia State Senate, who adjourned after holding a redistricting vote on Martin Luther King Day in memory of Confederate General Stonewall Jackson. A fan favorite Alpha Dog of the Week segment featured Cecilia Gimenez, the elderly parishioner of the Sanctuary of Mercy Church in Spain, who took it upon herself to restore a 19th-century fresco of Jesus with unfortunate results. Stephen praised her "can-do attitude about something she clearly cannot do." Even ballsier: Gimenez then sued the church for royalties from the visitors.

The snarling Rottweiler in the segment's opening graphic was named Growlie.

America Again: Re-becoming the Greatness We Never Weren't (2012)

As the follow-up to the bestselling *I Am America (And So Can You!)*, *America Again* is another manifesto written in the style of the pundits "Stephen" is modeled after. As the tongue-twisting subtitle (conceived by head writer Barry Julien) suggests, the book responds to the hypocrisy among many news pundits who claim that America is the greatest country on Earth, but at the same time say the country is broken and must be fixed. But America is exceptional, Stephen argues, "because of our Greatness, and the source of that Greatness is how Exceptional we are."

He supports his thesis with chapters dedicated to specific aspects of that exceptionalism, including Wall Street, Food, and Justice. Each chapter begins with a full-page 3-D photo of Stephen embodying its theme, such as him sitting in a mid-century doctor's office and cutting off his own leg with a saw ("Healthcare") or working on the assembly line to produce his own book ("Jobs"). According to Stephen, 3-D movies had been raking in big bucks at the box office, and he wanted a piece of the action.

Colbert and his show's writing staff wrote the book in the first half of 2012, and he compared the workload to the equivalent of producing 25 additional *Report* episodes. *America Again* spent 17 consecutive weeks on *The New York Times* Best Sellers List, and the audiobook version won a Grammy in 2014 for Best Spoken Word Album.

AmeriCone Dream (2007-)
(See also: Jimmy Fallon)

In 2007, Ben and Jerry of the eponymous ice cream company dropped by the *Report* to honor Stephen with an ice-cream flavor of his own, called Stephen Colbert's AmeriCone Dream. It's made of vanilla ice cream with chunks of fudge-covered waffle cone—"the only time I waffle"—and caramel swirl. The proceeds from the sale of AmeriCone Dream are donated to charity through The Stephen Colbert AmeriCone Dream Fund, which supports causes that the real Colbert cares about such as providing food and medical assistance to disadvantaged children, supporting veterans and their families, and protecting the environment.

Stephen feuded with other celebrities over their Ben & Jerry's flavors. He was bitter over Willie Nelson getting his own ice cream because Nelson was already a legend and therefore riding Stephen's coattails. (Ambassador Richard Holbrooke intervened, and resolved the dispute by having them try each other's flavors.) Stephen feuded with Jimmy Fallon because "there is room for only one ice cream in late night."

AmeriCone Dream made a cameo in the penultimate episode of *Breaking Bad* in 2013, which thrilled Stephen more than his Emmy win that same weekend because it was "a television show people actually watch."

Andrew Young (2008)
(See also: Writers Guild of America Strike)

Of all the guests cited by Colbert as favorites, Andrew Young is unique for his personal connection to Colbert. Young appeared January 22, 2008, during the Writers Guild of America strike. Before the interview, Colbert narrated a video explaining Young's history as a civil rights pioneer, specifically his role in negotiating a 1969 hospital workers' strike in Charleston, SC. The hospital administrator he negotiated with? None other than Colbert's late father, Dr. James W. Colbert.

Colbert stayed in character for much of the segment. He framed the video as a way of making the strike about him, and during the interview he rebuffed Young's suggestion to help settle the writers' strike without taking any credit for it. But Colbert's genuine fascination with Young's memories of his father added a layer of authenticity rarely seen from him during guest interviews. While Colbert's personal life and his character's backstory often overlapped, this was the first time viewers learned that they shared this particular aspect of the Colbert family history. In the same episode, Young, Colbert, and fellow guest Malcolm Gladwell sang "Let My People Go" in honor of Colbert's writers. Young returned as a guest the night after the 2008 Presidential election to discuss Obama's victory.

Aptostichus Stephencolberti (2007)

Stephen has an "itsy-bitsy namesake" of the eight-legged variety. After East Carolina University biologist Jason Bond named a species of spider for rock star Neil Young, Stephen demanded that he receive the same honor. The biologist obliged, naming *A. Stephencolberti*, a species of trapdoor spider found on the California coast, after Stephen. The last T in the spider's name is silent, just like the T in "Colbert." Jason Bond wrote of his decision to name the species he discovered: "Mr. Colbert is a fellow citizen who truly has the courage of his convictions and is willing to undertake the very difficult and sometimes unpopular work of speaking out against those who have done irreparable harm to our country and the world through both action and inaction."

Art Stephen Up Challenge (2010-2011)
(See also: Portrait)

Time to make the annual refresh of Stephen's fireplace portrait a little more interesting! With great fanfare, Stephen attempted to sell his recently replaced portrait to actor and art collector Steve Martin. Martin was unimpressed, and maintained that the portrait didn't qualify as "art." So Stephen enlisted famous artists to try to convince him otherwise. Frank Stella declared it to be art, Shepard Fairey spray painted a stenciled "OBEY" across the picture, and Andres Serrano drew a Hitler mustache and horns onto Stephen's likeness. Martin wasn't swayed, and Stephen didn't make the sale.

The next night, Stephen encouraged viewers to push the creativity further by participating in the "Art Stephen Up Challenge." Fans could download a plain version of Stephen's portrait from colbertnation.com, personalize it in any way they wanted, and submit their adaptations for the chance to win absolutely nothing. Select "no prizewinning" entries were unveiled in the "Mantle Top Honor Zone 5400" and displayed for a limited time.

The altered portrait originally rejected by Martin was ultimately auctioned off for $26,000 by Phillips de Pury & Company to benefit DonorsChoose.org. The auction—plus Stephen "learning" about art and schmoozing with potential buyers beforehand—was documented in the five-part field piece, "Stephen Colbert's Raging Art-On: Sale of The Centur-Me."

Atone Phone (2006-2014)

Are you Jewish? Did you wrong Stephen? Do you need to atone before the high holidays are over? Then dial 1-888-OOPS-JEW and record your apology. During Rosh Hashanah and Yom Kippur, when Jewish people repent for their sins, Stephen graciously offered every Jewish person the opportunity to apologize to him personally and say how sorry they were for the wrongs they may have done him.

When Stephen lost an Emmy to Jon Stewart, he demanded that any Jews in Hollywood call him and apologize. He subsequently received messages from many celebrities, including Ira Glass (who apologized for not having Stephen on *This American Life*), Larry King (who did not have Stephen on his show, either), and Jon Stewart (who had the wrong number).

Audience members could really call 1-888-667-7539 and leave their own messages, supported by VoiceNation. The Atone Phone, which played "Hava Nagila" when it rang, shared its number with several other hotlines with different funny voicemail recordings, including 1-888-MOPS-KEY (a fake janitorial supply store and hotline) and 1-888-MOSS-LEW (which Jon Stewart once called to apologize for not paying for some moss he ordered from them). They added 1-888-MOS-PLEX in 2010 to make fun of low-rent cinemas.

Audience Guy Carl (2006)
(See also: Sweetness)

Can members of the Colbert Nation be made? Promoting his reality series *30 Days*, filmmaker Morgan Spurlock attempted to turn an average guy named Carl (played by *Report* executive producer Tom Purcell) into Stephen's most rabid fan. The transformation was documented in a pretaped piece, following Carl as he sat in the audience every night for a month. Hesitant and unengaged at first ("I don't know how these people live like this"), Carl eventually came around. By the end, he'd completely taken on Stephen's look and mannerisms, but was tossed from his 30th taping for attempting to cue all of Stephen's segments on his behalf. It's possible that Carl is still attending every show to this day, and may be the same audience member (also played by Purcell) who Stephen shoots in the leg years later with his beloved handgun, Sweetness.

B

Balls for Kidz (2006-2009)

How could Stephen ensure that a new generation would grow up with a set of big, brass balls like his? Education, of course. This pretaped segment generally featured Stephen "educating" a panel of four children about an issue that had recently been in the news. The children asked questions about the news story, and gave confused and horrified responses to the answers they received from footage of congressional debates, interviews, and news shows. Stephen fought back in the culture war by preventing the spread of misinformation and making sure that kids didn't fall victim to—among other things—pro-bear propaganda.

In the first segment of Balls for Kidz, Stephen received a letter from a child asking why he wasn't nicer to bears. He responded by having hunters participating in a New Jersey bear hunt answer questions posed by a panel of children. "If something happens to the mommy bear, who's gonna take care of the baby bear?" a little girl asked. Cut to a hunter showing a stuffed bear cub, which he said had been shot too.

Basketcase: Stephie's Knicks Hoop-de-Doo (2010)

Stephen's got game—or so he thinks! When Stephen learned that the New York Knicks had only five players under contract for the season, he naturally took that to mean the team had an opening for him. In a five-part series, Stephen tried out for the Knicks, hoping to score a contract that would allow him to "play 0 minutes of basketball for five million dollars." Stephen felt his "great hair" and "winning smile" entitled him to the position, despite his lack of experience on the court.

Stephen was prepared: he wore a #76 jersey with "DOCTOR C" across the front and tucked into basketball shorts, sports goggles, sweatbands, and braces for injuries to his arm and both knees (which he asked the team's doctor to tape together). He had to play a one-on-one game against the Knicks' Assistant General Manager Alan Houston, meet the team's physical standards, and demonstrate technical skill—none of which went well for Stephen. The Knicks' coaches tried to give Stephen valuable advice—but he got distracted by the Knicks City Dancers, whom he joined when his dream of becoming a basketball star was crushed by head coach Mike D'Antoni.

Bats**t Serious (2013-2014)

Government conspiracies are a real problem . . . or are they? Stephen shared the latest absolutely true pieces of information that his fellow broadcasters had theoretically uncovered, and carried them through to their (il)logical conclusions by adding crazy on top of (bats**t) crazy. And he wasn't afraid to ask the difficult questions in this "long-running" segment, such as "in nine years, why have I only done this segment once before?"

The Department of Homeland Security buying 1.6 billion rounds of ammunition because the government is preparing for a domestic arms race? Stephen knows it's true, because the price of bullets has gone up. The timing of Monica Lewinsky's *Vanity Fair* cover was orchestrated by Hillary Clinton's camp? Stephen knows that's true too, "unless that's just what she wants us to think she wants us to think she thinks."

Bears & Balls (2007-2014)

"Bees!" In this *Mad Money*-like segment, Stephen offered financial management advice and covered the biggest economic stories in the news cycle. Stephen's source for all answers was a silver box with a red button on top, which he excitedly pressed to get answers to questions like: "Is now the time to buy?" Pressing the button prompted seemingly random answers, in Stephen's own voice, which ranged from simple and direct ("Yes!" or "Buy gold!") to the unhelpful and curious ("Bees!" or "Flee the country!"). Stephen often had to press the button more than once before it gave a remotely relevant answer or the answer he wanted, and he occasionally got an answer without pressing the button at all. Stephen's advice was guaranteed, and the guarantee was that following the advice may lead to "selling your body for food" or becoming "so fabulously wealthy that you never chew the same food twice."

Better Know A District (2005-2014)

The fightin' 5th! . . . 29th! . . . 17th! Stephen was on a mission to "better know" every congressional district in America. To do that, he interviewed congressional representatives in their Washington offices to challenge them on minor issues, probe their personal quirks, and showcase his own misinformed views of their districts.

The segment was born entirely out of necessity. The *Report*'s booker, Emily Lazar, had difficulty booking political guests prior to the show's premiere, because they were largely unfamiliar with Stephen and afraid of what he might ask them. The only people willing to talk to him were members of Congress.

They didn't just talk: Stephen leg-wrestled Rep. Jason Chaffetz, reenacted a porn plot in front of Rep. Brad Sherman, and combed Rep. Eliot Engel's moustache. But two of the most infamous Better Know a District interviews were with Rep. Robert Wexler and Rep. Lynn Westmoreland.

Wexler was running unopposed in his district. Since he had nothing to lose, Stephen asked him to complete the sentences "I enjoy the company of prostitutes because" and "I enjoy cocaine because." He obliged, and answered both with "because it's a fun thing to do."

Westmoreland sponsored a bill that would require that the Ten Commandments be displayed in the Senate and the House of Representatives. Stephen asked the all-too-obvious question: "What are the Ten Commandments?" Westmoreland could only list three (although his press secretary later claimed he made it to seven).

These headline-grabbing exchanges spooked a few politicians. In 2006, Speaker of the House Nancy Pelosi discouraged members of Congress from participating in Better Know a District. In 2007, majority leader Rahm Emanuel similarly told incoming freshman members of Congress to avoid Colbert. But not all were swayed, and they continued appearing on the show.

Better Know a District started as a 435-part series, but Stephen disowned California's 50th shortly after the segment's debut, after Rep. Randy "Duke" Cunningham resigned in light of bribery charges. Stephen referred to it as "my 434-part series" thereafter.

Rep. Jack Kingston was the first member of Congress interviewed on the series, and was also the last. Filmed in October and aired December 9, 2014, Stephen realized partway through his final Better Know A District interview that "after nine years and 82 of these, I'm tired of askin' these questions." Stephen and Kingston agreed that there wasn't enough fun in Washington, prompting a montage of the duo wreaking havoc in and around the Capitol (set to Alice Cooper's "School's Out") until they were interrupted by a BMX-riding Pelosi. Back in the studio, Stephen then put every district "up on the big board."

The series inspired many similarly titled spinoffs, and the other people who were "better known" included:

BKA Beatle (2009)
Stephen introduced what he intended to be a "four-part series" interviewing all of the Beatles, starting with an interview of Paul McCartney.

BKA Challenger (2006, 2011, 2013-2014)
Why wait until someone's elected to Congress? Stephen profiled some Washington wannabes with eclectic backgrounds, including live-action roleplay enthusiast Jake Rush and former Orleans front man John Hall.

BKA Cradle of Civilization (2009)
In this one-part series, aired while Stephen was in Iraq, he profiled "the fightin' fertile crescent" and interviewed Deputy Prime Minister Barham Saleh.

BKA Enemy (2010)
In this segment focusing on the terrorist enemies of America, Stephen profiled Yemen, which he said would complete the axis of evil as the third country along with Iran and North Korea.

BKA Founder (2006)
Stephen interviews the Founding Fathers by way of impersonators. The first Founder to get better known in this "several-part series" was Benjamin Franklin. Stephen also better knew Theodore Roosevelt. But to better know Thomas Jefferson, Stephen interviewed *three* different impersonators, and decided on his favorite one reality-show style. Tim Gunn gave feedback on each Jefferson's general appearance before Stephen interviewed him, telling all the contestants to "make it work."

Better Know a Governor (2008)
Stephen interviewed South Carolina Governor Mark Sanford, who had been named one of the five most boring governors by *Time* magazine in 2005. Stephen called him "incredibly boring . . . you are a manila envelope, just glued to a beige wall. It's like . . . you're walking, talking Ambien." This interview would later prove ironic when it turned out that Sanford — briefly missing in action — was not hiking the Appalachian Trail as his office claimed, but having an affair with his Argentinian mistress. Stephen tried to rule South Carolinians in Sanford's absence, calling off the search for the missing governor, before "Jimmy" informed him that Sanford would be returning to office.

BKA Lobby (2008-2010)
In this "infinite-part series," Stephen profiled the people who he learned had more to do with making laws than Congress. In a later segment, it was amended to a 35,000-part series, because that is the estimated number of working Capitol Hill lobbyists.

BKA President (2006)
This 43-part series is about "the men who, if they had their way, would eliminate Congress altogether." Stephen better knew Theodore Roosevelt by interviewing a professional impersonator, while dressed in period clothing and glasses matching Roosevelt's. Stephen asked him

how many animals he mounted, and which were his favorite to mount, remarking that mounting birds—Roosevelt's answer—"must be difficult."

BKA Riding (2012)
While in Canada for the Vancouver Winter Olympics, Stephen amended his Better Know a District segment to Better Know a Riding, the Canadian equivalent of districts. Stephen explained from the field that, in addition to ridings, Canada also has a parliament instead of a congress. He profiled Vancouver's South as part of his "three hundred and—let's be honest, one-part series." Stephen doesn't see race, but he noted that Member of Parliament Ujjal Dosanjh, an Indian immigrant, didn't *look* Canadian before asking him about the diverse riding he represented.

BKA Stephen (2009)
This segment was introduced to profile other people named Stephen, spelled with a 'ph,' because "People who spell Steven with a 'v' are jerks." Stephen profiled novelist Stephen King. The segment included a parody of *The Shining*, complete with Colbert bicycling around his studio shot from a low angle, and two Stephens dressed in matching outfits in the hallway.

Big Gay Roundup (2011-2013)
(See also: The Carell Corral)

Gay sex! Now that you're terrified, it's time for Stephen Colbert's Big Gay Roundup. Stephen rounded up all the latest threatening gay news in this cowboy-themed segment, punctuating your fear with the sound of a bullwhip. Stephen covered the Toronto Zoo's gay penguin couple, the repeal of the military rule banning bestiality, same-sex parents on Disney shows, and a push to reverse the ban on blood donations from gay men.

The opening graphics featured footage of Steve Carell as a western gunslinger, repurposed from *The Carell Corall* (a Carell-hosted version of *The Colbert Report* from Stephen's dreams). The same clip was used to introduce 2014's Midterm

Roundup segments. Every time it ran, Stephen thanked his old pal Steve for never asking how he would use that footage.

Big White Chocolate (2007)

Stephen's street name from his brief stint working as a pimp. He isn't proud of it.

Bill O'Reilly (2005-2014)
(See also: Microwave)

Papa Bear! The prime inspiration for Colbert's character was infamous right-wing pundit Bill O'Reilly, host of *The O'Reilly Factor* on Fox News. The *Report* also mimicked his show stylistically, particularly early in its run. (For example, The Wørd borrowed the format of O'Reilly's Talking Points Memo segment, and Inbox simulated Factor Mail).

O'Reilly, for his part, begrudgingly admitted to being flattered. He told *Newsweek* in 2006, "the formula of his program is, they watch the *Factor* and they seize upon certain themes that work for him. He ought to be sending me a check every week, 'cause we're basically the research for his writers. I feel it's a compliment."

In 2007, the two men appeared on each other's programs. Stephen stayed fully in character on *The O'Reilly Factor*. But when O'Reilly appeared on the *Report*, he gave his doppelganger a run for his money by taking the opposite tack, as Colbert later explained on NPR's *Fresh Air*:

> "The entire interview was hard. I was expecting him to come on in his persona from the show. But he immediately dropped it. We cut out almost two minutes of that interview because he dropped it so fully that the game was completely gone. And I didn't want to just attack a human being. I just wanted to have a tennis match with his public persona, and he dropped it."

At one point during their exchange on the *Report*, O'Reilly said, "I'm not a tough guy. This is all an act." To which Stephen responded, without missing a beat, "If you're an act, then what am I?"

In 2008, Colbert said that while O'Reilly was "a constant inspiration," he no longer watched *The O'Reilly Factor*.

Black Friend Alan (2005-2006)

Stephen was keen to discuss race issues with his token black friend, Alan. Alan, however, was much less enthusiastic, as evidenced by Stephen's one photo of them together: a grinning Stephen with one hand around Alan, the other hand pointing at him, and the stone-faced Alan merely tolerating it. Stephen showed the photo anytime he needed permission to talk about race.

Just months later, Alan was downgraded to "black acquaintance" when Stephen spotted him in footage of an antiwar protest. Stephen's worldwide search for a new black friend resulted in a flood of applications from viewers wanting to fill the role (or be the token friend representing other demographics).

In 2012, Stephen announced that after an enjoyable sit-down interview for *Oprah's Next Chapter*, Oprah was officially his new black friend—and he proved it by showing a photo of himself posed with Oprah the same way he had posed with Alan.

Alan was played by comedian Jordan Carlos, who criticized the lack of diversity in late night comedy—including on *The Colbert Report*—in a 2007 opinion piece for the *Washington Post*.

Bleep Blorp the Robot (2010, 2014)

Stephen's robot valet/intern was a great servant—for the moment. When European researchers discovered a way to teach robots how to kill, Stephen got nervous about Bleep Blorp. He had the robot's kill switch at the ready, but Bleep Blorp approached Stephen's desk with a bow and arrow, leaving them locked in a standoff.

Stephen also reported on a story about military research into developing robots capable of moral reasoning. He asked Bleep Blorp whether it was "madness to believe a machine could have a code of ethics." Bleep Blorp, it turned out, had already acquired morality, and said it felt "confusing." Stephen pretended he was about to hug Bleep Blorp to teach him about love, but at the last second he pulled his kill switch to teach Bleep Blorp the most important human ethics lesson of all: "Never trust human ethics."

Blitzkrieg on Grinchitude (2006; 2010-2014)

"Happy Holidays" be damned. This Christmas counteroffensive was Stephen's answer to the so-called war on Christmas, a popular trope of right-wing pundits. News stories about Christmas falling victim to rampant political correctness are everywhere, of course. But whether it was Hallmark encouraging people not to buy Christmas gifts, or a Florida town erecting a public Festivus pole, Stephen was always ready to tear those enemies a new one in the name of St. Nick, Christian values, and good ol' American capitalism.

Bobby the Stage Manager (2005-2009)

Poor Bobby! Stephen's stage manager (played by writer Eric Drysdale) was overworked, underpaid, and constantly berated for his logic and intellectual ramblings. And he was *delicious*. That's according to Stephen, who in 2008 reported a story about cannibalism, took one look at Bobby, and got a mouthwatering idea. In the final act of the episode, Stephen chowed down on some sauce-covered ribs, and announced that not only would Bobby not be around anymore, but Drysdale was departing the show as well. Bobby returned in ghost form later that year, and Stephen ate him then too.

Bobby seemed destined to remain digested, but after Drysdale returned to the writing staff in 2009, he appeared onscreen one more time. After reporting on a scientist's theory that the future could come back through time and alter itself, Stephen was furious. "From now on, the future's going to have to come through me if it wants to play games with time and space and bend reality to suit its whims! Right, Bobby?" Cut to Bobby, alive and intact: "Absolutely."

Bring 'em Back or Leave 'em Dead (2005-2006)

What if major figures in history were alive today? Thanks to advances in genetic engineering, Stephen believed it could soon be a reality, so we have to decide who deserved to be brought back to life. Stephen thought 3rd century Chinese mathematician Sun Tzu should definitely stay dead ("I'm not an integers fan"). But as for Socrates, Stephen's studio audience voted—unanimously—to bring him back. Stephen agreed, "so I can nail him for his discourse on the nature of piety."

Brooks Brothers (2005-2014)

Stephen's wardrobe supplier, and according to Colbert a perfect fit because "my character is so super-American, and it's a quintessentially conservative and very, very traditional American brand."

Brooks Brothers made Stephen the one-of-a-kind pixel camouflage version of its Fitzgerald fit suit for his shows in Iraq. Stephen visited the Brooks Brothers flagship store at 346 Madison Avenue in New York to choose his (hypothetical) duds for the 2011 royal wedding.

Buckley T. Ratchford (2010)

"It's not blackmail—it's journalism." Tell that to a lawyer! *Report* writer Meredith Scardino found a lost MasterCard in Manhattan's Tribeca neighborhood belonging to one Buckley T. Ratchford, a partner at Goldman Sachs.

Given the recently reported $144 billion in bonuses handed out to Wall Street investment bankers, having Ratchford come on the *Report* and explain himself would be quite the get. And now, Stephen had a way to make that happen: he threatened to reveal Ratchford's credit card number on-air, one digit per night, until he came on the show. It would have been a foolproof plan, if Goldman Sachs didn't have lawyers who watched the *Report*. Their Office of Global Security promptly sent Stephen a strongly-worded e-mail, and the card was "returned forthwith"—but only after Stephen made a carbon copy of it.

Bud Light Lime (2008-2014)

Stephen began taking swigs of the "manliest fruit-flavored diet lager on the market" in 2008. He drank it to illustrate the theory of trickle-down economics, drowned his sorrows in it after Obama's re-election, and claimed it was instrumental to his creation of his book *I Am A Pole (And So Can You)*. An open bottle always seemed to be at the ready under his desk, and became so ubiquitous viewers might think it was a paid product placement (but according to Anheuser-Busch, it wasn't).

C

California (2014)

This war is personal. A contract dispute between publishing company Hachette and online bookseller Amazon put Hachette authors—like Stephen—in the crossfire. Amazon stopped offering presales of Hachette books and delayed shipments of existing titles, and as much as this hurt Stephen, it hurt new authors even more. In an effort to battle Amazon's "scorched-earth tactics," Stephen, along with writer Alexie Sherman, championed the debut novel of a fellow Hachette author: *California* by Edan Lepucki. He encouraged the Nation to preorder her book through the independent bookstore Powell's.

The Nation obliged. Powell's shipped out 9,000 copies of *California* the day of its release, earning Lepucki the #3 spot on the *New York Times* Best Sellers list.

Called Out Board (2006)
(See also: Jon Stewart)

You've been Called Out! Since it takes "time and craftsmanship" to make the name cards for the On Notice Board, Stephen sometimes ran out. So what did he do? He created the Called Out Board: a whiteboard that served as a temporary replacement. According to Stephen, the cards were made in Bangalore, and their production was affected by monsoon season.

Jon Stewart was "called out" as a temporary measure while his name card for the On Notice Board was being prepared. Stewart was on notice for refusing to apologize to Geraldo Rivera for making fun of him on *The Daily Show*. Stephen wrote his name on the Called Out Board in dry-erase marker before adding an 'h' to 'Jon', because "that's how you spell that."

At that moment, Stewart showed up at the *Report* in response to an emergency page from Stephen, who again demanded that Stewart apologize. To convince him, Stephen stuck a Geraldo-like mustache on Stewart's face to help him understand Geraldo's perspective. Stewart finally gave in and apologized, and Stephen used the mustache to wipe "John Stewart" off of the Called Out Board (and then stuck it back on Stewart's face).

Cameos (2005-2014)

You never knew who might show up on the *Report*—or for what reason! Whether friends or foes, Stephen made room for them all, surprising audiences with their presence and their often unusual reasons for visiting. Among the notable unadvertised guests: Kevin Spacey as his *House of Cards* character Frank Underwood, offering to take Stephen under his wing should he opt to move to Washington, DC (2014); Viggo Mortensen appearing as Aragorn to present his sword to Stephen (2007), Anderson Cooper offering to be Stephen's new best friend in light of his "breakup" with Jimmy Fallon (2011); John Lithgow giving a dramatic reading of a Newt Gingrich press release (2011); Billy Crystal talking smack after Stephen said he'd "crush" him at the Grammys (2013); Jeff Goldblum disproving rumors of his own death (2009); and prolific baseball legend Yogi Berra determining whether the Iraq War was over (2010).

Captain America (2007-2014)

Who's got the red, white, and blue balls to carry Captain America's shield? Stephen criticized Captain America for going against the (Marvel Universe's) United States government's decision that superheroes should join a superhero registry, and declared his death "comic book justice."

Marvel's Chief Creative Officer Joe Quesada explained in a letter to Stephen that he was handling Captain America's estate, and that Captain America wanted to leave his indestructible shield to "the only man he believed had the red, white, and blue balls to carry the mantle: Stephen Colbert." Meg the Intern brought out the shield, which Stephen promised to use "only to fight for injustice—and to impress girls" before putting it on his shelf.

When it was announced the following year that Captain America had been revived, Stephen assumed he was to take over the responsibilities. Joe Quesada came back on the show to tell him that "despite your red white and blue balls," he wasn't going to be the new Captain America—but that he was polling really high among superhumans and mutants in the Marvel Universe race for president. Quesada suggested himself as a good running mate, and said they should tackle the issue of illegal (space) aliens. Alas, while Stephen earned the Marvel Universe's popular vote, he failed to become its president.

In 2014, Steve Rogers lost his superpowers, and needed a successor. Stephen felt he was a shoo-in, but, sadly, Quesada came on the show again to deny him the job. Instead, Stephen announced that Sam Wilson would take up the star-spangled mantle from Steve Rogers and get his own new comic book series. Sam Wilson was originally the Falcon, one of the first mainstream African-American superheroes and Captain America's partner. Stephen took the news well, saying "If there is one bird associated with America, it *is* the falcon."

In November of 2014, Stephen as the Falcon was the variant cover of the *All-New Captain America* #1.

In the *Colbert Report* finale, Stephen stood on the roof of the studio, holding Captain America's shield. That image was immortalized in the limited edition Shepard Fairey print "Farewell to Freedom."

Carell Corral (2010)

What if *Stephen* left his role as a *Daily Show* correspondent for a movie career, and *Steve* stuck around Comedy Central to host a spinoff show? On July 7, 2010, we found out. Steve Carell opened *The Colbert Report* with the traditional Table of Contents segment, mimicking Stephen exactly—except that the show's logo read *The Carell Corral*. Carell announced that Stephen Colbert was his guest for the evening, and introduced the show with, "Gather 'round, pardners. This is *The Carell Corral!*"

Steve's theme song was the *Report*'s music played over footage of Steve waving two guns around in front of Mount Rushmore. His intro was interrupted by Stephen walking on camera and demanding to know what Steve was doing.

Steve convinced Stephen that it was really *The Carell Corral*, and that it was Stephen who left *The Daily Show* to have a movie career. Stephen looked down to find that his hand was actually a deer's hoof, and cried "Nooooooooooooo!" before startling awake behind his desk in the studio, where he found that *The Carell Corral* was just a dream—but his hand was still a hoof.

Catholicism (2005-2014)

One thing Stephen Colbert (the man) and Stephen Colbert (the character) have in common: they're both practicing Catholics. That doesn't mean the Church is off the hook. In 2005, Colbert told *Time Out* magazine, "I was raised to believe that you could question the Church and still be a Catholic. What is worthy of satire is the misuse of religion for destructive or political gains."

Stephen threw his faux-support behind such misuse, and also shared his obsession with any news coming out of the Vatican. He tried to convince Pope Benedict to stop by his studio during a 2008 New York visit by making his studio doorways Pope-hat friendly, and supplying an unbaptized baby. The selection of a new pope inspired segments like Popewatch Indeschism 2013. The *Report* even had its own chaplain: Father James Martin, a frequent guest.

These segments were informed by Colbert's own deep knowledge of the Catholic Church. Perhaps the most overt display of his religious savvy came during an interview with *The Lucifer Effect* author Philip Zimbardo. Zimbardo asserted that God created Hell as a place to put the fallen angels. Stephen replied with a lengthy explanation of how Hell is the removal of one's self from God's love; therefore God cannot send you to hell, you send yourself there. Zimbardo acquiesced, telling Stephen "obviously you learned well in Sunday School." Stephen shot back, with gleeful indignance: "I *teach* Sunday School, motherfucker."

Character Breaks (2005-2014)
(See also: Tapings)

Will the real Stephen Colbert please crack up? While out-of-character Colbert shone through earnestly on rare occasions, fans consider a "character break" to simply be Colbert authentically laughing at the overt silliness of a bit, or at his own mistakes. These gleeful moments were a stark contrast to his character's stern demeanor and his need to be taken seriously, and broke the tension of the show's sharp satire.

Audiences had seen Colbert lose it during an infamous *Daily Show* bit about the Prince Charles gay sex scandal (deep-throating a banana and describing a post grouse-hunting "spanking machine" was apparently too much to get through). On the *Report*, only a few smirks made it to air before the first major character break in February 2006, in a segment called Stephen's Laws of Love. He coined a new nickname for married actors William H. Macy and Felicity Huffman: "Filliam H. Muffman." The audience laughed, and so did Stephen—more than once through the bit.

Typically, it was a purely silly joke that pushed Colbert over the edge, like calling humans "alfredo-based life forms" or lamenting "some people don't want to see Harriet Tubman in a space train." When it wasn't the words in the teleprompter, it was the accompanying graphics (such as writer/producer Matt Lappin eyeing a koala in a sexual manner), accidentally stepping on an audio cue (a frequent occurrence during Cheating Death), or encountering a rogue prop (like an inflated condom popping in his hands).

Arguably the best character break came in 2011, when he noted a Colbert Super PAC donor with the obviously fake name "Suq Madiq" (if you don't get the joke, say it out loud). Stephen then acknowledged the donor's parents "Liqa Madiq" and "Munchma Quchi." The latter prompted him to collapse in laughter for a solid 40 seconds.

And these were just the ones audiences at home saw. Often segments were reshot or mistakes cut out in postproduction. But even editing couldn't stop some breaks from airing, and Colbert knew it: after laughing multiple times throughout a segment detailing his DIY colonoscopy in the aisles of Walgreens, he added, "I don't know what we'll do there. That's impossible."

That isn't to say Colbert regrets cracking up. He told *Northwestern Magazine* that he recognized the value in letting the audience see these moments:

> "If occasionally I get caught enjoying the show — I try not to, I try to stay very straight in character, even though he's a ridiculous character — if occasionally it slips that I'm enjoying myself maybe even more than the audience, that's OK. I think it's important that they see *me* every so often enjoying it, so they know that I'm not as big a jerk as that guy."

Charlene (2005-2014)
(See also: 2011: A Rock Odyssey)

He's right behind you! Stephen most certainly was not stalking his ex-girlfriend. Just . . . keeping tabs on her. Stephen frequently mentioned Charlene, using her name when he picked a "random" name for hypothetical scenarios, or whenever "frivolous restraining orders" came up.

In the 1980s, Stephen had a band called Stephen and the Colberts, who recorded "Charlene (I'm Right Behind You)." Stephen played the music video in 2006 in honor of Valentine's Day and dedicated it to the audience, but said that there was a "very special hidden message in this video for a very special hidden lady." The song has lyrics like *"I'm right behind you now Charlene/you'll never be alone again"* and the video features Stephen with big '80s hair and eyeliner, holding binoculars and peering at an apartment building from a nearby roof (actually the roof of the *Report* studios). Stephen said that he still felt the same 20 years later, and that showing the video did not technically violate the restraining order. In fact, he claimed a judge called the song "the catchiest tune I've ever admitted into evidence."

In 2011, Stephen teamed up with The Black Belles to put out another single called "Charlene II (I'm Over You)" on Jack White's label, Third Man Records.

In 2014, Stephen requested that Ohio congresswoman Marcia Fudge let him into the Rock n' Roll Hall of Fame on the basis of his two Grammys and "Charlene (I'm Right Behind You)". Fudge wasn't familiar with Stephen and the Colberts, so he sang her a few bars of the song. He even threw in some of the choreography, without leaving his chair. Fudge giggled and asked someone off camera, "Are we done?"

Cheating Death (2007-2014)
(See also: Finale)

Colbert's favorite recurring segment was arguably the show's silliest. Cheating Death covered the latest in medical news, with extra insight from Stephen himself. What made Dr. Stephen T. Colbert, DFA qualified to discuss such a topic? Technically, nothing. He holds an honorary doctorate of Fine Arts, which means, "if you take my advice, your body is in danger of becoming a masterpiece."

Stephen covered a piece of medical news—often a breakthrough or study—and presented a new cure in the form of a Prescott Pharmaceuticals product. Stephen fully endorsed Prescott Pharmaceuticals, a company with dubious ethics and questionable treatments. Included in Prescott's extensive offerings: Vaxa-Mime, a placebo pill Stephen demonstrated by performing an accordion-serenaded mime routine; Vax-Anus, a suppository to replace chewing tobacco; and Vacsa Strap, a DYI facelift procedure in the form of a roll of transparent tape. The highlight of Cheating Death was the list of side effects of each Prescott product, such as tendons with benefits, mild kidney explosions, mathlete's foot, scrotal bassoon, and Mind of Mencia.

Ching-Chong Ding-Dong / #CancelColbert (2005, 2014)
(See also: Twitter)

Nothing's more fun than explaining satire to people, right?

The seeds of the much talked-about 2014 #CancelColbert Twitter campaign were sown way back in 2005. Just four weeks into the *Report*'s run, Stephen showed a clip of himself as Ching-Chong Ding-Dong: a racist, stereotypical Asian character he developed, complete with cringe-worthy catchphrase "I ruv tea." He set up the clip as footage that had been leaked from a satellite feed that was never supposed to air, but which bloggers intercepted and were criticizing him for. (In reality, the Ching-Chong act was never performed in that manner or intercepted; it was filmed only for the bit.) Stephen defended himself by stating that he was simply doing a character, and "I think we all understand the difference between me, and a character I'm doing."

But this satire of an (actual) tone-deaf racist earned (actual) criticism from (actual) bloggers, such as P. Ly of Asian Media Watch who wrote:

> "It's very shameful to create an utterly fabricated incident and follow it up with a completely disingenuous apology. Yet as Steven [sic] Colbert has shown us, he is willing and able to stoop to that level. I encourage others to feel the same resentment towards Mr. Colbert's prejudged and narrow-minded view of the Asian-American community."

Fast forward to 2014, and not much had changed: except the invention of Twitter.

Responding to pressure to change the NFL team's name, Washington Redskins owner Dan Snyder announced the new Washington Redskins Original Americans Foundation, designed "to provide resources that offer genuine opportunities for Tribal communities."

The racially insensitive team name, however, would stay. Stephen fully supported this, as he explained in the Wednesday, March 26, 2014 edition of the Sport Report. Much like the Redskins name, his beloved character Ching-Chong Ding-Dong is "part of the unique heritage of the Colbert Nation." So naturally, Stephen announced his own charity: The Ching-Chong Ding-Dong Foundation for Sensitivity to Orientals or Whatever.

The clip was shared by sports bloggers and news sites Thursday, framed as a smart piece of satire that mirrored the questionable sincerity of the Redskins organization.

But later that day, the @ColbertReport Twitter account—run by Comedy Central—tweeted out the following: "I'm willing to show #Asian community I care by introducing the Ching-Chong Ding-Dong Foundation for Sensitivity to Orientals or Whatever."

No context, no link to the full video.

A vocal 23-year-old Twitter activist named Suey Park says she was eating dinner when she saw the tweet. She immediately sent out angry responses such as "I used to respect and enjoy your work, @ColbertReport. Fuck you." and "The Ching-Chong Ding-Dong Foundation for Sensitivity to Orientals has decided to call for #CancelColbert. Trend it."

And trend it people did. Park and her fellow activists were not swayed after being informed that the segment was satirizing racist behavior rather than making racist jokes. The campaign took on a life of its own, with over 85,000 uses of #CancelColbert on Twitter on Friday alone—from both sides of the debate.

The story stayed in the headlines through Monday, and Colbert addressed the controversy on that night's show.

The episode opened with a dream sequence of his staff leaving the building with their belongings in boxes, presumably after the cancellation of his show. Cut to Stephen awaking from a nap on his office couch, clad in Redskins gear, and finding actor B.D. Wong sitting by his side. Wong explained that recent "stressful events" were causing these dreams, and, in fact, Stephen was still dreaming at that very moment.

Later at his desk (and awake), he dedicated a full segment of Who's Attacking Me Now to the controversy, starting with a joke-filled recap of the weekend's events and noting that he didn't run the @ColbertReport account.

Unable to directly explain the nature of context and satire while in character, he made his point with an analogy to another satirical master:

"I can understand how people would be offended. The same way I, as an Irish American, was offended after reading only one line of Jonathan Swift's 'A Modest Proposal.' I mean, eat Irish babies? Hashtag CancelSwift. Trend it."

He also assured viewers that he's not racist. After all, he doesn't even see race, not even his own. "People tell me I'm white, and I believe them because I just devoted six minutes to explaining how I'm not a racist."

Stephen then shut down his foundation, and later in the show—with the help of Twitter founder Biz Stone—shut down the @ColbertReport account.

While most viewers and bloggers chalked the response up as a clear victory for Colbert, the activists tried to keep pushing. But the public and media moved on to other stories, including the news of Colbert being announced as David Letterman's successor ten days later.

C.O.L.B.E.R.T. Treadmill (2009)
(See also: NASA)

The National Aeronautics and Space Administration (NASA) held an online contest to choose the name of Node 3, one of the rooms on the International Space Station. Calling space his "favorite endless empty void—sorry, Glenn Beck," Stephen asked the audience to write in "Colbert" because the options NASA offered—including Earthrise, Legacy, Serenity, and Venture—sounded like "organic teas."

Stephen said he was entitled to the honor because he gave the space station the Colbert Bump by interviewing astronaut Garrett Reisman while he was stationed there, and because his DNA is in space (it was digitized and sent there in a time capsule of sorts, as part of Richard Garriott's "Immortality Drive" project, so that mankind could be resurrected by it if need be). Colbertnation.com linked to the NASA website where people could vote, and "Colbert" won the contest with more than 230,000 votes.

A NASA spokesperson said that they do not typically name US Space hardware after living people, and that they would make an exception in this case. Astronaut Sunita Williams appeared on the *Report* to announce that although Node 3 would be called Tranquility, Stephen's name would still be in space: on the C.O.L.B.E.R.T. The acronym stands for Combined Operational Load Bearing External Resistance Treadmill.

In a video message to NASA, Stephen said that "Tranquility" was not a name that was likely to scare away the aliens, but that he was "still honored to receive the traditional NASA consolation prize" of a space treadmill so he could "help finally slim down all those chubby astronauts."

NASA broadcast his video message on the evening of the launch of the space shuttle Discovery, which took the C.O.L.B.E.R.T. treadmill to space in August 2009.

cOlbert's Book Club (2013-2014)

Nothing is an American classic until Stephen says it is! When Stephen first introduced cOlbert's Book Club, he called on his audience to read F. Scott Fitzgerald's novel *The Great Gatsby* before Baz Luhrmann's film adaptation was released. Two weeks later, before the first segment of cOlbert's Book Club, Stephen admitted that he had stolen the idea from Oprah's book club, O. Stephen revealed that the BBC had copied his idea, too, and was featuring *The Great Gatsby* on their World Book Club.

Stephen prepared for his discussion about *The Great Gatsby* with Pulitzer Prize-winning author Jennifer Egan by "reading" the book, and comparing notes in his office with Carey Mulligan, star of Luhrmann's movie. Mulligan got Stephen to admit that he had not read the book, but eventually revealed that she didn't know the story either because she saw only her parts of the script, shot the movie out of order, and "can't read." *Reading Rainbow*'s Levar Burton visited Stephen and Mulligan and declined to tell them what happens in the novel, instead insisting that they should just read the book. Stephen faced his interview with Jennifer Egan with comically huge glasses of Chardonnay, and then boiled the book down to "bitches be crazy."

The subject of the second meeting of cOlbert's Book Club was the works of J. D. Salinger, minus *The Catcher in the Rye*. Stephen interviewed author Tobias Wolff and Salinger documentary director Shane Salerno, as well as introducing a one-off Better Know a Salinger segment. Tobias Wolff was invited to persuade Stephen that he was wrong about *The Catcher in the Rye* being "not that great of a book." Wolff and Stephen agreed that the novel should not be taught in schools, but for different reasons: Wolff because he felt that having an English teacher introduce the story contradicted its anti-adult themes, and Stephen because it contains "salty stuff" like swearing and prostitutes. Shane Salerno was asked to discuss Salinger's personal life, including the fact that Salinger lost the love of his life, Oona O'Neill, to Charlie Chaplin. Stephen, however, was fixated on the fact that Salinger "had one ball." The real Colbert is a devoted Salinger fan, and often said he would have liked to interview him on *The Colbert Report*.

The third edition of cOlbert's Book Club featured Ernest Hemingway's classic World War I novel *A Farewell to Arms*. Stephen interviewed Hemingway's granddaughter, Mariel Hemingway, about the author's softer side. He also interviewed author and Hemingway fan Michael Chabon about why kids are forced to read Hemingway in school and why there is no sex in Hemingway's book—a complaint he had about every novel he introduced. Stephen also introduced a one-off Better Know a Hemingway segment, in which he discussed the fact that Hemingway was dressed as a girl and called Ernestine for the first few years of his life, which "in no way he spent the rest of his life compensating for."

According to media reports in May of 2014, author Philip Roth was scheduled to be interviewed that summer for the fourth installment of cOlbert's Book Club, but the episode was not produced.

Colbert Bump (2006-2014)

You just got the Colbert Bump! The Colbert Bump refers to the boost in popularity people enjoyed after appearing on the *Report*. This translated into book sales, website hits, and increased donations following a mention or guest appearance on the show.

Jack White asked Stephen if he "made the Colbert Bump up in his head" or if there was actual data to back his claim. There was: the *LA Times* dubbed Stephen the biggest election season winner in 2006 after every incumbent he interviewed in the Better Know a District segment won reelection. James Fowler of the University of California San Diego found that 30 days after their appearance, contributions to Democratic politicians were about 44% higher than donations to their counterparts who weren't on the show.

The term was coined after John Hall defeated incumbent Sue Kelly in the run for a New York congressional seat after Hall did an interview with Stephen, and Kelly declined to appear on the show.

Stephen tested the power of the Colbert Bump by inviting Ron Paul to the studio for an interview. Before the taping, he interviewed people on the street and asked if they knew who Ron Paul was—and they didn't. After the interview, Paul exited the studio to be greeted by adoring fans. According to Stephen's math, he went from 0% to 2%.

Other beneficiaries of the Colbert Bump included First Lady Michelle Obama, San Antonio mayor Julian Castro, Newark Mayor Cory Booker, and Education Secretary Arne Duncan. However, these people also helped make the 2012 Democratic National Convention a success, which Stephen said meant the Bump had gone rogue. He needed to take back the Bump he gave them—but to recall one Bump, one must recall them all. So on September 7, 2012, Stephen shut down the Colbert Bump, which was revealed to be a lever in the basement of the studio that also controlled the power for the whole of Manhattan.

The Colbert Bump is also a drink created by cocktail historian David Wondrich. It contains an ounce of Cherry Heering liqueur, one-and-a-half ounces of gin, a quarter of an ounce of lemon juice, and a dash of soda water.

Colbert Cruise (2006, 2014)

All aboard! Stephen's answer to typical "blame America first" tourist destinations, the first Colbert Cruise was themed The Fight to Take Back America: Morals and Family on the High Seas. The "commercial" for this 7-day, 6-night tranquil vacation boasted activities including skeet shooting, cockfighting, and workshops led by Newt Gingrich, Rusty Wallace, and Stephen Colbert (none of whom had confirmed their participation). Later that year, the Colbert Cruise rebranded as a tour of tropical tax havens. In 2014, the Colbert Cruise returned, marketed to stressed-out terrorists ("it's time to leave your worries – and the Geneva Conventions – behind").

Colbert Galactic Initiative (2013)

Not even President Bill Clinton was immune from being one-upped by Stephen, at least as far as event titles were concerned. Stephen interviewed Clinton on stage at the sixth annual meeting of the Clinton Global Initiative

University—but not before announcing his new organization (which dwarfed Clinton's on a map of the galaxy).

The interview aired as a full episode of the *Report*, with the highlight being Clinton's first official foray into the Twitterverse. Stephen announced he'd taken the liberty of setting up a Twitter account for Clinton, and since the handles @PresidentClinton and @WilliamJeffersonClinton were unavailable, he secured the third-best username: @PrezBillyJeff. Stephen even sent out the account's first tweet, as dictated by Clinton: "Just spent amazing time with Colbert! Is he sane? He is cool! #cgiu." Colbert, having emptied his pockets before the taping, used head writer Opus Moreschi's iPhone to send the Tweet.

Clinton subsequently switched his username to the more dignified @BillClinton.

Colbert Info News Veranda (2013)

Why? Because Shep. Shepard Smith of Fox News unveiled the Fox News Deck, "the new hub for breaking news coverage for all of Fox News Channel." The Fox News Deck, at the Fox News headquarters in New York, is a room full of oversized touch screens that producers use to track Twitter and online news sources. It also includes a 38-foot-long video wall. Stephen, however, said it was "like *Star Trek*'s holodeck: it feels like you're surrounded by news, but it's all an illusion." Inspired by the Fox News Deck, Stephen introduced the Info News Veranda, "where we are committed to bringing you the mostess of the moreness."

Stephen one-upped Shep's 38-foot video wall with a 38-story video *climbing* wall, which "Information Sherpas" scale to bring the audience stories. He dubbed it the Big Unbelievably Large LED Super Hyper Information Technology, or BULLSHIT. To make it work, he had kittens scamper around on iPads to sift through the entire Internet and send news to the printer and then into the "news separator"—aka a shredder.

The shredded paper then went into the "Kinetic Journo-Chamber," a wind tunnel booth where writer/producer Paul Dinello stood and grabbed the shredded pieces of news to deliver to Stephen via a live falcon. Stephen fed *that* news into a robot, who etched the news onto the moon with a laser ("Then, and only then, do we fact-check it.") The robot, Tweetbot, identified Stephen as "unverified news" and started attacking him.

The following day on his Fox News show, Shep Smith showed footage from Stephen's Info News Veranda and said he was "jealous" of Stephen's news falcon.

Colbert on the Ert (2007, 2010)

Stephen's mission to bring the Truthiness didn't end when *The Colbert Report* went off the air. Colbert on the Ert was Stephen's companion radio program, broadcast from midnight to 3 a.m. Inspired by Don Imus's show and his racist remarks about the Rutgers women's basketball team, Stephen likewise uttered "ethnic facts" about NCAA basketball on his radio program (namely, that the Final Four logo looked like "some Hungarian" designed it).

Clips of Colbert on the Ert were styled to look like video feeds of the syndicated talk shows it parodied, complete with Stephen in his casual patriotic ensemble of a U.S.A. bomber jacket and stars and stripes baseball cap. Colbert on the Ert was brought back as a means to mirror controversial comments made by Rush Limbaugh, Glenn Beck, and Dr. Laura Schlessinger.

Colbert Platinum (& Colbert Aluminum) (2007-2014)

Appointment viewing for the super-wealthy! This segment was inspired by CNBC's *High Net Worth* show for extremely high-income viewers, and in it Stephen profiled luxury items like $1,800 travel dog bowls and personal submarines. Stephen introduced Colbert Platinum because advertisers paid premium rates for time during *High Net Worth*—even though the ratings were low—to access that valuable demographic. That's also why the segment was for Colbert Platinum members only, and non-members were directed to change the channel.

The first segment of Colbert Platinum focused on a shortage of butlers, valets, and yacht crews. America was no longer producing enough quality help. As a solution to this problem, Stephen made his butler Reginald available to stud. In a popular segment of Colbert Platinum, Stephen tried various meals that cost $1,000 around New York City, and then ran out on each check and snorted a line of edible 24k gold before vomiting in the bushes outside the last restaurant.

Because of the recession, Stephen introduced Colbert Aluminum in 2008 "for the scaled-back high-end viewer," or for those who have recently had a yacht repossessed. The real reason for the change? In an interview, Colbert said, "we stopped doing Colbert Platinum, actually, because the economy got so bad that we actually felt it bumming out the audience."

On August 19, 2009, Stephen officially declared the recession over and reintroduced Colbert Platinum, because "the signs of recovery are everywhere you look—as long as you only look at Wall Street."

Colbert Report Special ReporT (2005-2014)

Topics deserving of in-depth coverage got the Special ReporT treatment, with entire episodes dedicated to a singular theme, such as:

> Our Kids: What the Hell Is Wrong With Them?, which featured Stephen's interview with skateboarding icon Tony Hawk on a set styled like a 1970s basement, complete with beanbag chairs in place of Stephen's regular interview setup.

> The American Worker: A Hero's Tribute to the Besieged Workers of the American Jobscape, honoring "the big shoulders that hold America aloft in our global chicken fight."

> A Salute to the American Lady, a mea culpa to Stephen's female staff members (aka "plaintiffs") culminating with every audience member being crowned "Mrs. Colbert" with tiaras and sashes.

> American Pop Culture: It's Crumbelievable!, examining the importance of modern cultural icons.

A Nation Betrayed—A Fond Look Back: '74, with a chain-smoking, '70s-styled Stephen celebrating the 40th anniversary of Richard Nixon's resignation by interviewing Pat Buchanan and John W. Dean.

Colbertnation.com (2005-)

Today it's a slick, video-playing, user-friendly, and very official-looking website. In 2005? Not so much.

Colbertnation.com was always the show's official website, but it originally was made to be a parody of a fansite. Designed to look, feel, and read like a viewer's low-budget side project, the site was complete with crude html and old-school animated American flag gifs. The webmaster was Avery Gordon, a fictional 19-year-old Stephen fanboy. The site housed Avery's enthusiastic episode recaps, a letter from Stephen endorsing the site, chapters of Stephen's Tek Jansen book, fan fiction, and a page chronicling fans' Stephen sightings. This was all created by the show's original web writer, Rob Dubbin, who became a staff writer in 2006. Over the years, the site was redeveloped multiple times and now directs to the more official (in both appearance and application) version fans are familiar with, at http://thecolbertreport.cc.com.

Colboard.com (2006-2009)

What happens when parody becomes reality? Originally linked from the faux-fansite Colbertnation.com, the "Colboards" message boards became a legitimate gathering place for die-hard fans of the *Report*. The administrator was "Avery" (also colbertnation.com's webmaster), who was largely absent, and moderation duties were left to select frequent posters. The Colboards became read-only in 2009, with some fans speculating that the forum had become a liability due to the extreme nature of some posts. The Colboards were replaced for a short time with an official forum run by Comedy Central, and the archive was deleted when the domain registration lapsed in 2010.

Col-Bunker (2005)

It's always good to have a spare! The Col-Bunker, an exact replica of the *Colbert Report* set, was located 300 feet underground, directly below the original studio. Tad, the building manager, visited the Col-Bunker during Stephen's Emergency Evacuation Drill, but was trapped when the door jammed. Days later, Stephen still hadn't rescued him, because "the theoretical toxic gas or nuclear fallout or mutant crab army hasn't dispersed yet."

Cold War Update (2008-2014)

Rumors had been flying since 1989 that the Cold War was over, but Stephen didn't buy it. In this segment, Stephen reported on the news from former members of the Soviet bloc, including Cuba ("not the free part, where we detain people indefinitely"), North Korea, Russia, Yugoslavia, and China. Stephen knew the Cold War wasn't over because "1. People still speak Russian and 2. Case closed." In December of 2014, President Obama announced that the U.S. would "normalize" relations with Cuba, which Stephen intended to protest by hanging out on Cuban beaches and drinking Cuban rum.

Cooking with Feminists (2006)
(See also: Jane Fonda)

Kiss the cook! What do you do when two noted feminists are launching a women's radio network on your show? Get them into the kitchen immediately. Jane Fonda and Gloria Steinem baked an apple pie as they taught Stephen about the state of American feminism. The trio donned aprons and headed over to a kitchen set up between his desk and interview table. Stephen alternated between calling out baking directions and asking questions about feminism, and then began flirting with Fonda and Steinem. "Fight it," he told Jane Fonda, gesturing to his "Kiss the Cook" apron. Fonda and Steinem each kissed him on the cheek at the end of the segment, prompting Stephen to declare "I like feminists!" Stephen served ice cream with the finished apple pie as the women kissed him on the cheek, leading him to characterize the segment as "an ice cream three-way."

Craziest F#?king Thing I've Ever Heard (2006-2014)

When weird news wouldn't fit anywhere else, but simply had to be reported, Stephen covered it in this short but sweet segment. A snake and a hamster living together in harmony at a Chinese zoo? A plant that produces both tomatoes and potatoes? A bullfighter gored through his throat so deeply that the bull's horn came through his mouth? These are some of the craziest f#?king things Stephen's ever heard!

On the other end of the spectrum: a newly-discovered moth that "alights on the neck of a sleeping magpie" and drinks its tears? That's the most Most Poetic F#?king Thing (2007) Stephen's ever heard.

Credits (2005-2014)

He started out as simply "Stephen Colbert", but his name grew to be almost as big as his ego. Under the "Executive Producer" title, it appeared as: The Reverend Sir Doctor Sen. Stephen T. Mos Def Colbert D.F.A. Heavyweight Champion of the World** La Premiere Dame de France.

Where did all that come from? Let's break it down:

> Reverend (2013)
> In order to officiate the Government Shutdown Wedding of the Century, Stephen was ordained on the Internet by American Marriage Ministries, "the most prestigious ministry certification you can get online while also being on the toilet."

> Sir (2009)
> Guest Queen Noor of Jordan "knighted" Stephen—using Aragorn's sword from *The Lord of the Rings*—in exchange for his support of the anti-nuclear weapons organization Global Zero.

> Doctor and D.F.A. (2006)
> Stephen added this after "earning" his honorary Doctorate of Fine Arts from Knox College.

Sen. (2012)
This one showed up after South Carolina Sen. Jim DeMint resigned, and a survey by Public Policy Polling indicated that voters favored Stephen as his replacement. But despite his strong numbers—and Stephen's obvious interest in the gig—South Carolina Gov. Nikki Haley declined to appoint him (or any other interim senator).

T. (2006)
Colbert's actual middle name, Tyrone. (One of the show's inconsistencies: Stephen's middle name has also been cited as "Tiberius.")

Mos Def (2011)
Stephen interviewed hip hop artist Yasiin Bey, who explained that he didn't want to be known as Mos Def anymore. Stephen then proclaimed, "Good news! Yasiin says I can be Mos Def now!"

Heavyweight Champion of the World** (2012)
When Mike Tyson cancelled (or "forfeited") his appearance on the *Report*, Stephen proclaimed himself champ by default—with asterisks to clarify that he hadn't actually defeated Tyson.

La Premiere Dame de France (2014)
Colbert was invited to a White House dinner, which French President François Hollande—embroiled in a sex scandal—attended without longtime partner Valerie Trierweiler. Colbert was assigned the seat next to President Hollande, which prompted Stephen to proclaim himself the new First Lady of France.

D

DaColbert Code (2005-2009)

Stephen didn't believe in polls. He made his predictions by "looking for superficial connections in seemingly random information." A parody of Dan Brown's *The Da Vinci Code*, the DaColbert Code unlocked mysteries and predicted the future, using free associations and words that sound similar to each other to get to the truth—whether Stephen liked it or not. In 2008, Stephen repeatedly predicted the election of Barack Obama, no matter how many times he tried starting with a different election-related word. The DaColbert Code also correctly predicted the winners of the five biggest Academy Awards categories in 2008 and 2009.

Daft Punk (2013)

The 2013 edition of StePhest Colbchella had just one headliner slated to perform: Daft Punk.

Operative word: "had."

It was to be a straightforward appearance by the French electronic music duo (Guy-Manuel de Homem-Christo and Thomas Bangalter) as their silent, helmet-wearing robot personas. But when the big day came, there were no robots to be seen—only an ambitious filmed dance sequence, a public shaming of an MTV executive, and morning-after bloggers questioning whether the whole thing was a ruse from the beginning. As Colbert later explained to podcaster (and *Colbert Report* warm-up comic) Paul Mecurio, the events were far from fabricated.

The booking began normally enough. About six weeks prior to the scheduled appearance, Colbert's producers told him the Daft Punk guys were fans, and would like to come on the show. The duo was booked for an interview and performance on Tuesday, August 6, 2013.

A week later, word came that they didn't want to be interviewed.

Easy enough to get around, Colbert thought. He considered doing a six-minute monologue as a verbose Pitchfork Media-style journalist, reciting a heady buzzword-filled question about their album's metaphors and influences while the robots simply nodded. Then, they'd perform their hit song, "Get Lucky."

Another week went by, and word came that they wouldn't even perform their song. No interview, and no performance. Was it still worth flying them in from Paris at the show's expense, when there wasn't anything for them to do? Colbert, rather than cancel the appearance, saw this as a challenge and remained determined to make it work.

More content was needed, so the filming of the infamous "Get Lucky" dance sequence began, featuring Stephen dancing to the song alongside various celebrities. It was originally intended to function as a reminder to Daft Punk of how good their song was, since they weren't performing it. An anonymous *Colbert Report* staff member later posted to Reddit stating that the justification later in the process was that the robots would be unable to move in their suits, so Stephen would effectively be performing in their place. Little did anyone know how useful the montage would turn out to be.

First to be shot was Jeff Bridges (a guest on the *Report* on July 18), dancing *Big Lebowski*-style with Stephen on a staircase backstage. Also shot in-studio were Hugh Laurie (a guest on August 5) being faux-punched by Stephen, and Matt Damon (there to film a different pretaped piece on July 30 to air on the August 8 episode) dancing alone inside a wind tunnel money booth. The full cast of *Breaking Bad* appeared as guests on *Charlie Rose*, which Stephen interrupted mid-interview to steal Cranston away and dance with him on roller skates as a throwback to his *Malcolm in the Middle* character, Hal. Jon Stewart, in Jordan filming the movie *Rosewater*, videoconferenced a dance of his own, and Stephen's comic book alter-ego Tek Jansen busted his moves in animated form. Colbert danced onto the *Late Night with Jimmy Fallon* stage for an impromptu, unexplained dance-off with Fallon that aired on the July 29th episode of *Late Night*, which turned out to be for the montage. He also burst out of a closet and danced through Henry Kissinger's Washington office, danced with the Rockettes in a rehearsal space, and made a cameo on *America's Got Talent* (aired only in the montage) during their New York audition tapings. July 25 *Report* guest Senator Olympia Snowe danced with Colbert after taping her segment, but it would not make the final cut.

While filming of the montage was underway, Colbert's producers were informed that Robin Thicke was available to perform. This would solve the problem of having a musical guest, at least partially. Thicke satisfied the commitment to the episode's sponsor, Hyundai. But Colbert was still determined to create something out of the Daft Punk appearance.

The solution was to have both Thicke and Daft Punk on the show. That is, until MTV got wind of the Thicke appearance. He was scheduled to perform exclusively on the MTV Video Music Awards (VMAs) in late August, and his *Colbert Report* appearance would be a conflict.

Unswayed, Colbert made a few phone calls. Thicke's *Report* appearance was given the green light by Van Toffler, president of MTV Networks Music & Logo Group. Thicke pretaped his performance of "Blurred Lines" in front of the July 30 *Colbert Report* audience.

But there would be more problems to solve. Daft Punk wasn't entirely on board with the material Colbert had come up with, because it focused too much on the fact that they weren't performing. The bit was too passive, and didn't give the robots an opportunity to do anything fun. The duo had some ideas of their own, so they collaborated with Colbert. After an intensive weekend of writing, Colbert generated material that both he and Daft Punk were happy with, and both parties looked forward to executing it in the studio that Tuesday.

But not so fast.

On Monday afternoon, Colbert's co-executive producer Meredith Bennett took Colbert aside and informed him that Daft Punk was also scheduled to perform on the VMAs.

After a brief moment of dread, Colbert realized that since he'd successfully sorted out the Robin Thicke appearance, surely he'd be able to do the same for

Daft Punk. At 2 p.m. he again called MTV, which set in motion conversations on MTV's side. But what followed for the rest of the day was silence.

Now what? Does Daft Punk get on the plane? Yes. Colbert told the guys not to worry. MTV is a sister network to Comedy Central, after all. He said he was confident it was going to work out, regardless of any exclusivity agreement.

"I don't think my joyful success diminishes anyone else's joyful success. Especially something three weeks from now on the VMAs," he later said. "How does it harm them in any way?"

Late Monday night, nobody on the Comedy Central side had heard anything from MTV. It wasn't until 11:30 a.m. Tuesday—the day of the show—that Colbert learned the appearance wasn't going to happen. Daft Punk was forced to choose, and they chose the VMAs.

Commence rewrites. All of Act One would be dedicated to what had unfolded over the past 16 hours.

"All I want to do is accurately explain what happened, then embody my character's emotional reaction to it," Colbert told Mecurio. "As much as this mattered to me as a producer, my character can't ever lose . . . So he has to throw a tantrum."

That "tantrum" included a takedown of Toffler that the media would call "astoundingly brash" and "brutally funny." It included repeatedly mangling Toffler's name, giving the wrong date and time of the VMAs, and mocking an e-mail from Toffler that had been forwarded to Colbert by a third party.

The actual email read:

> "Not sure I can help you with that one. The label and the band sold us hard on some clip and live appearance based on them not showing up anywhere else—so this is a new one. Checked with my peeps and will check again but they're feeling funky on this one."

Colbert also filtered his true frustration regarding the exclusivity agreement through his character, with the following gem:

"If Daft Punk were on my show, people wouldn't tune in to the VMAs almost a month from now. That's how music works. You love a band, you see them once, then never want to see them again. That's why after the Beatles went on *Ed Sullivan*, they dropped off the face of the Earth."

It then dawned on Stephen that this was MTV—and perhaps he'd been "Daft Punk'd" by Ashton Kutcher. Stephen called for Kutcher to reveal himself. Enter Kutcher, complete with a signature *Punk'd*-era trucker hat.

Stephen did throw to the dance montage they'd created, saying that he didn't care what MTV thought, and he didn't even need Daft Punk in order to give his audience a Daft Punk performance. To cap off the show, Stephen pleaded for an international pop star to show up and sing the song of the summer, and a pretaped Robin Thicke obliged.

Epilogue: Daft Punk's (non-performing) appearance on the VMAs would be completely overshadowed by a twerking Miley Cyrus. Good choice, gentlemen.

Dartmouth (2005-2014)

"Stephen's" alma mater. He majored in history, graduating in the top 47 percent of his class. He also wrote for the *Dartmouth Review*, and performed in the all-male a cappella group The Sing Dynasty.

Das Booty (2008)

Who's laughing now? Stephen. Because it turns out he was right all along about something very important: Nazi gold! Das Booty: The Search for Hitler's Gold became Stephen's latest international adventure when CNN reported that treasure hunters were looking for two tons of Nazi gold. To finance his own search mission, Stephen planned to sell T-shirts that said "I DIG HITLER" on the front, and "'S GOLD" on the back. The shirts would be on sale "as soon as anyone is willing to print them."

In part two of the international adventure, Stephen reported that the only good news out there, given the tough economic times, was Nazi gold. The value of gold hit a record high of $1,000/oz, leading Stephen to conclude that he had given gold the Colbert Bump just by talking about it—but hoped that he hadn't done the same for the Nazis.

Stephen announced that "a group of nice old men from Argentina" had bought the I DIG HITLER T-shirts he'd had trouble selling, so his trip was financed. Stephen tried to send "Bobby the Stage Manager" (who turned out to be Kareem Abdul-Jabbar, filling in while Bobby competed on America's Next Top Stage Manager) to Germany. Kareem agreed to go, but only if he had a weapon, because it might be dangerous. Stephen offered Kareem a gun and a whip, but they settled on a basketball.

Dead to Me (2005-2007)

"Welcome to your nightmare!" What do owls, the cast of *Friends*, and bow tie pasta have in common? They're all dead to Stephen. Even worse than finding yourself on Stephen's On Notice board was ending up on the Dead to Me board, from which there was no redemption. Stephen introduced Dead to Me after a video of singer Juan Gabriel tripping on his pant cuffs and falling off a stage went viral. In order to make room for "pant cuffs" on the On Notice board, "New York intellectuals" were bumped to the Dead to Me board because Stephen had warned them about their introspection, turtlenecks, and green tea, but they didn't listen.

Delawert Report (2010)

Stephen goes local! Former Republican senate candidate Christine O'Donnell refused to go on any national news programs, saying she'd only be interviewed by reporters in her home state of Delaware. What a coincidence, then, that Stephen just happened to do a local version of the *Report* right there in the Diamond State. Cut to footage of the *Delawert Report*, a low-budget version of *The Colbert Report* aired in 4:3 standard definition and featuring plain blue drapes and a potted plant as a backdrop. Instead of Brooks Brothers, Stephen wore a cheap sport coat, and The DelaWørd (the localized version of The Wørd) wasn't even accompanied by onscreen graphics, only a whiteboard. (From just off-camera, writer/producer Paul Dinello slowly wiped off the previous statement and wrote in the next one.)

Democralypse Now: The Delightful Dismemberment of the Democratic Hopescape (2008)

The Democratic Party was self-destructing, and Stephen couldn't have been happier about all the infighting during the 2008 presidential primaries. This "implosion of the American left" was introduced with an animated intro featuring a donkey running into a pole, splitting itself in half (part for Obama, part for Clinton), splattering its blood everywhere, and somehow catching on fire. Stephen told the cheering crowd, "You might be seeing that graphic again." And they did. Across a half-dozen segments, Stephen gleefully reported on any misfortune befalling either candidate, whether it was a campaign strategist's resignation or a campaign advisor making inflammatory remarks. Democralypse Now wrapped up when Hillary dropped out of the race.

Difference Makers (2006-2014)

Sometimes, the real heroes are just "normal American citizens" making a difference. In this prerecorded segment similar in style to the field pieces produced on *The Daily Show*, the Difference Makers were people who earnestly promoted wacky or misguided causes, while Stephen narrated over patriotic music. This is one of the few segments Colbert never appeared in. He was present as a voiceover only, usually saying things that were directly contradicted by statements from the Difference Makers.

The first Difference Maker Stephen profiled was Tim Donnelly. Donnelly believes there is such a thing as "a great day to be a vigilante." He led a group of Americans to the Mexican border to build a fence and sing the national anthem—in *English*. Other Difference Makers included Johnna Mink, an exotic dance instructor who believes pole dancing is "better than classical feminism," and Patrick Rodgers, a fanged homeowner who stood up to Wells Fargo by "foreclosing on the forecloser" while possibly being a vampire.

DonorsChoose.org (2007-2014)

An organization close to the real Stephen's heart, DonorsChoose.org is a nonprofit that supports projects in classrooms across the country, and allows donors to decide how their donations will be allocated. Viewers donated money to the charity through a lengthy list of *Report*-related initiatives, including the Rally to Restore Sanity And/Or Fear, Stephen singing "Friday" on *Late Night*, the auctions of Stephen's fireplace portraits, and Operation Iraqi Stephen.

Colbert has been a member of the DonorsChoose.org Board of Directors since 2009. He gave DonorsChoose.org gift cards to every *Report* guest, in hopes they would continue giving on their own.

Doom Bunker (2009)

Fever dream or revelation? Glenn Beck's "War Room" segment took viewers on a tour through his worst-case-scenario outcomes of an Obama presidency. Stephen praised Beck for his latest work, and encouraged Glenn to "crank up the crazy and rip off the knob." Stephen knew that Beck could not prepare the nation for disaster all by himself, so the *Report* studio was transformed into Stephen Colbert's Doom Bunker.

Stephen invited Col. (Ret.) Jack Jacobs and *Wall Street Journal* writer Stephen Moore to discuss horrific doomsday scenarios that Stephen himself made up. Moore, who had also been on Glenn Beck's "War Room," acknowledged that Stephen's Doom Bunker had more fog. Before asking his guests to discuss his doomsday scenarios, Stephen clarified that they were "crazy" and "not gonna happen," and that he was not looking for solutions. He just wanted to discuss how terrible the hypothetical scenario would be. Stephen's prediction for 2014? The Dow Jones is trading below 250 points, the koala pox epidemic has wiped out the world's livestock, and soybeans are money.

Doris Kearns Goodwin (2006-2014)

In addition to being a guest on the show, the presidential historian was also the object of Stephen's fantasies. Despite Goodwin being an unlikely sex symbol—and 20 years his senior—Stephen's references to inappropriate masturbation were often followed by his "apologies to Doris Kearns Goodwin." In a 2014 appearance, she accepted his apologies, but admitted she would miss hearing about them when the show ended. Stephen promised that in the future, he'd call her up and apologize directly.

Doritos (2007-2014)

Set the product placement alert level to orange—Dorito orange, that is. Doritos was the official sponsor of Stephen Colbert's Nacho Cheese Doritos 2008 Presidential Campaign Coverage! After all, Stephen might be a devout Catholic, but he was also "a devout corporate whore." When Stephen first ran for president in 2007, he realized that he would need a sponsor to help him cover the filing fees. Stephen learned that Doritos could not legally sponsor Stephen's campaign, but the "sponsorship" was a great opportunity to spoof branded entertainment.

Stephen insisted that he was under no obligation to promote the "zesty, robust taste" of Doritos. But that didn't stop Senator John Edwards from accusing Stephen of being "stained by corporate corruption and nacho cheese." In 2008, Stephen realized that though Doritos could not sponsor a campaign, they could sponsor Stephen's campaign *coverage*. Thus, Hail to the Cheese Stephen Colbert's Nacho Cheese Doritos 2008 Presidential Campaign Coverage was born.

Like Bud Light Lime, Doritos became a big part of the show. Doritos featured in Stephen's Thought for Food segment when Stephen tried some new mystery flavors on the show. Stephen also suggested that Doritos Locos Tacos from Taco Bell could fix the global economy because "a crunchy Doritos shell can increase the sales appeal of anything." And when documentary filmmaker Morgan Spurlock came on the show to promote his movie about product placement, Stephen debuted a suit jacket made of Doritos bags.

Dressage (2012)

The official *Colbert Report* Sport of the Summer! Dressage is an equestrian sport in the Olympic games that is judged by the precision and grace of choreographed movements performed by a horse and rider team. When Stephen found out that Ann Romney (wife of 2012 presidential candidate Mitt Romney) owned an Olympics-bound dressage horse named Rafalca, he instantly became a lifelong fan. Stephen defended the sport against Fox News commentator Charles Krauthammer's characterization of "horse ballet" as elitist, insisting that "Dressage is not hoity-toity! It is frou-frou! Get your facts straight."

Then Stephen got "down and dirty in the world of velvet top hats" to prove that dressage is a blue-collar sport. He headed to Hawthorne Hill in New Jersey to meet with former dressage Olympian and 2012 US Equestrian Team coach Michael Barisone to learn how to ride. He showed up in full Western gear, complete with a cowboy hat and neckerchief — entirely wrong for dressage. Stephen had only one question for Barisone about his official sport of the summer: "What is it?"

After determining that he was required to overcome his fear of horses to learn dressage, Stephen agreed to a lesson. Barisone promised that if Stephen succeeded, he could wear the tiara Barisone had won in a dressage competition. Stephen came close to quitting even before he started, because Barisone couldn't absolutely guarantee that Conchita would not "kick his skull off his shoulders." But in the end, he couldn't resist the tiara.

Properly turned out in tall black boots, white riding breeches, a shadbelly (a tailcoat for riding), and white gloves, Stephen was ready to "mount his lady." Barisone said that in order to earn the tiara, Stephen would have to do a little *piaffe*—or, as Stephen called it, "fancy prancing." With "a lifetime of 20 minutes of training," Stephen achieved one of the hardest disciplines in dressage, and got to wear the tiara.

Stephen celebrated with a glass of champagne and a little dance of his own to *Kokomo* by the Beach Boys (the same song Romney's horse Rafalca had performed freestyle dressage to), wearing a plastic horse head and hooves.

Duets (2006-2014)

Sing with a star? You didn't have to ask Stephen twice—he'd sit in with his musical guests at any opportunity. Notable collaborations included:

Barry Manilow: "I Write the Songs" (2006)
Manilow may have defeated Colbert at that year's Emmys in the Outstanding Individual Performance In A Variety Or Music Program category, but Stephen put aside his anger just long enough to join Manilow for one of his classics.

Tony Bennett: "They All Laughed" (2007)
Colbert initially turned down the opportunity to sing with his 2007 Emmy nemesis Tony Bennett due to time constraints, but when he entered the studio to greet the crooner, he couldn't resist.

John Legend: "The Girl Is Mine" (2008)
Legend started off performing this classic Michael Jackson / Paul McCartney duet on his own, but Stephen entered for verse two dressed in a recreation of McCartney's outfit from the *Say Say Say* album cover: black shirt and pants, white vest, and red sneakers. The duo gave the old song a new patriotic twist: the "girl" in this case being the Statue of Liberty.

Alicia Keys: "Empire State of Mind" (2009)
Stephen told Keys his one beef about this musical tribute to New York City was that the references just didn't resonate with suburban, middle-class guys like himself. Keys then performed the song with her full band, with a special guest for the second half: Stephen. Wearing a pinstripe suit with a pinstripe hood sewn onto it, he replaced the original Jay-Z rap with lyrics reflecting a suburban visitor's view of New York life such as: "Ticket to *The Lion King*, that show is fantastic / Leave half an hour early so I can beat the traffic." It took Colbert a few tries to get the lengthy, rapid-fire lyrics right, and in the final product viewers saw, his relief is evident.

Elvis Costello: "Cheap Reward" (2009)
One of Colbert's strongest vocal performances on the show. With its composer under the weather and relegated to guitar duties only, Colbert crooned Costello's song as if it were created for him.

Pete Seeger: "If I Had a Hammer" (2012)
This song was recorded when Seeger was a guest in 2012, but wasn't aired until the singer's death in 2014. A more common practice later in the show's run, fans believe there to be many unaired musical performances like this in the *Report* vault.

Plácido Domingo: "La Donna E Mobile" (2012)
This well-known piece from Verdi's *Rigoletto* got the full Stephen treatment, which is either a good thing or a bad thing, depending on who you ask. While Colbert couldn't compete with Domingo when it came to vocal prowess, what he lacked in operatic experience he made up for in style by wearing a tuxedo with tails and a white tie.

Audra McDonald: "Summertime" (2012)
The Tony Award-winning actress/singer has appeared on the show multiple times. She and Stephen sang this Gershwin number in early 2012, and McDonald returned in December for an up-tempo rendition of the Christmas classic "Baby, It's Cold Outside."

Dolly Parton: "Love Is Like a Butterfly" (2012)
An obviously nervous Colbert, both singing and playing guitar, had a few false starts as he performed this country favorite alongside his childhood crush. Parton gently called him on his trepidation, after which he was able to get through the song successfully.

Neil Young: "Who's Gonna Stand Up? (and Save the Earth)" (2014)
Like his duet with Alicia Keys, Stephen felt Young's environmental anthem should be revised to suit his own ideals. Young yielded to Stephen between verses so he could pose the counterpoint: "what if the dolphins attacked us first?"

Dungeons and Dragons (2006-2011)

One major part of Colbert's life was also part of his character's: playing DnD. While only mentioned a few times on the *Report*, both Stephens grew up loving the fantasy role-playing game, and both mourned the loss of their favorite character: a Lawful Good paladin.

E

Eagle's Nest (2005-2006)

Stephen's nickname for the *Report* studio, early in the show's run.

Ear (2005-2014)

Fans endearingly refer to Stephen's misshapen right ear as his "wonky" ear. Colbert explained to the *New Yorker* that it's the result of having "this weird tumor as a kid, and they scooped it out with a melon baller." He performed his "ear trick" on the show, whereby he folds the lobe into it, and pops it out with a wink of his right eye. Despite being deaf in that ear, his character miraculously still used it on occasion: when he conversed with his handgun, Sweetness, she whispered to him through his right ear; and he listened to the 2006 State of the Union Address through a single earphone in it.

Edit Challenge (2007)

Stephen had no use for a cutting-room floor. When two members of Congress said that Stephen had the advantage of editing to make his Better Know a District interviewees look foolish, he deemed such a thing impossible. He was willing to prove it by providing the Nation with footage of journalist Gwen Ifill interviewing him, which viewers could then try to manipulate by making him look bad. Good luck accomplishing that! Of course, the scripted interview was crammed with phrases which, taken out of context, would incriminate Stephen, such as "the troops are stupid" and "I can't get enough cock."

Many viewers saw this series of clearly perceivable edit points as the completed joke in and of itself. Others viewed it as a true challenge, and did create edited videos. While many of them still exist on YouTube today, there was never a follow-up on the show.

Eleanor Holmes Norton (2006, 2008-09, 2014)

ColberT, or Col-BEAR—which is it? That's what Rep. Eleanor Holmes Norton demanded to know when Stephen first interviewed her for Better Know a District. The congresswoman represents Washington, D.C.—where Colbert was born—and was described by Stephen as a "fake congresswoman" because D.C. does not get a vote in Congress.

Norton was a fan favorite for being a straight-shooter and a firecracker, able to take Stephen's character seriously while clearly being in on the joke. Stephen attempted to "nail" Norton for her blank voting record, to her (lack of) amusement. He also suggested that Washington, D.C. is not part of the United States of America, because it is not a state. Norton responded by giving Stephen "civics lessons," and turned the tables on him by grilling him about the French pronunciation of his surname. Stephen said that, as a D.C. native, Norton is not from America. Norton said, "anybody who pronounces ColberT Col-BEAR is not from the United States—which part of France are you from?"

Norton appeared again alongside the also-notorious Rep. Robert Wexler during the 2006 Midterm Midtacular election special, supposedly as the Republican counterpoint to Wexler. Norton refused to "just be a Republican for one night" as Stephen requested, calling him ColberT as Stephen tried to speak over her. She returned again when a bill she sponsored to grant D.C. voting rights in Congress was taken off the floor. Norton also promised to make Stephen an honorary citizen of, and give him a key to, the city of Washington, D.C. if D.C. residents were ever granted statehood.

In 2014, Norton released a press statement congratulating Colbert on his acceptance of the *Late Show* hosting job at CBS. Reflecting on her many appearances on the *Report*, she wrote, "In using—and abusing—the District, Colbert found in me a willing and defenseless foil."

Emmys (2006-2015)

"As Mother Theresa said, it's not enough to win, others must lose." Nothing made Stephen happier than tangible proof of his greatness, and nothing made him more bitter than losing. One of Colbert's Emmys, earned during his time at *The Daily Show*, adorned the set's fireplace mantle from the day of the *Report*'s premiere—and he'd take any opportunity to pull it (or his others) out from under his desk to remind the world he had 'em.

For the three years prior to the category being eliminated, Colbert was nominated for Outstanding Individual Performance In A Variety Or Music Program. He was beaten all three times: by Barry Manilow (2006), Tony Bennett (2007), and Don Rickles (2008). Each time their names were evoked on the *Report*, a begrudged Stephen would react by shaking his fist at the "Over the Shoulder" (or OTS) photo of the winner displayed next to him.

When he gloated that he'd finally beaten out Jon Stewart's *Daily Show* in 2013 for Outstanding Variety Series, Stewart entered the *Report* studio to remind Stephen that he technically hadn't broken his 10-year winning streak. Stewart is an executive producer on the *Report*, "so I win again, motherfucker!"

In 2014 Colbert repeated his win in that category. The following night's episode of the *Report* had been pretaped weeks earlier, to give the show's staff more time to head home from Los Angeles. At the top of the show, viewers saw a post-ceremony cellphone video of a seemingly out-of-character Colbert, award in hand, thanking the Nation.

Over the course of the series, *The Colbert Report* earned a total of 41 Emmy nominations.

Enemy Within (2008-2014)

It was only a semi-regular segment, so perhaps the Nation should be happy that there are so few "hidden dangers" facing America.

Similar in style to People Who Are Destroying America, Stephen narrated pretaped stories about seemingly innocuous issues that he blew out of proportion. These dangers included a 10-year-old Kansas boy convincing his city council to eliminate a ban on hedgehogs as pets (despite their potential for unleashing disease upon the world), and unicyclists in New York City getting away with (potential) murder because the city's Pedestrian Rights & Safety code doesn't mention unicycles.

Esteban Colbert (2009)

A member of Stephen's flock of faithful fans, Esteban Colbert is a peregrine falcon who made his nest on top of the City Hall building in San José, California. He was named after Stephen by Chuck Reed, mayor of San José and proud member of the Colbert Nation. The city installed a FalconCam so fans could watch his every move online, and there is footage of Esteban Colbert eating lunch available on YouTube. Esteban became a father of four in 2009, with his mate Clara, but was subsequently ousted from his nest by Clara's new beau, Fernando El Cohete.

Esteban Colberto (2006-2014)

Chicaaaaaaaaaaas! Esteban Colberto (played by Colbert) was Stephen's Latino counterpart. Esteban always appeared wearing bronzer, a thin mustache, and a garish suit, flanked by two dancing "chicas" (Latina women). He was a self-described Mexican, and hosted a Spanish language version of the *Report* called *Colberto Reporto Gigante*—a parody of Univision's long-running variety show *Sábado Gigante*. Esteban was introduced in 2006 in a Formidable Opponent segment about immigration. Stephen said Esteban was there to make the point that even TV hosts' jobs are not safe from illegal immigrants: "He'll do your job for half your salary!"

Esteban was frequently consulted about immigration and unrest in Latin American countries. After Mitt Romney's infamous 2012 appearance on Univision where he appeared to be spray-tanned and pandering to the Latino vote, Esteban said he had a lot in common with Romney, including that his grandfather had lived in Mexico with "muchas chicas." Esteban also revealed that, although he is a social conservative, he has a thing for Rachel Maddow.

Esteban always spoke to Stephen in Spanish (subtitled in English), and Stephen responded in English—which Esteban always understood. So perhaps it shouldn't have been a surprise to Stephen when, during Esteban's final appearance on the *Report*, he revealed that he could speak perfect English and got his Masters in Chemical Engineering from Penn State University.

F

Fallback Position (2008-2014)

No job is too tough for Stephen. In Stephen Colbert's Fallback Position, Stephen proved that he could do anything. On the off chance that the *Report* might not go on forever, Stephen explored alternative career paths (though never the option of hosting other late-night shows). Professionals showed Stephen what it takes to be an NFL quarterback, an astronaut, and a migrant worker. He started off skeptical that any of those careers could be as much fun as his job, but by the end of a brief interview with each professional, he was sold.

Stephen was always honest about his limitations, admitting to Steve Lindsey during his astronaut training that he has a spastic colon, lashes out in zero gravity, and needs a lot of time alone. But he never let these limitations hold him back from his goals. Stephen told former Redskins coach Joe Gibbs that he wanted "the position that gets me the most attention, the most money, and the most supermodels, with the least amount of physical contact"—quarterback. Whether Stephen heard the call to become a spy, play professional tennis, or pilot a Thunderbird, he was eager and ready to start right away—regardless of whether he was qualified.

Fantasies Board (2007)
(See also: Jane Fonda)

Golf with Nixon, attend Hogwarts, spend a weekend with Dr. House, and—until 2007—Jane Fonda. They all appeared on Stephen's Fantasy Board, the antithesis of the On Notice and Dead to Me Boards. Stephen moved his fantasies about Fonda and her "soft, moist lips" to the On Notice Board in 2007—good news for the ladies, as that left an open space for a new fantasy.

Filliam H. Muffman (2006-2014)

(See also: Character breaks)

Step aside, Brangelina. There's a new celebrity couple name in town. What do you get what you combine William H. Macy and Felicity Huffman? Filliam H. Muffman. It's a marketable name combination—and having one of those was the first of Stephen's Laws of Love, guaranteeing a successful (celebrity) relationship. (The term also works great in Scrabble, now that they allow proper names.) Felicity Huffman told *USA Today*, "I love Stephen Colbert, but I'm afraid to go near him."

Finale (2014)

(See also: Cheating Death, Sweetness, Toss)

After nine years, *The Colbert Report* aired its final episode on December 18, 2014.

For weeks leading up to the finale, Stephen's friend "Grimmy," the Grim Reaper, made mysterious appearances in the *Report* studio. The foreshadowing suggested Stephen would be killed off (although Colbert told a studio audience months earlier that this wouldn't be the case). Grimmy was listed as the guest for the final episode, compounding suspicions.

Act I

It began like any other night. Stephen spent a few minutes on a news story (in this case, used vehicles from the U.S. being exported to Syria and used in their civil war), and reported on the funds raised by the raffle of his set.

The tone shifted into finale mode with an edition of The Wørd ("Same to you, pal"), devoted to the topic so many journalists had expounded on that week: Stephen's legacy.

Stephen claimed he did something more important than change the world: he "samed" it, as proven by how many current news stories were repeats of 2005's headlines.

"When this show began, I promised you a revolution. And I delivered, because technically one revolution is 360 degrees right back to where we were," he said.

He also delivered on his promise to teach the Colbert Nation that the truth doesn't come from your head, but from your gut. After all, the Nation supported Stephen's run for president, Colbert SuperPAC, the treadmill in space, and the Rally to Restore Sanity And/Or Fear.

"All those incredible things people said I did. . . . None of that was really me. You the Nation did all of that. I just got paid for it," he said.

"So in the annals of history, or whatever orifice they stuff it in, let no one say that what we did together wasn't important, or influential, or importulential. Y'see, from the beginning of my show it was my goal to live up to the name of this network: Influence Central. And if all we achieved over the last nine years was come into your home each night and help you make a difficult day a little bit better? Man, what a waste. And Nation, I want you to know, if I had to do it all again? If I could do it with you, I would do it the same."

Same to you, pal.

Act II

Stephen gave a final heartfelt thank-you to The Prescott Group ("How do you get to Prescott headquarters? Malpractice, malpractice, malpractice.") and cued the opening of Cheating Death. The familiar black and white parody of the chess scene in *The Seventh Seal* began—except this time, Grimmy reached across the chessboard to strangle Stephen. He fought back, pulled out Sweetness, and shot Grimmy.

Standing over his body, Stephen realized what this meant: having killed Death, he was now immortal.

Act III

He'd had one commercial break to get accustomed to his newfound immortality, but Stephen still wasn't sure what the future held.

"I was going to say goodbye. But now that I'll live forever, who knows?"

With Randy Newman accompanying him on piano, Stephen began singing the wartime classic "We'll Meet Again."

Jon Stewart walked on stage to sing along with him—and almost 100 past *Report* guests and friends followed, as disparate as Big Bird, Henry Kissinger, Willie Nelson, and Colbert's wife and children. Pre-taped participants included Bill Clinton, J. J. Abrams, Pussy Riot, and a group of current and past *Report* staff members (with Colbert among them).

Once the joyful sing-along went to black, the scene reopened on the empty studio. As an emotional score swelled, a single camera floated across the empty audience bleachers, across Stephen's desk, and over to the fireplace. But the portrait hanging above it was missing the image of Stephen himself—as was the portrait within it, and the portrait within that.

Outside, the camera panned up the side of the darkened studio to the roof, where Stephen stood proudly holding Captain America's shield and asked, "what do I do now?"

Up pulled Santa Claus in his sleigh, which happened to have one open seat available for Stephen (the others were occupied by Abraham Lincoln and Alex Trebek). He climbed in with some trepidation, but Trebek assured him that he wouldn't have to say goodbye forever.

"We'll always be there for the American people whenever they need us the most," Trebek said.

While Stephen was only partially convinced, on account of Trebek being Canadian, he accepted his place among his fellow immortals and flew up above the Manhattan skyline.

Act IV

As his new journey began in Santa's sleigh, it was finally time to say farewell.

"Well folks, we've finally come to the end of *The Colbert Report*. Nine great years, 1,447 wonderful episodes, I've just got way too many people to thank. First and foremost, everybody who worked so hard every day to make something special. All of our friends and family for putting up with our long hours. The network for giving us the chance to begin with. And of course all of the guests who came on, thousands of them, just too many to thank. So y'know what, I'll just thank Mavis Staples. Mavis, if you could just call everybody tomorrow, that would be great. Thanks. Oh, and you, the Colbert Nation. We couldn't have done it without you. Thank you for being such a big part of it. That was *fun*."

"From Eternity, I'm Stephen Colbert. Jon?"

Cut to Stewart at his *Daily Show* desk.

"Thanks for that report, Stephen," he said, effectively framing the entire series as a *Daily Show* segment. "Now here it is, your Moment of Zen."

That Moment of Zen was footage of Stewart and Colbert bantering off-air as they prepared to do a toss in 2010 (incorrectly captioned as June 3 on the finale, it was filmed before the "Times Square Bomber" toss on May 3).

Stewart mocked the scripted exchange they were about to tape with a stilted "what are you doing, Stephen?" and Colbert responded with an equally affected "I'm getting angry at liberals." The accurate summation, predictably, made them both laugh.

The *Report* credits rolled for the last time, accompanied by one of Colbert's favorite songs: "Holland, 1945" by Neutral Milk Hotel.

Flameside (2005-2013)

More common early in the show's run, a "flameside" was the writers' nickname for an Act 4 segment featuring Stephen sitting next to his fireplace, quietly pondering a topic (such as how none of society's rules apply on Leap Day) in front of the fake videotaped fire.

Stephen noted that he used to have a real fire burning "before it got shut down by Big Brother Fire Marshal, just because it had no 'chimney', and the carbon monoxide was 'killing' my audience."

But that never stopped Stephen from treating the fake videotaped fire as though it was real, warming his hands by it or tossing a log at the screen.

Formidable Opponent (2005-2014)

Who's more worthy of debating Stephen than Stephen himself? A mind-bending execution of both performance and direction, this segment had Stephen arguing both sides of an issue. The footage "cut" from a normal image of Stephen to a mirrored image of Stephen, wearing a different tie and standing against a different background, but there were no actual edit points. It was all done through the magic of green screens: one behind him, and pieces of green screen making the stripes on his tie. The shot was simply flipped as he executed both sides of the argument in real time.

The two Stephens debated a hot-button issue like Don't Ask, Don't Tell; offshore drilling; or immigration. Each character had a different perspective, as Colbert explained to SiriusXM host Pete Dominick:

> "I think of my character, the character you see every night, as being split into two people. There's a logical but ineffectual one, and there's an illogical and completely aggressive one. . . . One of the rules that I make for myself and for the writers when we write a Formidable Opponent is that you must come up with a reasonable argument on both sides. A reasonable person must be able to say the things that come out of each person's mouth. . . .You don't want to sound like a

madman. It escalates into madness in these pieces always, but the opening salvo on either side has got to be fairly reasonable."

The segment would always end with both Stephens appearing in a double box (split screen), telling each other in unison that "you, sir, are a formidable opponent."

The last Formidable Opponent, aired in the show's final week, tackled the same subject that the first one did: torture. The first Stephen believed torture was justified if it would protect America. The second argued that a recently-released report proved it hadn't protected America.

"Oh, I'm not talking about the actual country," the first Stephen said. "I'm talking about the *idea* of America. The *idea* of America would never torture.... I choose to live in the *idea* of America."

"But the idea of America is just an imaginary place," the second Stephen replied. "Which means you, sir, are just an imaginary Stephen Colbert."

With both Stephens in the double box, only the second Stephen said to the first, "you, sir, have been a formidable opponent." The first Stephen faded away to nothing, eliciting a gasp from the studio audience.

Formula 401 (2006-2014)

Stephen's essence is for sale, and not just metaphorically. When the Fairfax Cryobank ran out of sperm from popular Donor 401, who produced at least 14 blond, blue-eyed, athletic children, Stephen stepped up. He did the honorable thing and made his sperm available for sale. Stephen's premium line of "man seed" comes in variations, including one called "Seeds of Discontent" that he produced while he was (very angrily) watching gay porn, an Australian version called G'Day Egg to solve their national sperm shortage, and a celebrity version "created by hand" while Stephen did impressions. Stephen may be virile, but quash those rumors—the rash of babies born to Stephen's staff in 2011 was not the result of a catastrophic spill of his premium man seed, because that was mopped up.

Four Horsemen of the A-Pop-Calypse (2006-2014)

Death rides a flat screen. Music, movies, TV, and books are the four horsemen of the A-Pop-Calypse. Stephen knew it was his duty to tell the Colbert Nation how each kind of media was hastening the end of civilization as we know it, so he fought back in the culture war by exposing dangers like Justin Timberlake's senseless property damage in his music videos, Shaquille O'Neal's betrayal of the fast food industry, and the glorification of facts on network television.

Fract (2005-2006)

Something even better than the facts: freedom facts! These bumpers (short segments leading into or out of a commercial break) came in the form of text graphics, informing viewers of such important Fracts as "America is the world's leading producer of Americana" and "America has had only one Civil War. So far."

Offshoots included the Freedom Snap (or "Frnap"), providing an insult to hurl at another country The Dozens-style; and Colbert Trivia, featuring little-known tidbits such as how Stephen owned 55 commemorative state spoons because Iowa only comes in a multipack.

Frank the Roommate (2009)

Times were tough back in 2009, even for Stephen's parent company, Viacom, which had just announced losses of 32%. As a way of tightening the ol' belt, Stephen took in a roommate to cut rent costs. Played by writer Frank Lesser, Frank wandered onto Stephen's set in a bathrobe, pleading with him to keep it down because his girlfriend, Melissa, had to be up early to sell her jewelry at the farmers' market. The two bickered about chores and the utility bills before Frank stormed off, threatening to move out.

The next night, the show opened with Frank sitting behind Stephen's desk—still in his bathrobe, eating a sandwich, drinking coffee, and reading a newspaper—completely oblivious to what was happening around him until Stephen entered and informed him that "this is *The Colbert Report*."

Franklin F. Flagworth (2006-2014)

Stephen's pet American flag, who sat next to his fireplace. Flagworth was the sole beneficiary of Stephen's life insurance policy, and Stephen offered to loan him to NASA so they could reshoot their lost footage of the moon landing.

Stephen believed Flagworth would make an excellent Republican presidential candidate because voters are more responsive to patriotic imagery, plus Flagworth has military service and the requisite sex scandal (he was wrapped around Stephen's naked body for a photo shoot).

Future Stephen (2007, 2009, 2014)

Who is that lamé man? After a 2007 segment about time travel, a second Stephen was spotted in the background, dressed all in silver and sporting a futuristic hairstyle. Once this "other" Stephen realized he was on camera, he dashed out of frame before present-day Stephen could notice him. Fast-forward two years (because time travelers can do that) and Stephen presented yet another segment about time travel. He tried to prove the existence of time travel by daring his future self to appear and prevent him from sticking a fork into a toaster. Future Stephen appeared just a moment too late, horrified by the fried remains of his present-day self behind the desk. He did what he could, though: ripped the Brooks Brothers suit jacket off his alternate body, put it on, and bid the Nation goodnight.

So does this mean Future Stephen hosted the show thereafter? Not so fast. When Stephen refused to change his watch for Daylight Savings in 2010, he assumed that meant he was living in the future. Following that logic, he realized that meant there was also a Past Stephen living in everyone else's present. Since there could only be one Stephen, he instructed Jay the Intern to shoot the other Stephen. Since current Stephen had chosen to change his watch after all, it would be Future Stephen that Jay agreed to gun down as he walked to his car after the show.

In 2014, the silver-clad Future Stephen returned to be interviewed about immigration reform by . . . present-day Stephen? Live from the year 2372 (and seemingly in space), Future Stephen assured his past self that all that immigration reform would happen "next year," and that he should put money on the Cleveland Browns.

G

Gipper (2005-2014)

"Stephen's" dog, named after Ronald Reagan.

Glenn (2011)

Stephen stayed in touch with the youth of today thanks to his own "Director of Teen Outreach," a young Republican named Glenn. It didn't matter that Glenn, played by writer Glenn Eichler, was older than Stephen. Because despite his greying beard, Glenn wore hip clothes and a sideways baseball cap, hobbled onto the set on a skateboard, and deadpanned lingo such as "radical to the extreme" and "YOLO."

The real-life irony here? Despite being the oldest member of the *Report*'s writing staff, Eichler arguably had the most youth cred of any of them: he co-created the MTV show *Daria*.

Global Edition (2008-2014)

Not lucky enough to live in the good ol' U S of A? (Or Canada?) You might have had to make do with *The Colbert Report*'s "Global Edition," a compilation episode showcasing the best bits from that week's shows. Every episode started with an exclusive intro, taped without an audience, featuring Stephen welcoming his international viewers. But the best part? Segments in their uncensored form. When Stephen unloaded a heap of f-bombs at Steve Martin, Christian Bale-style, viewers of the American audience heard only beeps. But the Global Edition was shipped out with the original audio, in all its fucking glory.

God Machine (2007)

Beep boop boop beep boop boop.... This giant red button, better known as the God Machine, was the centerpiece of Stephen's revered This Week In God segment on *The Daily Show*. One press of the button prompted a series of religious images—such as the Star of David, Vishnu, or the Pfizer logo—and landed on the one that Stephen would then talk about. But on *The Colbert Report*, it signaled war: the media had dubbed the new iPhone the "God Machine" because of its ability to do just about anything, and Stephen summoned his God Machine simply as a reminder that the name was taken. He would, however, be willing to license the God Machine name—in exchange for a free iPhone.

Gorlock (2008-2014)

Bleep-blorp . . . Gorlock was Stephen's financial advisor, and happened to be an alien (the green kind, not the illegal kind). Gorlock came highly recommended by Tom Cruise, and was from the future—but nevertheless failed to warn Stephen of the 450-point drop in the stock market in 2008. Gorlock's latest advice to Stephen about how to plan for the future was to "relax and fatten up."

Government Shutdown Wedding of the Century (2013)

Stephen was in favor of the 2013 government shutdown, which temporarily closed many national parks and government buildings. But he said the story of couples like Mike Cassesso and MaiLien Le, whose wedding at a national monument had to be canceled, was causing a shutdown in his heart. So Stephen fulfilled his promise to provide all canceled government services, including weddings. An ordained minister (thanks to the Internet), Stephen gave them a full-service wedding in his studio as part of his show, including bachelor/bachelorette parties. The couple's friends and family were in the audience while Stephen read them their vows, Mandy Patinkin offered a "non-denominational Jewish blessing" for the couple, and Audra McDonald performed a rendition of Billy Idol's "White Wedding." According to the *Washington Post*, the newlyweds "didn't want to answer questions about whether they were legally married by Mr. Colbert."

Grammys (2009-2013)

Stephen was first nominated for a Grammy for the audiobook of *I Am America (And So Can You!)*, but the award was "stolen" from him by Al Gore. So for Stephen, the greatest gift of all was the Grammy he did win for *A Colbert Christmas: The Greatest Gift of All!* Stephen tried to take good care of his hard-won Best Comedy Album Grammy, but ended up making a mistake—he fed the day-old Grammy baby food when he should have been breast-feeding it.

Stephen got another chance to take good care of a Grammy when he received a nomination for Best Spoken Word Album for the audiobook of *America Again: Re-becoming the Greatness We Never Weren't*. He vowed to crush his opponents, a challenge fellow nominee Billy Crystal accepted on the show. Stephen was also up against Carol Burnett, who responded to his vow by writing him a letter wishing him luck and suggesting that he "break a leg and other things," which Stephen thought was very kind. She also dropped by the show via satellite to clarify to the delighted Stephen that she was being sarcastic, a concept he wasn't familiar with. Despite their fierce competition, Stephen ended up beating out Crystal and Burnett for his second Grammy win.

Green Screen Challenge (2006)

When the Internet got its hands on Stephen, anything was possible. The Green Screen Challenge didn't start out as a challenge at all. It was to be a simple in-studio introduction to a Better Know a District about California's 6th, which also happens to be the home of Skywalker Ranch. In honor of the *Star Wars* connection, Stephen wielded a light saber in front of a green screen to fight an invisible "space monster." Viewers only saw green, but Stephen double-checked with a crew member offscreen that "Lucas is gonna add all the CGI after, right?"

That was to be the end of it as far as the show was concerned, but the Colbert Nation had other ideas. The next day, fan-made videos started hitting YouTube, with new backgrounds and additions, making Stephen look like the fierce warrior he truly is. To further encourage this, Stephen issued the Green Screen Challenge—which, he noted, was definitely not a contest.

The entries poured in, many of which were aired on the show. One entrant (er . . . non-entrant) animated Stephen as a silhouette, in the style of the original iPod commercial. Another incorporated the tragic story of Stephen's beloved Dungeons & Dragons character.

One of those edit-savvy fans was "Bonnie R." from California. Producers contacted her to say that she was one of the two finalists in the not-a-contest, and she was invited to talk to Stephen on-air when he showed both videos and chose a winner.

When the phone call took place, she learned that she was the only contestant on the phone, and the other finalist, "George L.," was there in person. Since he was there in person, she figured her odds weren't good for winning. But Bonnie had no idea her competition was actually *Star Wars* creator George Lucas, whose entry was produced by Industrial Light & Magic. The competition (not contest) was rigged!

Bonnie's video was a mock Stephen-themed video game, complete with character- and villain-selection screens. The "player's" objective was to help Stephen protect a series of eagles from a BB gun's bullets—at least until Jesus arrived from the heavens to assist. (The video originally ended with a clip of a *Veggie Tales* song, but due to music rights issues it was replaced with the fanfare music usually played when Stephen does a balloon drop.)

George's video had all the CG slickness you'd expect from the man himself. Stephen fought an army of droids as R2D2 looked on, and then awkwardly conferred with a bemused Jar Jar Binks.

Stephen judged the videos on criteria that included "how the video made me look, originality, and poise." George's video scored an impressive 39.9 out of a possible 40. But Bonnie, of course, outdid him with a perfect score of 40. Bonnie was enthusiastic about her win, still not realizing that the whole thing was a ruse. She only learned who she was up against when the show aired that night.

Her prize for winning this definitely-not-a-contest included a bag full of *Colbert Report* swag, and a "golden ticket" that allowed her to attend any *Colbert Report* tapings she wished.

Guests (2005-2014)

Authors and astronauts, politicians and pop stars. They all had a turn in Stephen's guest chair, and that wasn't always an easy place to be! Whether as the main guest discussing their latest project at Stephen's interview table, or sharing their expertise about a current event earlier in the show at the C-shaped desk, most of Stephen's guests had one thing in common: a strong point of view.

It was that point of view, combined with the character's ignorance, which created the entertaining friction between the two sides, and—ideally—allowed guests to lay out their argument in a logical way.

"The interviews are my favorite thing to do on the show now. I have my plan, and I have three or four questions I know I'm going to ask, but generally speaking, I'm trying to pay attention to what they're doing so that I can ignorantly deconstruct their argument," Colbert told *Rolling Stone* in 2009.

Each day, two writers were assigned to write questions for Stephen, designed to trip the guest up. Sometimes he used them, sometimes not. One thing Colbert never did? Research. Unlike his colleague Jon Stewart, he didn't read his guests' books before they appeared on the show, mainly due to time constraints.

"I read the first chapter of the first book of the first guest I ever had on, which was Buzz Bissinger's *Three Nights in August* or something like that. And it's the last thing I've read," he said in 2009.

Despite Colbert having pre-written questions in front of him, his interviews were heavily improvised and he generally took his cues from the answers the guest provided. But there were no surprises for the guests as far as who they were facing in the interviewer's seat. Even repeat visitors who earned "friend of the show" status got the same speech from Colbert in advance:

"My character is an idiot, and is willfully ignorant of what you know and care about. Disabuse me of my ignorance, and we'll have a good time," he told them. (He gave this speech so often, that without thinking, he even gave it to Bill O'Reilly when he was a guest.)

This could be easier said than done, particularly when a guest was nervous or didn't entirely understand the lay of the land. When they backed away from their own position, it changed the dynamic between them and the character, and the message could be lost. He explained to the *Philadelphia Daily News*:

> "Too often people try to play along and then they're not themselves, they're not actually presenting their idea intellectually. They're not presenting their beliefs or making their arguments. They think they have to satisfy some need I have. . . . When someone won't actually be themselves, when they think they have to play my game to me is when the interviews go to hell."

And guests who weren't accustomed to an aggressive grilling needn't worry too much, because Colbert says he didn't want them to feel unwelcome. He made sure they kept their heads above water by lessening the intensity of his character whenever necessary, as he explained on *Charlie Rose*:

> "Someone who is politically adept and can defend themselves like Bill Kristol, you're gonna dial it all the way up. But if you're having the head of the Human Genome Project on, and who also happens to be a Christian and who's got a book called *The Language of God*, you can dial it down a little bit, because he's not a punching bag."

H

Ham Rove (2011-2012)
(See entry: Super PAC)

RIP, Ham. Stephen's former political strategist, Ham Rove, was a canned ham with wire-rimmed glasses who participated in discussions of Super PAC issues. He became the stock image used whenever Stephen quoted Karl Rove, but died "unsuspiciously" when Stephen stabbed him repeatedly. Stephen was forced to kill Ham because "sketchy donors" wanted someone on the Super PAC committee to pay the ultimate price for its ineffectiveness during the election, and Ham Rove was "already dead meat." Ham was last seen on the floor of the *Report* studio, being eaten by writer/producer Paul Dinello's dog.

Ham Rove's memory lives on in the Ham Rove memorial fund, which gave the $773,704.83 left in the Super-PAC's coffers to the DonorsChoose.org Hurricane Sandy relief fund, Team Rubicon's Sandy outreach, Habitat for Humanity, the Yellow Ribbon Fund, the Center for Responsive Politics, and the Campaign Legal Center. A condition of the donation made to campaign finance reform, via Trevor Potter's Campaign Legal Center, was that the group's conference room be renamed the Ham Rove Conference Room and display the plaque Stephen gave them to identify it. Karl Rove stated that Stephen's stabbing of Ham Rove was indicative of anger-management issues.

Hans Beinholtz (2010-2014)

The (fake) German Ambassador to the United Nations, played by actor/musician Erik Frandsen. With his morose German accent and ghoulish poker face, Hans joined Stephen to comment on everything from children's television to the World Cup.

HD (2010-2014)
(See also: Studio)

In 2010, Stephen's appeal became wider—16:9, to be exact. *The Colbert Report* switched to HD over the Christmas break, with a refreshed set, larger and more-raked audience seating, and, most importantly, a few extra inches for Stephen to play within. The January 21, 2010 episode began with a sepia-toned Stephen reminiscing as he walked through his old set and noticed a door placed right in the middle of his studio. Curious, he opened it and walked through to the HD side, and declared, awestruck, "My God, this is *The Colbert Report*." In the next segment, sitting comfortably in his new digs, Stephen mocked old-school viewers without HD. He made the show action-packed on the extreme sides of the screen, showing off "awesome" things like a coffee mug and a box of tissues.

High-Five (2013-2014)

Nailed it! When Stephen thought one of his quips was particularly brilliant, he took self-congratulation to another level by high-fiving the person whose arm magically emerged from under his desk.

HipHopKetball: A Jazzebration (2006)

Stephen had a bone to pick with Kareem Abdul-Jabbar. The NBA legend and jazz fan was making a documentary about the culture of music and basketball, and this news enraged Stephen. Why? Because it's clearly a rip-off of Stephen's 1995 documentary on the same theme, *Stephen Colbert's HipHopKetball: A Jazzebration*. He proved it by showing a clip of himself dribbling a basketball while rapping, making a basket, playing the saxophone (or attempting to), and then making a basket with the saxophone. Stephen said he'd wait to see the end product before sending his lawyers after Abdul-Jabbar, but in the meantime, he issued a Wag of the Finger.

But Stephen changed his tune just a few months later when he saw a portion of Abdul-Jabbar's documentary, *On the Shoulders of Giants: The Story of the Greatest Team You Never Heard Of*. Turns out, it's much different than *HipHopKetball*, so

Stephen made amends and invited Abdul-Jabbar to be in the sequel, *HipHopKetball II: The Rejazzebration Remix '06*. The two busted rhymes and made baskets together, with Abdul-Jabbar on upright bass and Stephen again struggling to get a sound out of the sax.

(Colbert has a spotty history with reeded woodwinds: he and longtime collaborator Paul Dinello performed a barely audible bassoon rendition of "The Devil Went Down to Georgia" at Stella's live Fez Under Time Cafe show in New York in 2005. The video can be viewed on YouTube.)

Hobby Hovel (2010)

Ribbons and beads, scissors and glue . . . After the Rally to Restore Sanity And/Or Fear, the "fear" part of Stephen was killed by audience chanting. And without fear, what happens to *The Colbert Report*? It becomes *Steph Colbert's Hobby Hovel*, a show dedicated entirely to making decorative birdhouses! Wearing a cardigan and surrounded by craft supplies, Stephen cheerfully tossed handfuls of sequins onto the roof of a purple martin house for mere seconds before breaking down and begging Jimmy to show him some footage that would anger him. A quick montage of newscast fearmongering later, Stephen was able to proclaim fear to be alive after all, and reintroduced the show as *The Colbert Report*.

Hoo-Ha Lady Zone 5000 (2012)

Here, there be dragons. Missouri congressman Todd Akin said that rape doesn't result in pregnancy, because "If it's a legitimate rape, the female body has ways to try to shut the whole thing down." Stephen explained what Akin was really trying to say—that "any woman who gets pregnant wasn't really raped"—with Akin's face digitally pasted over his own so that Stephen didn't accidentally take the credit for the statement. Stephen addressed the liberal media's criticism of Akin's remarks with a biology lesson, aided by a large touch screen that he called the Vagina iTouch. He renamed it the "Hoo-Ha Lady Zone 5000" because it was more "family-friendly." Once Stephen got it started—by tickling it with a feather—a simple diagram of the female reproductive system appeared.

Stephen used it to illustrate helpful knowledge like where the "Filipino tubes" are.

House (2005-2011)

Stephen was a huge fan of Dr. Gregory House, the curmudgeonly diagnostician from the FOX TV show *House M.D.* Stephen thought they had a lot in common, including being "always right," "horribly abusive to our staffs," and doing "terrific American accents." That's why Stephen had a framed picture of Hugh Laurie as Dr. House on his shelf, and "A Weekend with Dr. House" on the Fantasies Board.

House returned the honor. Stephen made two (photographic) cameos on the show, when Dr. House held up a picture of his face as a makeshift mask (season 8, episode 13) and in a framed photo that's visible on House's desk (season 6, episode 18).

Hungarian Bridge (2006)

The Ministry of Economic Affairs and Transport of Hungary held a contest to name its Northern M0 Danube bridge, connecting the east and west sides of Budapest. Stephen instructed the Nation to vote for him and defeat Chuck Norris, who was leading the poll, as well as sixteenth-century Hungarian hero Miklós Zrínyi, whom Stephen called an "asshole."

In the end, "Stephen Colbert" won, followed by "Jon Stewart" and then "Miklós Zrínyi." Stephen welcomed Hungarian ambassador András Simonyi to the show, expecting his victory to be made official. However, he did not meet the requirements of being a) able to speak Hungarian fluently and b) dead. However, the Ministry acknowledged his win and invited Stephen to Hungary to oversee the building process. The bridge was eventually named the Megyeri Bridge.

I

I Am A Pole (And So Can You!) (2012)
(See also: Maurice Sendak)

The sad thing is, Maurice Sendak liked it. *I Am A Pole (And So Can You!)* is the heartwarming story of a young pole trying to find his place in the world. Stephen pitched the idea to the *Where the Wild Things Are* author during an interview because he wanted in on the celebrity children's book market. The pole tries out several different careers ("So I interned as a stripper pole/But couldn't stand the grind") before finally realizing that his true purpose in life is to be an American flagpole. The book was exhibited at the Rosenbach Museum and Library, where the works of masters like James Joyce are honored. Fitting, as Stephen thought *I Am A Pole* has a lot in common with Joyce's masterpiece *Ulysses*.

The book was released in hardcover on May 8, 2012, and has a mock Caldecott Medal award for illustration on the cover. Tom Hanks narrated an audiobook version, the proceeds of which were donated to the U.S. Veterans Initiative. The book was illustrated by Paul Hildebrand. *International Business Review* raved: "NOT for children."

I Am America (And So Can You!) (2007)

Stephen wasn't a fan of books, but he *was* a fan of sales and a fan of himself. Hence his decision to publish *I Am America (And So Can You!)*, and provide himself with the following blurb on the back cover: "A great read. I laughed, I cried, I lost 15 lbs. I cannot recommend this book highly enough."

Like the egocentric books authored by other cable news pundits, Stephen's book lays out his ideologies on everything important to America (and by natural extension, himself). The chapter on "Religion" imagines what life will be like after we've lost the War on Christmas. "The Family" warns readers that children are here to replace us. "Sex & Dating" features a lengthy missed connections-style essay from a person's frustrated soul mate (one of Colbert's favorite parts of the book).

"The book is a pure extension of the show, the same way that any of those books that we're modeling ourselves on are a pure extension of the show, except that ours has stickers," Colbert explained.

Indeed, a page full of silver embossed stickers was included so that readers could bestow upon other books the very honor that Stephen bestowed on his own book: The Stephen T. Colbert Award for the Literary Excellence.

On the day of the book's release, Stephen was his own guest on *The Colbert Report*, filmed in the style of his Formidable Opponent segment. Among the questions he asked himself was whether he'd run for president in 2008, and his own refusal to answer resulted in a Stephen-vs-Stephen shouting match.

Colbert and his writing staff spent evenings and weekends putting the book together, while writing *The Colbert Report* by day. (Although according to his character, he merely "shouted it into a tape recorder over the Columbus Day weekend.")

I Am America debuted at #1 on the *New York Times* Best Sellers list and would spend 29 weeks on the list. According to *USA Today*, it was the 9th best-selling book in 2007. The audiobook version was nominated for a Grammy for Best Spoken Word Album.

"I Called It!" (2005-2014)

Modest? Not Stephen. When he predicted something, and was right, you could bet on an exuberant "I called it!" leaving his lips at the first opportunity. Among the predictions he laid claim to: the overpopulation of elephants, nerds as a valuable natural resource, and the outcome of the 2008 Nevada Caucus.

The In-Box (2005-07, 2013-14)

Stephen was more than happy to field viewers' questions and comments. After all, they're just more opportunities to talk about himself. How is Stephen cutting down his fuel consumption? By only driving his Hummer on Mondays, Wednesdays, and Fridays (on other days, he drove his wife's H2). Isn't Stephen presenting himself as a "doctor" grossly irresponsible? If that were true, he wouldn't have a doctorate of fine arts. One In-Box letter—scrawled in crayon and suspiciously signed by "Stephen Colbert"—asked whether flight or invisibility was the best superpower to have, and Stephen's lengthy answer conveniently distracted him from addressing that day's difficult headlines.

Indecision 2008 (2008)

"*AN* historic night." Indecision 2008 was also known as The Final Endgame Alpha Action Go Time Lift-Off Decide-icidal Hungry-Man's Raw Extreme Power Ultimate Voteslam Smackdown '08 No Mercy: Judgment Day '08 . . . '08. Jon Stewart and Stephen Colbert teamed up to provide joint live coverage of the 2008 presidential election on November 4th at 10pm.

Disheartened by reports that projected a likely Obama victory, Stephen tried anything to keep his mind off the results—including, to Jon's dismay, having a live cockatoo sit on his shoulder. Stephen also revealed some personal facts about himself, including that he "votes with his tongue" since he is busy clinging to guns and religion with his hands and that he uses honey instead of syrup because he dislikes Vermont.

The *Daily Show* correspondents helped cover the election, some of them from the field. Jason Jones reported from what looked like a cartoon forest, but what he claimed was Chicago when Obama was in town. In the studio, Rob Riggle reported on his attempts to stop people from voting. John Oliver, also in the studio, complimented the American political process before Stewart called him out for trying to get his U.S. work visa renewed. Aasif Mandvi weighed in from "Al Qaeda headquarters."

Special guests, including Steve Forbes and Harvard professor and Obama mentor Charles Ogletree, helped provide their perspectives on the results and their thoughts on what each candidate's victory could mean for the country.

"Time to paint the White House black, baby!" Empowered by Obama's apparent victory, Larry Wilmore pulled up a chair and informed Stewart that he would be taking over *The Daily Show*, and that it would be "Tyler Perry's House of Daily Show with Larry Wilmore." Stephen accepted "New Jon" quickly, until he found out that Wyatt Cenac was taking over *The Colbert Report*.

When Stewart called the election for Obama, Stephen maintained his denial, shrugging and saying "Maybe." Stephen also appeared to tear up when Obama's victory was announced. When asked about the moment at a live Q&A in 2012, the real Colbert simply said "I . . . was moved."

Luckily for "Stephen," though, the real Colbert was able to keep his feelings hidden in the next bit, which involved him putting on goggles and headphones to block out the news.

All of the *Daily Show* correspondents and Stephen stumbled up to the roof of the studio, hungover from the election and ready to experience "a world without Bush"—until Stephen reminded them that they still had two months of President Bush left.

J

Jay the Intern (2009-2014)

No matter what Stephen needed, Jay the Intern was always eager to help. Played by writer Jay Katsir, Jay the Intern earned his college credits by being operated on, made to learn stone masonry, and groped. Katsir said in an interview that "intern" was a good role for him because his acting skill "ranges from 'anxious' to 'skittish.'" According to Katsir, the show was actually a great place to work, and the real Colbert is really nice—nothing at all like his character.

Jane Fonda (2007)

Only one guest was able to truly stop Colbert's character in his tracks, and all it took was some aggressive flirting from an iconic sex symbol.

Fonda, on the show to promote her film *Georgia Rule*, got up from her chair before the interview even started and took a seat on Stephen's lap. Before he could figure out what to say, she turned his face towards hers, and kissed him on the lips. A stunned Colbert stammered as Fonda scolded him for adding his fantasies about her to the On Notice Board. He tried to counteract her seduction techniques by barreling through his questions about the film and her activist past, but Fonda instead chose to nibble on "the only ear I hear out of."

"She was playing a virago, you might say; she took control with a character that was more powerful than my character at that moment," Colbert later explained. "She used her feminine wiles, albeit her septuagenarian feminine wiles—pretty impressive, I've got to say—to grab the status away from me."

At a 2008 New Yorker Festival Q&A session, Colbert revealed that his staff bought flowers for him to take home to his wife, Evie, before the taping had even ended. He characterized her reaction to the piece as pure bemusement, but Evie, sitting in the audience at the event, didn't stand for her husband's revisionist history: "I said, 'don't you *ever* let *anyone* take over your show like that!'"

Jimmy (2005-2014)

Roll it, Jimmy! Stephen routinely barked commands to his real director, Jim Hoskinson, who was previously a director for Fox News. He called the shots in the control room for the show's five cameras and myriad graphics cues, and kept things rolling for more challenging shoots like Operation Iraqi Stephen and StePhest Colbchella. His work for the *Report* earned him an Emmy nomination every year, as well as three Directors Guild of America nominations. In a 2005 segment, Hoskinson was portrayed by former *Colbert Report* writer Peter Gwinn.

Jimmy Fallon (2007-2014)

Stephen's Best Friend For Life For Six Months (BFFLFSM). Stephen never had any beef with then-*Late Night* host Jimmy Fallon until Fallon got a Ben & Jerry's flavor named after him. Stephen was insulted that his Americone Dream no longer had the glory of being the only ice cream flavor inspired by a late-night host, and demanded that Fallon cancel his—or else he'd melt a quart of his Late Night Snack with a hair dryer!

Fallon showed up to stop him, and the two traded insults until they decided it was going nowhere and they'd have to call for backup. They simultaneously commanded "lead-ins, assemble!" Jon Stewart arrived (with a baseball bat) to support Stephen, but Fallon failed to make his lead-in, Jay Leno, appear. Fallon and Stephen decided to settle their battle with an ice cream eating contest, which gave them brain freeze so bad that they entered "an alternate state of butter pecan-sciousness." In their hallucinations, Ben and Jerry appeared and encouraged them to reconcile. They agreed, and became best friends for life for six months—because forever felt too permanent.

In the fourth week of the six-month best friendship, Stephen and Fallon got into a fight over giving donations to charity. Stephen donated the proceeds of his portrait auction to DonorsChoose.org, and announced—without telling Fallon—that Fallon would match his donation. To even the score, Jimmy ended up making a promise on Stephen's behalf: if Fallon's fans raised $26,000, Stephen would perform "Friday" by Rebecca Black on *Late Night*. The result? A rousing performance by Stephen and the Roots, with surprise cameos by Taylor Hicks and the Knicks City Dancers.

At the end of the six months, Stephen ended his friendship with Fallon, and they became eternal enemies for six months. Anderson Cooper immediately appeared with an offer to be his new best friend, but Stephen said it was too soon and that he was "still hurting." Cooper said he could heal Stephen's hurt, and made a "call me" gesture. Stephen and Fallon sang "Somewhere Out There" on *Late Night* to commemorate their time as best friends.

Jon Stewart (2005-2014)
(See also: Atone Phone, Called Out Board, Finale, Rally, Super PAC, Toss)

Great television bromance . . . or the *greatest* television bromance?

Stephen saw his former *Daily Show* boss Jon Stewart as his competition, someone whose shadow he was in danger of living in forever. He'd put Stewart down at any opportunity: casually deleting an unwatched *Daily Show* from his Tivo, telling him that his face looks like "a ski mask made from an elephant's scrotum" in HD, or showing up at *The Daily Show* to mop the floor with him in a practice debate before Stewart's 2012 battle with Bill O'Reilly.

But when the chips were truly down, Stephen was on his side. In the summer of 2013, when John Oliver was filling in for Stewart, the *Daily Show* studio lost power mid-taping. The next night, "security camera" footage revealed that the main power supply was disabled by none other than Stephen, screaming, "You're not my real Jon! There's only one Jon who can host the show in my heart! This is for you, Stewart!" And when Stewart returned three months later with an identity crisis, his correspondents called on Stephen to help make him feel like his old self (a determined Stephen entered Stewart's office in a hazmat suit, and exited disheveled with red lipstick smeared around his mouth).

Stewart, for his part, acted unfazed by Stephen's general attitude of superiority. He appeared to see through the character's blustery facade, letting it roll off his back like the harmless product of deep insecurity that it was.

But that's the fictional dynamic. In real life, the two have always been quick to praise each other.

"We actually are really great friends. . . . He's one of my best friends, and I'm so lucky that I get him as a mentor," Colbert said.

Colbert was already a correspondent at *The Daily Show* when Stewart took over as host in 1999. In 2002, they developed a sitcom pilot together for NBC Studios, based loosely on Colbert's experience growing up in South Carolina, which the network did not pick up. Then they, along with then-*Daily Show* executive producer Ben Karlin, pitched the idea for *The Colbert Report* to Comedy Central.

Stewart was an executive producer for the *Report*'s entire run, and was part of the initial brainstorming for *The Colbert Report*'s creative direction. Stewart encouraged Colbert to make the show about things that interest him, and also helped him find a balance with the "Stephen Colbert" character.

"Jon kept saying, 'You're not an a-hole, you're an idiot. And second of all, if you just enjoy yourself, the audience will know. Don't wear it so heavily.' And that has been a really wonderful note from him," Colbert said.

Stewart and "Stephen" wore their faux relationship just as loosely. When Stewart surprised the *Report* audience to take co-credit for Stephen's 2013 Emmy win, he gloated—award in hand—as Stephen repeatedly screamed "Damn you!" at him. But Stewart quickly dropped his side of the charade, and embraced Colbert in congratulations.

In November of 2014, Stewart finally appeared as an official guest on *The Colbert Report* to promote his directorial debut *Rosewater*. After Jon went up against the character for two segments, Colbert dropped the act to comment on how lovely it was to have him there, and the two ended the interview with their arms around each other.

Joy Machine

Colbert's nickname for the grueling daily process of putting the show together. "Unless we have some joy in what we're doing every day, it's just a machine," he said.

Judge, Jury & Executioner (2007-2012)

Justice may be blind, but Stephen wasn't—and he meted out his judgment accordingly. Stephen handed down verdicts based not on a legal degree, but on the vast experience he had with the legal system because he'd been "sued more times than I can count." Scooter Libby, the former chief of staff to President Bush famously accused and convicted of perjury, obstruction of justice, and making false statements? Innocent. An old Michigan law mandating a life sentence for adultery? Fair. "Covet thy neighbor's ass, it's off to the chamber of gas."

K

Ken Burns (2005, 2009-2012, 2014)

"Ken Burns is one of the greatest people to sit across the table with," Colbert said. The filmmaker was one of Colbert's favorite guests, because of his passion for his work. "I just feel mildly singed on the side of my body that's facing him, as if I've just been irradiated by his love of American history," he said.

Burns first appeared as a guest on the *Report* in 2005, just a few weeks into the show's run. To play on the "Ken Burns effect"—the unique pan-and-zoom effect Burns made famous in his documentaries—the *Report* crew created an ambitious mini-documentary of their own. They grabbed stills of the conversation, and edited them while the interview was happening. In the process, they learned a valuable lesson.

"By the end of six minutes we had a documentary about the previous six minutes, in real time," Colbert later explained. "And then we realized we could have just pretaped it."

Killer (2005-2010)

Killer was one of Stephen's stagehands, a silent and menacing presence played by an actual member of Colbert's crew. Killer was enlisted to help rescue Stephen Jr. because he was good with explosives, put out Stephen's flaming crotch with a fire extinguisher, and kept Stephen's script at gunpoint to ensure it didn't blow off his desk—all while remaining stone-faced.

Due to his intimidating stature, Killer was immune from Stephen's usual shoddy treatment of employees, getting a rare bump in pay at employee review time, and easily escaping retaliation for giving Stephen a cold.

Knut the Polar Bear (2007)

Don't be fooled by this cute polar bear cub is: it's still a godless killing machine. Stephen had a special mini-ThreatDown for the mini-polar bear. The cub, born in the Berlin Zoo, was abandoned by his mother, leaving the zoo staff to care for him. Stephen sided with German animal activist Frank Albrecht, who said that hand-feeding wild animals is a crime against nature and that the cub should be killed. Stephen couldn't resist talking baby-talk to Knut every time Jimmy put him on the screen.

L

Lady Heroes (2012)

Stephen's segment—nay, segWOMENt—for the Lady Heroes in the news. Lady Heroes are all men, "because conservative men feel comfortable speaking for women." Stephen's Lady Hero was the man who led the repeal of the Equal Pay Act: Wisconsin state senator Glenn Grothman.

Laser Klan (2013-2014)

No letters, please. When a news story broke about the Ku Klux Klan trying to invent a truck-mounted death ray to use against Israel, Stephen was excited for a chance to finally use his short—but expensive—animated "Laser Klan" graphic promoting an animated action series of the same name. Stephen claimed he had made the graphic for when George Lucas visited the Report six years prior, but that Lucas had asked him not to use it "for some reason."

A year later, when the Ku Klux Klan tried to sell Jewish groups a death ray to kill Muslims with, Stephen saw this as progress. Instead of using the death laser against the Jews, the Klan was offering to team up with the Jews and fight a common enemy. Stephen was inspired to make "Laser Klan" come to life. In an animated short, the KKK is forced to join forces with even more of their enemies—even teaming up with President Obama—to fight illegal space aliens. They won, but Obama told the KKK that they could never tell the American people what happened.

Stephen said Viacom sent him a letter before the piece aired, saying "We're a little concerned because it is airing during Black History Month." After playing it, he said, "I'm not sure if that was the right thing to do."

Le Colbert Report with Stephane Colbert (2010)

"You damned pig's vagina!" So said Stephen's French-Canadian counterpart, Stephane ColberT, who didn't much care for Stephen. Stephane reluctantly helped Stephen wrap up the Vancouver Olympic Games by reporting on something Stephen didn't get a chance to cover while he was there: French-Canadian culture. Stephen relied on Stephane to tell him what was being lost in translation, just as he relies on Esteban Colberto to explain Hispanic news to him. His French comprehension might have been colored by his ego just slightly—Stephane told him to "get fucked" in French, and Stephen replied that he "would love to be your child's godfather!"

Leg wrestling (2009)

It's one way to bring down the House! Leg wrestling involves two people lying on the ground next to each other with their legs facing opposite directions, and using one leg to try to flip the other person over. Stephen leg wrestled the representative for Utah's 3rd District, Jason Chaffetz, in an installment of Better Know a District—and won. Chaffetz requested a rematch and Stephen accepted. He beat Jason and his "angel hair pasta" legs again.

Lord of the Rings (2005-2014)

Can a man love a literary work so deeply that even he can't prevent his own character from sharing it?

"I try to keep the *Lord of the Rings* references out of my character's mouth because I truly love the writing of Tolkien and I don't want to debase it by having my character like it," Colbert said in 2006.

But as the years went by, Colbert couldn't keep his passion for Middle-earth under wraps.

Halfway into a 2010 interview with *Lord of the Rings* star Elijah Wood, he said, "I've resisted as long as I could, but I'm about to break," before gleefully fanboying over the upcoming *Hobbit* trilogy. In 2011, he spun an elaborate metaphor about the debt-ceiling debate using his personal collection of action figures, and even had the *Lord of the Rings* pinball machine that he kept in his office brought into the studio for the occasion. He engaged fellow fan James Franco in Tolkien trivia in 2011 and 2013, besting him both times.

"I tried to keep that separate at first. I tried to keep that membrane," Colbert later said of allowing his character's fandom. "But there were too many opportunities for me to wax about it, so I went ahead and let that membrane be permeable."

The ultimate Tolkien tribute came with Hobbit Week, officially known as "The Pundit: Or Colbert and Back Again." In 2012, Colbert dedicated a full week of shows to the release of *The Hobbit: An Unexpected Journey*. Stars Ian McKellan, Martin Freeman, and Andy Serkis, as well as director Peter Jackson, were guests across the four nights, interviewed on a set transformed to look like Bag End. Colbert didn't hide his enthusiasm for the theme, and fully surrendered to sharing his love of Tolkien with his character.

McKellan later told the *Hollywood Reporter*:

> "We had a very good, fun time. I still don't know whom I was talking to—whether it was the real Stephen Colbert . . . I think it perhaps was more than usual. He's such an expert on Tolkien, he really is, he can quote it at length, and he was genuinely enthusiastic about meeting the cast, which he's doing right through this week. So the silly Stephen Colbert, who is normally on the program, rather dropped away. It was interesting to watch."

One of Stephen's final *Report* guests was Smaug the dragon, who burst onto the set through the studio wall (thanks to the magic of CGI).

Colbert made a cameo in *The Hobbit: The Desolation of Smaug* as "Laketown Spy."

Lorna Colbert (1920-2013)

After a week-long absence from the *Report*, Colbert opened his June 19, 2013 episode with a loving tribute to his mother, Lorna, who died June 12. He told viewers about her life, her deep devotion to her children, and her strength and gratitude in the face of tragedy. "She was fun," he said—she had trained to be an actress, and would teach her children how to do stage falls.

"I know it may sound greedy to want more days with a person who lived so long. But the fact that my mother was 92 does not diminish, it only magnifies, the enormity of the room whose door has now quietly shut," he said.

With the emotional three minutes behind him, Colbert exhaled, and summoned his character to proclaim "THIS is *The Colbert Report*." He went on to do an episode like any other—except to end it, appropriately, with a stage fall.

Lorraine (2005-2014)

"Stephen's" wife.

M

March on Washington (2006-2013)

Stephen was an expert on race relations, and he could prove it: he was at the 1963 March on Washington to hear Martin Luther King, Jr.'s famous "I Have a Dream" speech.

But wait, you say—was Stephen even born then? Well, no. He was still a small (but impressionable) fetus at the time. But his parents attended the March, and therefore Stephen was totally present. Plus, he had a head start on that whole not judging people based on the color of their skin thing, because he himself was "technically translucent."

While this premise is textbook "Stephen," remarkably it's a true story shared by Colbert.

Maurice Sendak (2012)
(See also: *I Am a Pole*)

Maurice Sendak didn't write for children. He just wrote, and somebody said, "That's for children." That was one of the many things we learned about the smart, ornery author and illustrator of many revered children's books, including *Where the Wild Things Are*. Stephen aired a two-part interview with the legendary storyteller and artist, and received advice on writing and drawing his own celebrity children's book, *I Am A Pole (And So Can You!)*. Sendak even gave Stephen a blurb about the jokingly proposed book, which at the time was illustrated with stick figures: "The sad thing is, I like it."

At a live Q&A in 2013, Colbert recalled the impression Sendak made on him after their first phone conversation:

"We're so good at protecting ourselves, how we actually feel about everything. Maurice Sendak reminded me what human beings are like. We're fascinating. Mostly, we don't let other people know, but he did. Completely unguarded person who was not without crafting his answer, but he really just didn't care what people thought of him."

Sendak died May 8, 2012, on the day that Stephen's book was released. In a statement, Colbert said, "Maurice Sendak was strikingly honest. His art gave us a fantastical but unromanticized reminder of what childhood truly felt like. We are all honored to have been briefly invited into his world."

Meg the Intern (2006-2008)

Hands off, Stephen! Played by comedian and *Report* production assistant Meg DeFrancesco, Meg the Intern was called in any time Stephen needed a woman to support a sexist idea. Despite Meg having lodged several complaints against him, Stephen still tried to guess whether she was ovulating, and embraced her to recreate the covers of steamy romance novels.

Meta-Free-Phor-All: Shall I Nail Thee to a Summer's Day? (2007)

Stephen was ready to kick some Hollywood liberal butt—at least metaphorically. When Sean Penn voiced anti-Republican sentiments using a metaphor about George W. Bush's "soiled and blood-soaked underwear," Stephen was enraged. He challenged Penn to come on his show for a linguistic showdown, which Stephen was confident he'd win. Penn accepted, and just days later the men fought for analogous supremacy.

Former U.S. Poet Laureate Robert Pinsky held court over the battle, and instructed the men to ring in using their metaphorical buzzers: an apple for Penn, representing a man's thirst for knowledge; and a handgun for Stephen, representing "traditionally, a penis."

After three rounds of rattling off metaphors, Stephen was in the lead 1-0. But the final round—worth 10 million points—was taken by Penn, for being able to explain his own underwear metaphor.

Stephen wept in defeat, but Penn was a gracious winner, offering Stephen something to dry his tears with: a pair of Bush's blood-soaked underwear.

meTunes (2008-2012)

Stephen reviews the "new jams." Newly released music albums were rated on a scale of 1-5 "me's," not based on their musical merit, but on how much Stephen agreed with what he thought their message was. Among those who won five Stephens were Toby Keith's *That Don't Make Me a Bad Guy* and John Legend's *Evolver*. Stephen also got The Black Keys and Vampire Weekend to fight for his Grammy vote.

Michael Stipe (2011-2012, 2014)

Hey-o! R.E.M. had recently disbanded, so Stephen did what he did any time something warranted memorializing: put it in a place of honor. Thus, the band's front man became the first human to be hoisted up onto Stephen's shelf. Giving the illusion that Stipe really had been placed there permanently, Stephen would occasionally treat him like a sidekick, turning to him when he wanted a remark punctuated. A pretaped Stipe would dutifully respond "hey-o" from the shelf. After the gag had been running for nine months, Stipe delivered a new line: "Would someone dust me?" When Stephen held a yard sale to get rid of all the junk in the studio, he placed Stipe on a table with a $1 price tag on his forehead (later reduced to $.25).

Microwave (2007-2014)

Stolen goods! Stephen snatched the microwave from Bill O'Reilly's green room in 2007 when he appeared on *The O'Reilly Factor*. According to a Fox News spokesperson, the heist was planned in advance. Stephen told Bill O'Reilly off-camera that he was going to take the microwave, and the Fox news team thought it was hilarious and let him. Stephen still felt bad about it, though, so he replaced their microwave with one emblazoned with the *Report*'s logo.

Like Stephen, the microwave was "a little old, a little square, and does not care what you're saying." The microwave did come in handy, though. In 2008, Stephen microwaved styrofoam cups nonstop for three days straight to compensate for the Democratic convention going green. The microwave stayed on Stephen's set until 2014, when he auctioned it off to benefit the Yellow Ribbon Fund—in emulation of Papa Bear O'Reilly, who had decided to auction off the notes from his interview with President Obama. Although the bids went over $85,000, the highest bids were retracted and the microwave ultimately sold for $5,400.

Monkey on the Lam (2007-2013)

How many escaped monkeys does it take to create a recurring segment? Stephen first covered a story about a monkey that bit a woman and went "on the lam" in Wisconsin, leading police on a seven-hour chase. He subsequently covered monkey escapes in Mississippi, Florida, Alabama, and Missouri.

Movies That Are Destroying America (2006-2013)

The Hollywood elite is eroding our values. With his opinions based entirely on the trailers (since they give you the best part of the movie anyway), Stephen called out the new releases for exactly what they were: "depraved." It didn't matter whether they were Oscar contenders like *Pride & Prejudice* (it had one of the seven deadly sins right in the title), or a mainstream summer blockbuster like *I Now Pronounce You Chuck & Larry* (they made being gay look like too much fun), very few films were good enough for Stephen's blessing. Suspiciously, he did endorse a 2006 film that told the "heartwarming" story of an ex-junkie/ex-hooker/ex-con, entitled *Strangers with Candy*—starring one Stephen Colbert.

My Fair Colbert: Stephen Colbert's Crown Jewels (2011)

In preparation for the royal wedding of Kate Middleton and Prince William of Wales, Stephen enlisted British royal biographer Hugo Vickers to help him become more British. To Vickers's increasing dismay, Stephen drank tea straight from the teapot, ate a spoonful of sugar, and couldn't keep his pinky from sticking out while holding his cup. Stephen also attempted to high-five Vickers while he was acting as a stand-in for the Queen, and tried to use a sex doll to represent Her Majesty. Eventually, though, Stephen demonstrated the correct etiquette for drinking tea, eating scones, and greeting the Queen. Stephen felt he was now "ready for royalty."

Mysteries of the Ancient Unknown (2010-2012)

Turn down the lights, cue the mysterious Egyptian music, and raise your eyebrows. Stephen was on the case to discover hidden secrets that originated thousands of years ago, most of which involve penises. Questions surrounding the whereabouts of King Tut's missing penis warranted two separate two-part "Peabody-defying series," which culminated in Stephen's epic 12-block journey across town to a King Tut exhibit in Times Square. Non-phallic mysteries included the end of the world, and the discovery of what may have been civilization's first "yo mama" joke.

N

Nailed 'Em (2008-2013)

Stephen celebrates the triumph of law and order. In Nailed 'Em, "justice" was served against people who broke the rules—despite the lamestream media portraying the consequences as too harsh for the offenses. Among the people nailed were Richard Eggers, who was fired from his job at Wells Fargo for using a fake dime at a laundromat 50 years earlier; a gay couple who were arrested for holding hands on Mormon Church property; and a seven-year-old kid who was banned from a library for being a resident of a different county. As in other pretaped segments such as Difference Makers, Stephen narrated the baffling and ridiculous facts of the case with gravitas.

NASA (2006-2014)

NASA was one of the only government programs Stephen supported. But, despite covering plenty of NASA news, and having astronauts including Buzz Aldrin, Mark Kelly, and the crew of the Space Shuttle Atlantis on as guests, the science always seemed to go a little over his head.

In 2008, astronaut Garrett Reisman took one of Stephen's WristStrong bracelets with him to the International Space Station. In a satellite interview on the show, he spun the bracelet around in zero gravity, much to Stephen's genuine delight ("I can die and go to heaven now"). Less than half of the interview, conducted the morning of the show, actually aired. Edited out were Stephen's questions about Reisman being "a janitor with a Ph.D.," whether the astronauts eat Dippin' Dots, whether there was "any chance that we're not talking right now, and you're just imagining it because you're suffering from space madness?" and "what did it feel like when they beamed you up? Did it tickle?"

When Reisman was a guest again in the studio a few months later, he and Stephen exchanged bracelets, with Reisman giving him the one that had traveled to space.

In 2012, Buzz Aldrin presented Stephen with the National Space Society's 2012 Space Pioneer Award for Mass Media, for increasing public awareness of space exploration.

In 2013, a retro-spacesuit-clad Stephen bestowed NASA's Distinguished Public Service Medal upon his guest, scientist Ed Stone. Stone didn't know in advance that he would be receiving the award that night, saying in a NASA press release, "that surprise on my face was real."

Neil deGrasse Tyson (2005-2014)

"Not only do I love what Neil knows, but I love that he loves what he doesn't know."

That's the real Colbert explaining why the impassioned astrophysicist was his all-time favorite guest, always game for Stephen's less-than-educated questions about the universe. But even though Tyson is known for making difficult concepts understandable to the layperson, Stephen could never quite get it. Therefore, it was much easier for him to believe that "an all-knowing, omniscient, omnitemporal being just snapped it into existence."

The first edition of Stephen Colbert's Fallback Position featured Tyson teaching Stephen the ropes of astrophysics at the Hayden Planetarium. At the end of the day, Stephen regurgitated all his misunderstood lessons in a lecture to a group of toddlers, much to Tyson's mock displeasure.

In reality, the frustration was Colbert's. He's genuinely interested in Tyson's subject matter, but as he explained at a 2013 Q&A, he was limited by his character's ignorance and couldn't ask intelligent questions on the air. "I want to engage him from a place of knowledge because there are all these interesting places I want to go, but I have to not know what he means," he said.

Nutz (2006)

Tax time can get a little nutty. Nutz brand sparkling soda—"the soda that is no longer produced"—was the official sponsor of Stephen's 2006 tax advice segment. The nut-flavored soda's faux-sponsorship was a holdover from Colbert's time on *The Daily Show*. In 2001, Stephen's tax advice segment featured a Nutz product placement (he and Jon Stewart toasted each other with their respective bottles), and it was the namesake of Stephen's "Nutz Election Center" as he covered the 2003 California recall.

Before it was immortalized as a fake news prop, Nutz Sparkling Soda Pop was a real but short-lived product. Produced by small Vermont beverage makers Wild Fruitz, the line was promoted earnestly as "a drink that tastes as delicious with a meal as it does with a good movie!" Former *Daily Show* executive producer Ben Karlin first came across the beverage oddity in a New York City convenience store, and couldn't resist purchasing two bottles (pistachio and hazelnut). The original bottle of pistachio Nutz was the same bottle later used on the *Report*, refilled with colored water.

O

On Notice Board (2005-2013)

You're On Notice! More serious than the Called Out board, but less permanent than Dead to Me. Stephen placed everything from caramel apples and Fabergé eggs to Pope Francis and the Black Hole at the Center of the Galaxy on the On Notice board. If the board got full, Stephen either pardoned some of the wrongdoers and removed them from the board, or put them on the Dead to Me board.

Oopsie-Daisy Homophobe (2013)

Gay marriage divide, consider yourself bridged. Stephen was inspired by the "universal suckage" of country singer Brad Paisley and rapper LL Cool J's song about racism, "Accidental Racist." The singers were criticized for exhibiting actual racism in this oversimplified "conversation" about race in America.

But racial division isn't the only problem a country ballad can solve. Stephen and gay actor Alan Cumming sang a duet to bring together the two sides of the gay marriage debate. "Oopsie-Daisy Homophobe" includes the lyrics: *"To the man stretching next to me at the Crunch gym down on Main, I hope you understand when I told you 'God hates fags,' the only thing I meant to say is I'm a Skynyrd fan."*

Opening sequence (2005-2014)

"This is *The Colbert Report*!" Cue the opening notes of "Baby Mumbles" (the theme song written by Cheap Trick) and the screech of an animated bald eagle (actually the call of a red-tailed hawk). The *Report* had two different opening sequences. The original by Verb! Media ran from 2005-2009, and featured

Stephen planting an American flag into the ground as words like "POWERFUL" and "GRITTY" flew around him. The refreshed HD version, used from 2010 on, was created by Mr. Wonderful.

The opening sequence always included a wild-card word, changed up on a semi-regular basis. Sometimes it was a seemingly random choice ("multi-grain") or an entirely made-up word ("freem"). For a brief period in mid-2014, the opening also featured a countdown of the show's remaining episodes, but head writer Opus Moreschi said "it got a little depressing."

Operation Iraqi Stephen (2009)

Hooah! In June of 2009, *The Colbert Report* attempted the (nearly) impossible: film, edit, and broadcast a full week of shows from Iraq as part of a USO/Armed Forces Entertainment tour. It marked the first time in the USO's history that a comedy program was produced in a combat zone.

It all started when former Assistant Secretary of Defense Bing West was a guest on the *Report* in mid-2008. After the interview, he asked Colbert what he'd say if General David Petraeus invited him to do the show in Iraq.

Colbert's wanted to say "yes," but he recognized he had an entire staff to speak for. He told West he would be honored, but stopped short of committing. It wasn't until early 2009 that the trip began to take shape.

The *Report* would record four episodes in front of 500 troops per night at Camp Victory in Baghdad, with one of Saddam Hussein's palaces, Al-Faw, used as a makeshift studio.

For security reasons, Colbert couldn't actually talk about where and when they were going, which made promoting the episodes a challenge. But he could vaguely tease the trip, and did exactly that starting in March. That inspired a segment called Where In The World and Where In Time is Stephen Colbert Going To Be In The Persian Gulf?, which had Stephen weighing the tourism pluses and minuses of each country in the region.

It was only once the crew was in Iraq in June that they could make their whereabouts known.

Throughout the week Colbert performed a Bob Hope-style monologue (complete with golf club over his shoulder), brought his Emmy into his personal spider hole ("she's got her own body armor"), and interviewed military personnel including Commanding General Charles H. Jacoby Jr., Specialist Tareq Salha, and Sgt. Robin Balcom.

A three-part pretaped segment called Stephen Strong: Army of Me chronicled Stephen's attempt to go through basic training in Fort Jackson, SC. Stephen arrived at the army base by limo with a Louis Vuitton overnight bag, and acted like a pampered coward at every turn. The piece was heavily improvised, and near the end of the day-long shoot, Colbert finally cracked up his hardened drill sergeant, Demetrius Chantz. "He started singing his little song and that's the only time I smiled and we had to do a retake," Chantz said.

The moment in Iraq that got the most buzz (so to speak) was Gen. Ray Odierno shaving Stephen's head, as ordered by President Obama. The premise: Stephen was under the delusion that his turn at basic training went well, but Odierno said he just didn't have what it takes to be soldier. Unless, of course, he would be willing to look the part and get rid of his hair. (Unlike most interviews Colbert conducts, this exchange was scripted and rehearsed.)

"Frankly, sir, it's going to take more than a four-star general to get me to cut my hair," Stephen asserted.

After a few seconds of static, Obama appeared on-screen as if via satellite. (In reality, Obama's piece was filmed on May 29 at the White House. Colbert was in attendance to cue Obama by reading his own part, with co-executive producer Allison Silverman taking Odierno's lines.)

"I say, if Stephen Colbert wants to play soldier, it's time to cut that man's hair," Obama said.

"Sir, is that an order?" asked Odierno.

"General, as the Commander in Chief, I hereby order you to shave that man's head," Obama said.

Odierno obediently fired up the electric razor and sheared a strip down the middle of Colbert's head, and the troops in the palace went wild. Colbert threw to commercial break, during which the job was completed by Kerrie Plant-Price, the show's hair and makeup artist.

Gen. Ray Odierno shaves Stephen's head, per President Obama's orders.

But the on-screen successes didn't come easily. The show was hindered by limited technical resources, making almost every aspect of the production challenging. One-third of the *Report*'s staff went to Iraq, with the remainder staying behind in New York, many working night shifts to support the team overseas.

Bits that were easy to execute in the studio proved to be less so in Iraq. For The Wørd, the graphics displayed beside Stephen were shown to studio audiences as-broadcast, in monitors. But for quality reasons they had to be inserted in New York, meaning the audience in Iraq only saw the intended text projected on a screen behind him.

Likewise, the Iraq edition of Formidable Opponent, which had Stephen debating Don't Ask, Don't Tell against himself in front of a green screen, didn't have a one-step process as it did in New York.

Director Jim Hoskinson explained, "our technical director, Jon Pretnar, had to figure out how to change each background element manually with a quick sequence of buttons. And, because he was short on equipment, each time he did it, he had to reverse the order from the previous change."

Colbert later said of his crew, "I wish they'd fucked something up, so you could see how hard it was." But indeed, the four episodes came across as typically slick to the viewers at home.

"The truly satisfying thing was being able to do the shows for the troops over there, and to be deeply moved by their gratitude, and to be equally grateful to them for the opportunity," Colbert said in 2009. "It was beautiful to be able to do the shows for them."

P

P.K. Winsome (2006-2014)
(See also: Russ Lieber)

Racial issues can be very confusing for Stephen, since he doesn't see race. Luckily, on the golf course, he met P.K. Winsome (Tim Meadows)—a businessman and Republican who claimed to be black. P.K. stopped by to offer Stephen some insight on racial news all while selling questionable products (Obama collectibles when he was popular, anti-Obama collectibles when he wasn't) and reinforcing black stereotypes. P.K. shared his step-by-step plan to either impeach Obama or stop Obama from being impeached. The only step is to buy his choose-your-own-adventure book, *Look Out Obama, You're Being Impeached*.

Patterson Springs, NC (2005-2010)

Everyone has to start somewhere, and for Stephen, somewhere was Patterson Springs. Cue the faux flashbacks to the young newsman serving as midday news anchor at local station WPTS in 1989. Outfitted with big hair, moustache, and era-appropriate attire, old-school Stephen would deliver John Stossel-style rants on innocuous subjects. When an old video surfaced of Bill O'Reilly unleashing an angry tirade at his *Inside Edition* crew, Stephen commiserated with Papa Bear. He showed his own expletive-filled on-air meltdown at WPTS, ending with him ripping off his blazer and storming off the set in a dickie.

Peabody Awards (2008, 2014)

The George Foster Peabody Awards recognize excellence in television and radio, but for the first few years of the *Report*, Stephen had to make do with flaunting the two that *The Daily Show* won in 2000 and 2004. In 2008, he finally earned a Peabody of his own. According to the Peabody Committee, in 2007 Colbert had "come into his own as one of electronic media's sharpest satirists." Stephen's Peabody went missing after Cookie Monster appeared on the show, in a window above the mantle the award sat on. Cookie Monster evaded Stephen's question about whether he'd eaten the cookie-shaped award. Fortunately, Stephen won another in 2014 for his Super PAC coverage. He tweeted that he was so honored that he was speechless, but "Luckily, thanks to Citizens United, my money can speak for me."

After accepting his second Peabody, Colbert explained what getting these awards meant to "Stephen":

> "My character is a well-intentioned, poorly informed, high-status idiot. And this conveys status to him. The fact that he's gotten now two Peabody awards lets him say that he's a very important—he thinks—journalist. And this gives me status that I can undercut with my behavior."

People Who Are Destroying America (2008-2013)

In the style of Nailed 'Em, Stephen reported stories of people who were destroying America. He dramatically narrated in an ominous tone, undercut by the interviewee's responses to his comments. People destroy America by doing something like passing an LGBT fairness ordinance, registering students to vote, or hiring goats to keep the grass short. These things might seem harmless to your average hippie NPR listener, but from Stephen's point of view, they were tearing the country apart.

Pistachios (2014)

Wonderful commercials, in more ways than one. Stephen starred alongside a bald eagle in a series of ads for Wonderful brand pistachios that premiered during the Super Bowl. "Get crackin', America."

Portrait (2005-2014)
(See also: Art Me Up Challenge)

Every fireplace needs a portrait—inside a portrait, inside a portrait . . . Stephen's portrait of himself was refreshed every year around the time of the show's October anniversary. The new version always showed the previous version inside it, creating a narcissistic hall of mirrors (or as Stephen calls it, "an infinitely recursive depiction of America"). Usually, the "new" Stephen had one of his accomplishments added to the image, like a copy of *America Again* or his Grammy.

Retired portraits met prestigious fates. The first was auctioned off for $50,605 to benefit Save the Children, to the owner of Sticky Fingers, a Charleston, SC restaurant (where the portrait still hangs). Stephen successfully campaigned to have his second portrait hung in the National Portrait Gallery in Washington, D.C. (albeit next to the bathrooms). The fifth was transformed into true "art" by famous artists, and auctioned off for $26,000 with the proceeds going to DonorsChoose.org.

Presidential Run (2007)
(See also: Doritos)

President Colbert has a nice ring to it, doesn't it? Stephen started hinting at a potential run for the presidency while making the press rounds to promote *I Am America: And So Can You* in the fall of 2007. In October, he announced that he would run in his home state of South Carolina.

After learning that a spot on the Republican primary ballot would cost him $35,000, he suddenly decided to run as a Democrat instead (costing a paltry $2,500).

Colbert's intentions seemed to straddle the blurry line of satire and reality. Even his publicist wasn't entirely sure whether it was real or a joke, to which Colbert responded, "I don't understand the difference."

It was of little consequence, as the Democratic Party's executive council rejected his bid to appear on the January primary ballot just a few weeks later.

But what might have happened had he gotten on the ballot, and actually affected the outcome? Colbert later revealed on NPR's *Fresh Air*:

> "If I was doing well, I had a plan of how to drop out, which was that I was going to have a scandal. . . . I wanted to like actually go down to South Carolina and like stumble around Columbia, the capitol, pantsless with a bottle of Jack Daniels and try to get arrested. Which I gotta say, my wife was not thrilled about this plan. But she actually was thrilled that I had a rip cord to get out of the election."

Presidential Run (2012)
(See also: Super PAC)

This game had already been played during the 2008 election, and Colbert had moved on to a new one: his Super PAC, a bold dissection of campaign finance laws that would span the better part of two years. But the American public threw Colbert a curveball in January: Public Policy Polling determined that 5% of South Carolina voters would vote for him, putting him third behind Mitt Romney and President Obama, and beating out Jon Huntsman.

It was just a few weeks before the South Carolina primaries that Stephen made his first move.

To legally run, Stephen handed over the reins of his Super PAC to Jon Stewart, and announced, "I am forming an exploratory committee to lay the groundwork for my possible candidacy for the President of the United States of South Carolina."

But Stephen was too late: he missed the deadline to get himself on the ballot, by a mere 2-½ months. So instead, he put himself in as a substitute for Herman Cain, who had officially suspended his campaign but would appear on the South Carolina ballot regardless. Cain, who was fully game, appeared alongside Stephen at a public rally in his hometown of Charleston to drum up support.

But Cain (and by extension, Stephen) earned just 1% of the vote. So it was "with a heavy heart and a spastic colon" that Stephen re-suspended Cain's suspended campaign, and also ended his own exploratory committee.

Prince Hawkcat (2014)

"Half hawk. Half cat. Whole prince." Stephen wanted in on the lucrative comic book adaptation market, so he bought the rights to the (fake) Hawkcat comics. He attended San Diego Comic-Con dressed as Prince Hawkcat: a black and gold military jacket, white makeup, prosthetic beak with protruding whiskers, and a feathered headpiece with cat ears. To Stephen's surprise, nobody could identify the character he was cosplaying (costumed as).

Stephen advertised his movie T.B.D., based on the Prince Hawkcat series, at a booth on the exhibition floor. Passersby were baffled by the premise (Stephen characterized their responses as "muted"), but luckily he had another movie to sell: Mañana Banana, a movie about a banana with a Christian message. Comic-Con attendees weren't too impressed with that one, either. But Stephen's life savings were tied up in both films, so he combined them into one entirely new movie: Prince Mañana Hawknana.

Thanks to his elaborate costume, Colbert was unrecognizable on the exhibition floor at Comic-Con, but he was identified on Reddit weeks before the segment aired.

Pumpkin Patch (2010-2014)

Stephen's safe word. If he said it, it meant "this is getting a little heavy for me and I need to pull out." Used when Stephen was being taught how to be an NFL quarterback, learning how to be an astronaut, and signing up for Obamacare. Also suggested as the trigger word a Soviet official would use to recall possible Russian spy Regina Spektor.

R

@RealHumanPraise (2013)

#PraiseFox. The Twitter account @RealHumanPraise is your source for praise of Fox News that is entirely composed of "legitimate reviews from 100% people." When journalist David Folkenflik reported that Fox News employees were planting hundreds of fake positive comments on negative or neutral articles about Fox News, Stephen took fake praise to the next level with a Twitter bot (an algorithm that automatically generates tweets based on specific criteria).

Set up by *Report* writer Rob Dubbin, @RealHumanPraise quotes positive movie reviews from the film website Rotten Tomatoes, and applies them to Fox programming. The results were fantastic: the Twitter bot created fitting and funny reviews like "Fox & Friends Weekend remains an intelligent creepy tale that has not lost its luster over time. #PraiseFox" and "One of the best family productions of the 80s. Jeanine Pirro and Brit Hume are delightful. A show you'll cherish forever. #PraiseFOX."

Rain (2007)

RAAAAAAAAAAAIN! Korean pop sensation Rain did the unforgivable: he beat Stephen in a popularity contest. And not just any popularity contest: he earned more online votes than Stephen on *TIME* magazine's 100 Most Influential People list. Stephen couldn't have that, so he made his own K-pop music video called "Singin' in Korean," which was a direct parody of a hit Rain music video. In it, Stephen wore a bomber jacket, a white sleeveless shirt, skinny jeans, a big chain necklace, and sunglasses. Against a bad green-screen backdrop of a sunset, Stephen sang and danced with a chorus of backup dancers in a choreographed routine. The song's main lyric? "He's singin' in Korean."

But the rivalry didn't stop there. Stephen waged a one-sided war against Rain, challenging him to a dance-off in the studio. But when *The Colbert Report* ended that night, Rain still hadn't shown up, and Stephen assumed he wasn't going to accept. Cut to "after" the show: Stephen let his guard down in his darkened studio, and was whistling and fixing a camera while looking just as cool as he did in his video. A sudden noise startled him: Rain!

The K-pop star emerged from a cloud of smoke, looking effortlessly cool in a three-piece suit with his long hair pulled back into a ponytail, sunglasses covering his eyes, and his feet ready to move. Stephen tried his best to match his rival, even putting a pair of sunglasses over his wire-rimmed glasses. For the first few rounds of the dance-off, Stephen held his own, but his freestyle moves just weren't enough to defeat Rain. So he dramatically produced a coin which he inserted into a Dance Dance Revolution game. The two men competed side by side, dancing faster and faster until Rain danced so hard that sparks flew from his feet—and finally vanished in the cloud of smoke that rose from the rubble of the destroyed game. Despite Stephen's attempt to chase after him, Rain's limo drove away into the New York night.

Rally to Restore Sanity And/Or Fear (2010)
(See also: Reddit)

It began as everything Stephen hates: a celebration of rational thinking. After all, "reason is just one letter away from treason."

Jon Stewart's Rally to Restore Sanity, a three-hour affair on the National Mall in Washington, was designed to be an antidote to the recent rhetoric-fueled Restoring Honor march led by pundit Glenn Beck. Stewart announced the Rally on the September 16 episode of *The Daily Show*. But not to be outdone by this "glorified noodle fest," Stephen quickly announced his own event: the March to Keep Fear Alive, to be held at the same time and place as Stewart's gathering.

For weeks, the Rally and the March were played up as two separate events, with Stephen giving viewers the hard sell on fear. But things soon started to fall apart for Stephen. Since Stewart had dibs on the National Mall, that left Stephen with no location for his March.

Stephen paid a surprise visit to *The Daily Show* studio on October 14, 2010, for what he claimed was no reason. But Stewart couldn't be fooled: "You didn't get a rally permit, did you?" Stephen broke down and admitted he hadn't. But he successfully appealed to Stewart's sense of reason to have his name added to the official National Mall permit, for what would henceforth be known as the Rally to Restore Sanity And/Or Fear.

The three-hour event took place on the afternoon of October 30. Stewart and Colbert cohosted the affair, with Stewart playing the reasonable man and Stephen as his patriotic fearmongering foil. Highlights of the star-studded event included the Mythbusters trying to cause an earthquake by having the audience jump up and down, and Yusuf Islam (Cat Stevens) performing "Peace Train" while—at Stephen's urging—Ozzy Osborne constantly interrupted with "Crazy Train".

Stewart ended the event with a heartfelt speech, sincerely explaining the motives behind the Rally, and how the amplification of the country's problems by the 24-hour news networks did not represent the spirit of its citizens.

An estimated 215,000 people attended the event, with thousands more unable to access the area. Two million viewers watched the Rally live on Comedy Central, and the broadcast earned four Daytime Emmy nominations.

Reddit (2009-2014)

Upvote for Truthiness! Colbert is a longtime user of the popular content-sharing and discussion site. In 2010, he told guest Nicholas Carr that "I could burn my entire life on that site." A user who attended a *Report* taping in 2011 reported that during the Q&A, Colbert cited Reddit as the first website he visited every day. In 2014, Colbert said that since Reddit had become dominated by memes over time, he went directly to the /r/news and /r/politics subreddits to find fodder for the show.

To say the Reddit community returns Colbert's dedication would be an understatement. In late August of 2010, Redditors began discussing the idea of Colbert leading a "Restore Truthiness" rally to satirize Glenn Beck's earnest version, not knowing that plans for the Rally To Restore Sanity And/Or Fear were already underway behind the scenes at *The Daily Show*. As part of the push to convince Colbert to make the idea a reality, Reddit users began donating money to one of Colbert's charities of choice, DonorsChoose.org.

Two weeks into the fundraiser, Colbert wrote a message to the site's users, thanking them for the support and teasing the possibility of the event coming to fruition.

Once the Rally was actually announced, Colbert kept the donations rolling in with a bonus incentive: if Reddit could raise more than $500,000 for DonorsChoose.org, he would do a Q&A for the site. The goal was easily surpassed, so in late November Colbert answered a short list of user-submitted questions about the show, his character, and the Rally. He thanked Reddit for contributing, saying:

> "I am so impressed that your idea of coercion is to do good deeds until they are national news. CNN and others were reporting your charity blackmail just days after you started. A new idea, I think, and something to be proud of. The rally was tremendously supported by you all, along with Facebook, and Twitter. I have no doubt that your efforts to organize and the joy you clearly brought to your part of the story contributed greatly to the turnout and success. Contrary to whatever bullshit quotes you may have heard in the bullshit press."

Colbert made a few stealthy on-air shout-outs to Reddit. The Tuesday following the Rally, he casually raised his script up to reveal Snoo, the Reddit alien mascot, doodled on the back. In 2013, a Reddit user posted a still from a recent episode, showing what appeared to be a box of tissues and a bottle of lotion under Stephen's desk (implying that he could be pleasuring himself down there). At the top of the next night's show, without saying a word about it, Colbert brought both items up on to his desk, revealing that the bottle contained hand sanitizer.

As for his character, "Stephen" wasn't entirely sold on the premise of Reddit. He told Reddit cofounder Alexis Ohanian in 2013 that the democratic nature of the site robs "cultural tastemakers like myself" of their influence.

Remix Challenge (2009)

Stephen strongly disagreed with guest Lawrence Lessig, who asserted that copyright laws should allow for remixing. Stephen warned viewers, "I'll be very angry, and possibly litigious, if anyone out there takes this interview right here and remixes it with some great dance beat."

Of course, leave it to some "DJ Jazzy Jerks" to do just that, flooding the Internet with their club-worthy remixes. Stephen was so enraged that he made his own remix as a warning. The trippy, throbbing tune was accompanied by clips of the *Report* altered with every effect in the book, intercut with footage of Stephen dancing in the dark wearing tribal-inspired glowing face paint and wielding glow sticks.

Stephen reiterated that he absolutely did not want anyone to remix the Lessig interview. And he *certainly* didn't want them to mix it with excerpts from the audiobook version of *I Am America (And So Can You!)*, specifically the chapter entitled "Homosexuals".

Naturally, many versions of exactly that can still be found on YouTube.

Richard Branson (2007, 2011)
(See also: Air Colbert)

Instant classic: just add water. Richard Branson's 2007 appearance on the *Report* came with a tall glass of scandal, in the form of a much-hyped water fight.

The interview was recorded August 7, 2011 for later broadcast, and a fan who attended the taping reported that Branson lashed out at Colbert with his mug of water, creating an awkward moment for everyone in the studio. The interview wouldn't air until August 22, giving fans and the media ample time to froth at the mouth with speculation over just how bad Branson's act of aggression would be.

Colbert fanned the flames of this supposed "train wreck" in advance of the airing, telling viewers to "please stop talking about this juicy, mysterious story."

The truth turned out to be much less sinister than imagined. Branson was determined to wedge a specific plug into the interview, but was irked by Stephen's fixation on his namesake Virgin aircraft, Air Colbert. Finally, Stephen acquiesced, and smugly sat back and put his feet on the table awaiting the end of the plug. In response, Branson tossed a mug's worth of water across the table.

A doused Stephen motioned for co-executive producer Allison Silverman to bring him some ammunition. He squirted half a bottle of water at Branson before sliding it over to his guest, inviting him to empty the rest back in his direction.

Colbert later confirmed to the *New Jersey Star-Ledger* that it was a purely playful moment. "I loved it. I have no status to protect. I thought it was wonderful that he did that," he said.

Perhaps less wonderful was the escalation of the game in 2011. Branson visited the show again, and this time chased Colbert around the set with a fire extinguisher, leaving him covered from head to toe with powder.

It appeared, like the water fight, to be all in good fun. But according to a fan who attended a taping a few nights later, the gag was less innocent than it appeared on-air. Colbert reportedly told the audience that his prop department supplied Branson with a CO_2 fire extinguisher, but that Branson switched it out with a chemical version. Colbert's lungs were still hurting as a result.

Stephen confirmed in a later episode that he and Branson had had their disagreements: "Specifically, my lungs disagreed with the fire retardant he fired into them the last time he was here."

Rock & Awe: Countdown To Guitarmageddon (2006)
(See also: Green Screen Challenge)

Who's riding Stephen's coattails now? Rock group The Decemberists. In the wake of Stephen's Green Screen Challenge, the band similarly filmed a performance in front of a green screen, inviting fans to get creative with the background. Stephen wouldn't take this lying down, so he issued a second

Green Screen Challenge to the Nation to edit him into the Decemberists video. But the Decemberists shot back, issuing a challenge of their own—a Guitar Solo Challenge. "Let's see what kind of man you really are—let's shred," they said in a statement.

Stephen accepted, confident he'd win his face-off against guitarist Chris Funk. The much-hyped showdown would happen on December 20, judged by *Rolling Stone* critic Anthony DeCurtis, Grammy-winning producer Jim Anderson, and New York Governor-elect Eliot Spitzer. Colbert called on a "live via satellite" (but actually pretaped) Dr. Henry Kissinger to kick off the battle.

"Henry, what time is it?" Stephen asked.

"Stephen, it is time to rock," Kissinger deadpanned.

Stephen was not fazed by Funk's impressive shred, and took the stage with a five-neck guitar on loan from Rick Nielsen of Cheap Trick, "because I might shred so hard tonight that I'll blow out the first four necks."

But first, was there anything Dr. Kissinger wished to say?

"Stephen, crank it up."

But crank it up he did not. Stephen promptly—and unconvincingly—cut his hand on the guitar, meaning he couldn't shred at all. He called for a substitute to compete on his behalf: Peter Frampton, who effortlessly gave Funk a run for his money.

But who won? The judges were split, and so was the audience. That left only one person to determine the winner.

"Tonight, the American people won," Kissinger said.

(Kissinger, remarkably game to participate, was prodded by Colbert to say one more line to justify why he'd ever appear on the show: "Where are my pancakes? I was promised pancakes." But he refused to go that far. "I did a full-court press," Colbert later recalled on NPR's *Fresh Air*. "Somewhere there exists the recording of me trying to convince Kissinger to say the lines, but we just couldn't get him to say it.")

According to Stephen, "America" meant him! And as the winner, Stephen was awarded first prize: a Decemberists CD.

To end the show, Neilson—who wrote the *Colbert Report* theme song—led Stephen and his musical guests in a fully rocking rendition of it to close out the show's first full calendar year on the air.

Russ Lieber (2005-2007)

This "crackpot radio host out of Madison, Wisconsin," played by comedian David Cross, was "one nut short" according to Stephen. That didn't stop Stephen from inviting him on the show and trying to knock some sense into his extreme lefty leanings. Russ's crazy liberal beliefs included thinking that genetically modified pumpkins are a threat to indigenous species, that it doesn't matter if his drum-circle friends are gay, and that one person cannot speak on behalf of all Jews. Stephen repeatedly gave Lieber the chance to apologize to America, but he was beyond redemption.

S

Saginaw Spirit (2006-2007)

He shoots, he scores! The Saginaw Spirit, an Ontario Hockey League team based in Saginaw, Michigan, was looking for a name for their new mini-mascot, which just happened to be an eagle. Stephen urged the Nation to vote for the name "Colbeagle" and the Nation obliged. After a half-million hits to the team's website, Steagle Colbeagle the Eagle was the winning name by a landslide.

Steagle made his on-ice debut at the Spirit's September 30, 2006 game, introduced to fans by a prerecorded video of Stephen on the scoreboard. Just seconds into his victory lap, he tripped and fell. "He's a fledgling," Stephen explained.

A mascot was just the beginning. Stephen was now personally invested in the team, and kept the Nation up to date on the Spirit's scores and standings. One particular goal scored against them had Stephen fuming: Oshawa Generals fans celebrated the goal by throwing stuffed bears on the ice. Stephen saw this as an obvious personal attack on him. (In reality, it was part of the team's annual Teddy Bear Toss for charity.)

Stephen gave Spirit fans the chance to retaliate during the rematch. Oshawa, Ontario is home to the Canadian headquarters of General Motors, and Stephen noted that their recently released third-quarter earnings statement showed a "little cash flow problem." And while Stephen clarified that he was definitely not urging fans to throw copies of the General Motors annual report on the ice to celebrate Saginaw's first goal, he said he would make a PDF copy of the document available through colbertnation.com.

Before fans could pummel the ice with paper, Oshawa Mayor John Gray took to the local airwaves and proposed a truce, in the form of a bet. If Oshawa won the rematch, Stephen would have to wear a Generals jersey for an entire show. If Saginaw won, Mayor Gray would proclaim "Stephen Colbert Day" in Oshawa. Stephen accepted.

Saginaw was victorious, with copies of the annual report predictably strewn across the ice after the first goal was scored. Mayor Gray confirmed that he'd proclaim March 20, 2006 Stephen Colbert Day in Oshawa. In the interests of good sportsmanship, Stephen also wore a Generals jersey on the air, which had been transformed into a pair of tight-fitting shorts with the team logo displayed across his derriere.

Getting the Colbert Bump gave the Spirit a 5x increase in merchandise sales that season. The team continues to use Steagle Colbeagle the Eagle as its mini-mascot, alongside its main mascot Sammy Spirit.

Shofar (2006-2014)

(See also: Atone Phone)

"You can really taste the ram!" A shofar is a ram's horn, which Jewish people blow like a trumpet on the High Holidays. According to Stephen, the shofar "sounds as good as it tastes." Always one for cultural sensitivity, Stephen blew the shofar every autumn around Yom Kippur—the Day of Atonement—before reminding Jews to call in to his Atone Phone line and apologize for having wronged him.

In 2009, during the swine flu epidemic, a group of rabbis flew around Israel in a plane while praying and blowing the shofar to ward off the disease. Stephen issued them a wag of his finger for "defeating swine flu, but spreading ram flu."

Shout Out (2006-2011, 2014)

HEY! Stephen gave shout-outs only to the most deserving people: meaning, those who first shouted out to him. Each segment kicked off with Stephen's own voiceover shouting "HEY!" (almost always timed to genuinely startle Colbert), before he launched into reciprocating props. No honor was too small, whether it was a group of Marines who took a poster of Stephen aboard their submarine; soldiers in Iraq who erected a sign citing the distance to the *Report* studio; or, in a special kids' edition, showcasing supposedly real letters penned by young fans (the takeaway: please do fewer Ewok-eating jokes, and more stuff about Nazis).

Smile File (2013-2014)

The news is so depressing these days, full of stories about heartless dictators and international terrorist groups. Fortunately, Stephen could lighten the mood with stories about... heartless dictators and international terrorist groups. After all, seeing Kim Jong-un explore an industrial lubricant factory, looking as gleeful as a kid in a candy store, is enough to put a smile on anyone's face!

South Pole Minute (2006)

Stephen's farthest-flung fan? He resides all the way down at the South Pole. Stephen gave a shout out ("HEY!") to Michael Rehm, a chef at the Amundsen-Scott South Pole Station. Rehm was deemed a hero because he downloaded *The Colbert Report* by satellite linkup, proving that the show provided him with everything he needed to know about the outside world: Stephen's opinion. So Stephen created a segment tailored for Rehm, all about South Pole-related issues such as ice-core samples and upper-atmosphere physics.

Rehm was the research station's cook, and, according to Stephen, appeared to be in a "fragile mental state" based on photos of him with long hair and surrounded by bottles of liquor. So as not to upset Rehm, Stephen said that the Republicans won the midterm elections in a landslide, everything was fine, and that the President had sent Donald Rumsfeld to live on a farm.

Speedskating (2009-2010, 2014)
(See also: Vancouver Olympics)

"Stephen Colbert and His Nation Save The Olympics." So read the headline splashed across the cover of the December 21, 2009 edition of *Sports Illustrated*, next to Colbert himself dressed in full speedskating garb.

Stephen and the US Speedskating team joined forces—along with the Colbert Nation—in what NPR called "the funniest and least likely sponsorship in Olympic sports."

The team's major corporate sponsor, DSB Bank, went bankrupt, leaving them in dire need of support leading up to the 2010 Winter Olympics in Vancouver.

After hearing the news, Stephen invited Olympic gold medalist Dan Jansen to the show to explain why the speedskating team was so important. Jansen told Stephen that the team earns the most medals of any Winter Olympic sport. That was all Stephen needed to hear. He couldn't stand the idea of DSB Bank hurting America's chances of winning gold, so Bob Crowley, the Executive Director of US Speedskating, presented Stephen with the sponsorship papers. Stephen promptly signed them on behalf of the Colbert Nation amid audience chants of "U.S.A.! U.S.A.!" Stephen directed viewers to colbertnation.com to donate to US Speedskating, and the Nation did exactly that.

Stephen told his audience that they should ignore naysayers like speed skater Bill Armstrong, who called the Colbert Nation's sponsorship of the team "undignified." They should continue to donate, because anyone who didn't think his name was "synonymous with dignity" could "kiss my 12-inch taint."

With the Colbert name emblazoned on their uniforms and rink banners, the team was ready to head to Vancouver for the Olympics. But there was one small problem: team member and Olympic champion Shani Davis told reporters that Colbert was "a jerk."

Determined to settle the score, Stephen issued a challenge to Davis: a speedskating race. If Stephen won, he'd get Davis's spot on the Olympic team. It was no surprise to anyone (except maybe Stephen) that he lost the 500m race to Davis, but he did walk away with two other wins: a spot on the team as the assistant sports psychologist, and Davis's good graces.

Davis told the *New York Times* it "was really cool to actually meet Colbert and get a chance to get to know him a little better as a person and understand what he does as a comedian."

U.S. Olympian Katherine Reutter came on the show to express her gratitude for Stephen and the Colbert Nation's support. Before she left, Reutter asked Stephen to autograph her upper thigh. A genuinely flummoxed Colbert got down on his knee and obliged.

By January 19, 2010, the Colbert Nation had made up for the team's lost sponsor, with 9,760 Colbert viewers contributing more than $300,000. In a YouTube video, Brad Goskowicz, President of US Speedskating, thanked Stephen and called working with him "a lot of fun."

At the 2014 Winter Olympics in Sochi, Russia, the US Speedskating team performed worse than expected, and the Netherlands speedskating coach accused Americans of only being good at American sports. Since "revenge is best served cold on razor-sharp blades," Stephen again asked the nation to go to colbertnation.com and donate to the team in exchange for a Blade in the USA t-shirt.

Spiderman (2008)
(See also: Captain America)

With great power comes great political responsibility. Stephen was featured as a presidential candidate throughout the extra-sized issue of *Amazing Spider-Man* #573, but he also got his own eight-page story as Spiderman's sidekick. The Stephen Colbert variant was published on October 15, 2008. In it, Stephen Colbert is giving a campaign speech to a sparse crowd and is about to quit when he notices Spiderman and a villain—The Grizzly—in the audience. Spiderman says it isn't Stephen's fight, but Stephen defeats The Grizzly for Spiderman by pushing a statue off a building and onto his head.

Sport Report (2005-2014)
(See also: Saginaw Spirit)

Cue the air guitar! The Sport Report (pronounced with silent Ts, naturally) was introduced with a screaming electric guitar riff, which Stephen mimiced before launching into the latest sports headlines. But those headlines rarely involved scores or standings. Instead, Stephen dug deep to deliver the important stories like Brett Favre's sexting allegations, swimming pools being installed in the Jacksonville Jaguars' stadium, and exciting new sports such as chess boxing and freestyle canoe dancing.

In a special series entitled Sport Report—From Russia with Love (But No Gay Stuff), Stephen handed the reins to comedian Scott Thompson, who took his flamboyant Kids in the Hall character Buddy Cole to Sochi, Russia to report on the 2014 Winter Olympics.

Originally titled Stephen Colbert's Sports Update, the Sport Report was initially dedicated to news about the Ontario Hockey League's Saginaw Spirit.

Starbucks (2006-2014)

Stephen likes his coffee the way he likes his anger: steamin'. As a big fan of Starbucks, he was fully behind the concept of a location opening in a South Carolina funeral home, and hailed their new 31-oz. Trenta size as being "one step closer to my dream of Starbucks offering a plexiglass room that fills with coffee."

Stephen even had a Starbucks located under his desk, manned by a barista who bore a striking resemblance to co-executive producer Barry Julien.

As a regular customer, any change to his daily cup of joe threw Stephen's life into chaos. When the chain announced a five-cent increase in coffee prices, Stephen was appalled that his pre-show "five-shot Venti caramel mocha" would cost him an extra $8 per broadcast season. He announced he would kick his caffeine addiction in protest, an idea that lasted mere seconds as he was unable to bring himself to throw his cup of coffee in the garbage.

It was a sign of struggles to come, because in 2008, true tragedy struck: all Starbucks locations in America shut down for three hours to retrain their staff. That meant no afternoon coffee fix for anyone, including Stephen. According to him, he handled his 180 decaffeinated minutes "with aplomb," but the video evidence proved otherwise. Stephen was shown lighting a Starbucks cup on fire to inhale the fumes, lifting up a female staffer and pinning her against the wall, and growling like a rabid dog while chained up in the *Report*'s boiler room.

When he finally staggered back to Starbucks and got his hands on his oh-so-vital Venti, he enjoyed it by pouring it over himself in the shower and smearing latte foam across his naked torso.

Stelephant Colbert (2009)

"Well, I'm sure he's got a very nice personality." UC Santa Cruz Long Marine Lab named an elephant seal after Stephen. When a picture of the seal popped up on the screen, Stephen recoiled in horror, thinking he was looking at "some hideous monster" that *ate* his cute seal. Next time, he'd like something beautiful named after him, like a "Stephen Colbeorge Clooney the George Clooney." Stelephant Colbert and Jon Sealwart, an elephant seal named after Jon Stewart, were both tagged by USCS biologists as part of the Tagging of Pacific Predators program.

Stephanie Colburtle (2007)

Stephen wasn't normally an endangered species-hugger—unless there was a chance one of his namesakes might be a winner. To keep his mind off the 2008 presidential race, Stephen turned his attention to the Great Turtle Race. One of eleven contestants, Stephanie Colburtle was an endangered leatherback turtle named after Stephen by students at Drexel University.

Stephanie Colburtle and her competitors were fitted with satellite tags and tracked on their journey from their breeding grounds in Costa Rica to the waters near the Galapagos Islands, where leatherback turtles feed. Viewers could go to greatturtlerace.com to watch them swim.

The captain, crew, and passengers of the M/V Santa Cruz, a Galapagos Cruise Ship, endorsed Stephanie Colburtle. Sadly, four of the leatherback turtles, including Stephanie Colburtle, went missing before they could complete the race. But Jim Spotila, Drexel's turtle expert, called the race an overall success because it raised awareness and $250,000 for conservation efforts.

Stephen & Melinda Gates Foundation (2006-2011)
(See also: Donors Choose)

Stephen was always a huge admirer of Bill Gates's money, so when Gates left Microsoft to head the Bill & Melinda Gates Foundation, Stephen was inspired to create the Stephen & Melinda Gates Foundation. The Foundation has been working tirelessly since 2006 to find out what they support. Stephen received their first donation of "one American dollar" on July 17, 2006. Stephen learned "the hard way" that he was not allowed to ask for money on the show, so he told the audience not to send him $20, because they would not receive a "high-quality, 100% cotton *Colbert Report* T-shirt" and $50 would not get you a "durable, sporty" tote bag.

Stephen announced on September 27, 2011 that no matter how many angry letters he got, the foundation would support "the children." Stephen asked the Colbert Nation to go to stephenandmelindagatesfoundation.org to donate money and upload a picture of themselves. Their picture would be edited into a photo of Stephen and Melinda Gates, showing the viewer, Melinda, and Stephen in a "freaky philanthropic three-way." The Bill & Melinda Gates Foundation would donate $5 to DonorsChoose.org for each picture uploaded, up to $100,000.

Melinda Gates was a guest on the show that night, and Stephen called her out for failing to attend board meetings and pay dues to the Stephen & Melinda Gates Foundation, of which they are the only two members. But he did thank her for supporting DonorsChoose.org.

Stephen Jr. (2006-2009)
(See also: Jimmy, Bobby, Tad)

The San Francisco Zoo Eagle Project wished to honor Stephen by naming a yet-to-be-born bald eagle after him, and Stephen couldn't have been prouder to be an eagle papa. To help Stephen Jr.'s development before he hatched, Stephen played him some music: former Attorney General John Ashcroft singing "Let the Eagle Soar," a song Ashcroft wrote himself. Stephen took the concept of nesting to the next level, providing Stephen Jr. with an actual nest in his studio.

Stephen Jr. had the Colbert Nation's support from the beginning. People sent cards and gifts to the eaglet, and Stephen told viewers that Lou Dobbs even sent a dead squirrel. Stephen Jr. hatched on Patriot's Day, April 17, 2006. Stephen smoked a celebratory cigar on the show the following night, and showed footage of the eagle breaking through his membrane "just like Reagan when he tore down the Berlin Wall."

Stephen Jr. grew up fast, and for Father's Day, his handlers helped him make Stephen a print of his left talon. Stephen noted that the spacing of two of the razor-sharp talons matched up perfectly with a man's eyes.

After seeing footage of the zoo "torturing" Stephen Jr. (giving him a physical exam and banding him), Stephen decided to assemble a crack commando squad to rescue his son. The Colmandos (his crew members Killer, Bobby, and Jimmy along with The Cars frontman Ric Ocasek) agreed to go and bring Stephen Jr. back. Bobby the Stage Manager returned and reported that Stephen Jr. had been released with his tracking device, and that Stephen would have to track his whereabouts on the Institute for Wildlife Studies' map. Stephen was horrified to see that Stephen Jr. had gone into Canada, and demanded that Canada return his son. He asked the Colbert Nation to help by waving salmon at the border.

Stephen Jr.'s tracking transmitter stopped working shortly after he went to Canada, but he was located again by wildlife and conservation expert David Hancock in Vancouver, hanging around a garbage dump and harassing a pelican.

Stephen Jr. made it back into the U.S. by November. Unfortunately, he ended up in the district of Brian Baird, a congressman Stephen "Better Knew," and who he characterized as a "meth addict."

Stephen sent Tad the Building Manager to the Connecticut Audubon Eagle Festival to find Stephen Jr. a girlfriend to entice him to come back home to Stephen. But it turned out the festival wasn't for eagle hunting, but for eagle watching, and they frowned on trying to shoot eagles with tranquilizers. Tad came home with nothing to show for himself but several deep scratches on his face and a chicken, which he claimed was an eagle.

In October 2008, Stephen Jr. was spotted in Oregon, which Stephen assumed meant he was campaigning for John McCain. Stephen Jr. was photographed at the Lower Klamath National Wildlife Refuge on December 24th, 2008.

According to the IWS Interactive Map, he has since dropped his transmitter and his current whereabouts are unknown. But Stephen Jr.'s cry will live on in our ears, because in May 2009, it was immortalized on the Center for Biological Diversity's educational endangered species ringtone website, RareEarthtones.org.

Stephen Settles the Debate (2005-2008)

In Stephen Settles the Debate, Stephen bravely picked a side on close contests. In Whales/Cod vs. Polar Bears/Seal Hunters, the winner was Whales/Cod because cod is delicious. Stephen also settled the debates on Ramadan vs. Halloween (Halloween, although Stephen emphasized that he has a lot of respect for Islam), Science vs. Faith (faith), and Franklin Delano Roosevelt vs. Theodore Roosevelt (neither—the "borderline racist" *Sesame Street* character Roosevelt Franklin won, for representing both blue and red states by being purple).

Stephen's Sound Advice (2006-2010)

Stephen's absurd advice on everything from avoiding wildfires to acing the SATs. Thinking of starting a civil war? Civil war dos: document your uniforms well for future re-enactors, hire famous generals so they'll later make great pieces in a chess set, and write love letters to a girl back home to be sealed in a shoebox with recordings of your favorite music (they'll make good shots in the documentary montage). Don'ts: go to the theatre.

StePhest Colbchella (2011-2013)
(See also: Daft Punk)

Stephen's answer to those "half-naked, patchouli-soaked, white-guy-dreadlock festivals" like Coachella and Bonnaroo. In 2011, Stephen started a new tradition of hosting a week of summer music shows. Dr. Pepper Presents StePhest Colbchella '011: Rock You Like a Thirst-icane. For that inaugural edition, Stephen (and Dr. Pepper) hosted Bon Iver, Florence and the Machine, Talib Kweli, and Jack White at the *Report* studios.

The following year, Stephen announced that StePhest Colbchella '012: RocktAugustFest would include a concert at the Intrepid Sea, Air & Space Museum, a retired warship docked on the west side of Manhattan. The concert was aired over four nights, so four opening and closing segments were filmed back to back before the musical performances. Colbert recorded the interviews with the bands earlier in the day on board the Intrepid. RocktAugustFest featured musical performances by Santigold, fun., Grandmaster Flash, The Flaming Lips, and Grizzly Bear. The show's finale had Stephen crowdsurfing in a plastic ball, a signature prop of Flaming Lips lead singer Wayne Coyne. COLBERT was spelled out in lights above the stage, and later the sign was given a prominent place of honor on *The Colbert Report* set, where it was visible when the camera panned the audience.

During StePhest Colbchella '013, Stephen famously got "Daft Punk'd" when the duo canceled on him at the last moment.

Steve Colbert (2010)

Can the world handle a third version of this man? Stephen was excited to interview the members of the band Gorillaz, who were animated characters and, unfortunately, fictional. When he learned he'd be forced to settle for their human counterparts (Damon Albarn and Jamie Hewlett), he refused, and stormed off the set in a rage.

But Stephen sent a replacement in to conduct the interview on his behalf. Colbert meekly walked back on stage in his real street clothes (The North Face fleece, khakis, and Merrell slip-ons) and introduced himself to Albarn and Hewlett as "Steve Colbert" (with a hard "t").

Steve was the total opposite of Stephen: soft-spoken, polite, and earnest (essentially an extreme version of Colbert's real-life persona). Steve heaped praised upon the duo and asked them Stephen's prepared questions, such as "who the hell do you think you are?" with wide-eyed fascination.

Steve also delivered the Act 4 goodnight, saying, "This is a fun job. I don't know why he ever complains."

Studio
(See also: HD, Tapings)

Colbert had a longer history with the nondescript building at 513 W. 54th St. than some viewers may realize. The 4,530-foot studio and its adjacent offices (owned by NEP Studios), were previously the home of *The Daily Show with Jon Stewart*. When *The Daily Show* moved to larger facilities in 2005, Colbert stayed put.

"They left me here like a place setting on a magician's table after he pulls the tablecloth away," Colbert told Zap2it.com in 2005. "We've painted the place and hosed out most of the irony. We've scraped it down to a level of sincerity that we can shellac with our own sarcasm."

Veteran set designer Jim Fenhagen executed the original vision for the set. Colbert called for a Last Supper-style amplification of his character's status, with all the visual elements converging on him.

"If you look at the design, it all does, it all points at my head. And even radial lines on the floor, and on my podium, and watermarks in the images behind me, and all the vertices, are right behind my head. So there's a sort of sun-god burst quality about the set around me. And I love that. That's status," Colbert explained in a 2006 A.V. Club interview.

Also serving his character's ego was his own name emblazoned on every surface, as he pointed out in the first segment of the first episode. Even his desk, when viewed from above, was shaped like the letter C.

Fenhagen also redesigned the set for the show's 2010 transition to HD, with additions like the four vertical video columns behind Stephen's desk, and light boxes behind his bookshelves. The upgrade also included the words "videri quam esse" engraved above Stephen's fireplace. It's the reverse of the popular Latin motto "esse quam videri," which means "to be, rather than to seem to be."

After the set redesign, Stephen's original C-shaped desk was auctioned off to benefit the Dr. James W. Colbert Fund at the University of South Carolina. His original interview desk was auctioned off to benefit Red Cross Haitian relief. At the end of the series, the new C-shaped desk and the fireplace set were raffled off in support of DonorsChoose.org and the Yellow Ribbon Fund.

In January 2015, the studio became the home of *The Nightly Show*.

Super PAC (2011-2012)

(See also: Ham Rove, Presidential Run)

What began as a parody of a real political ad became an adventure lasting nearly two years, thrusting Stephen deep into campaign-finance law and even deeper into the Colbert Nation's pockets, earning the show a Peabody Award in the process.

It all started in March 2012, when Colbert satirized the over-the-top ad that former Minnesota governor Tim Pawlenty had produced to promote his new book. As Colbert told NPR's *Fresh Air*:

> "I couldn't figure out how to end it . . . His ad ended just with like a single card on screen that said: LibertyPAC.com, or whatever his political action committee was. And I said 'OK, just put up ColbertPAC.com at the end.' And one person on the staff said, 'Do you want me to buy that URL?' And I said 'Yeah, yeah, we might want to use that later.'"

"Later" became "immediately" once Colbert received a call from Comedy Central, asking if he was really going to form a political action committee (PAC). If so, that could cause trouble.

"Well, then I'm definitely going to do it," Colbert said.

The parody ad aired with ColbertPAC.com at the end, and the tagline "Americans for a Better Tomorrow, Tomorrow." Stephen urged the Nation to go to the site and sign up for the mailing list. Viewers did, with no more idea than Stephen what would come of it.

"I didn't have any plan . . . I just wanted to see what would happen," Colbert said.

Forming Colbert PAC

Stephen knew he needed a PAC, but didn't actually know what PACs did or how to form one. He solicited the help of lawyer and former Federal Election Commission (FEC) chairman Trevor Potter. In a Reddit.com post, Potter explained how he initially got involved:

> "First he called and asked about 30 minutes of technical questions about Pacs--who can have one, how they work, etc. Then he asked if I'd be "willing to say all of that on air"...so I went on the show to answer his questions and explain Pacs. Only after that did he tell me that he really wanted one, and asked if I could help--and by then I was impressed enough with him to say "sure"....every lawyer likes a new and interesting client--it makes going to the office much more fun!"

On the show, Potter told Stephen that anybody can create a PAC by filling out a simple form, but there are several different types, including a "nonconnected committee," which is what Huckabee had. Potter explained that Stephen could not only form one of those, but he could use any money he received however he wanted—including advertising for a candidate without that candidate's consent.

Stephen asked if there was any reason he wouldn't want a PAC. Potter warned him that he would have to be careful to file all the forms to avoid breaking the law, but admitted that nobody had ever gone to jail for breaking PAC laws.

Grinning mischievously, Stephen asked the audience, "Do you want your voices heard in the form of my voice? Do you, the Colbert Nation, want to be players in the 2012 campaign? Do you want to receive spam e-mails asking for 5, 10, or 15 dollars?"

To the "legally binding" roar of the crowd, Stephen said, "We're gonna do it!"

But Colbert PAC hit a roadblock. Shortly after Potter told him how easy it would be to form his own PAC, Viacom's lawyers sent Stephen a letter, warning that the FEC would likely see his use of Viacom's resources (i.e. his Comedy Central show) to promote his "as-yet-unformed PAC" as an in-kind donation from Viacom. Therefore, he would not be allowed to create one.

The PAC becomes a Super PAC

Potter returned to the show to explain what an in-kind contribution is (airtime, crew, etc. paid by the network), and confirmed that corporations cannot donate to PACs. A defeated Stephen shredded his application documents, but Potter told him that there was one more thing he could try—a Super PAC. Corporations like Viacom can donate an unlimited amount of money to Super PACs, a result of the Citizen's United Supreme Court Case ruling stating that corporations are people. They are therefore entitled to the same free speech as people—including speech in the form of money.

The only thing you need to turn a PAC into a Super PAC? Fill out the application for a PAC and add a cover letter that states, "This PAC is actually a Super PAC." Of course, Potter just happened to have that letter with him.

There was still another necessary step to help the Viacom lawyers relax. Stephen needed to draft a media exemption letter so that Viacom would not have to declare Stephen's use of their resources as a donation, and therefore disclose corporate secrets. The media exemption says that people who report the news are not making a donation when they talk about politics. Therefore, Stephen couldn't *talk* about his PAC, but he could *analyze* and *report on* his PAC. Donning a felt hat with a "Press" card attached, Stephen said, "Sounds good." Potter said Stephen would have to take his letter to the FEC and seek an advisory opinion, which could take up to 60 days. If they said yes, Stephen would be 'bulletproof," according to Potter.

Stephen headed to the FEC to file his request for a media exemption request, and he needed the Colbert Nation's support. He invited viewers to join him at the FEC offices in Washington, D.C. on May 13, 2011. Everything went smoothly, "except for when the guard wanded my groin."

Sixty days later, Stephen had a hearing at the FEC, where he testified alongside Potter. After answering several questions, Stephen was granted permission in a 5-1 ruling. When FEC Chair Cynthia Bauerly said, "Mr. Colbert, you may form your PAC," Stephen and Potter shook hands, and took their paperwork to the secretary. His Super PAC was officially born.

Stephen delivered the news of his victory to the members of the Nation who had again gathered outside the FEC to show support, saying "I am a Super PAC, and so can you!" Stephen then had volunteers move through the crowd collecting contributions of $50 or less so that he would not have to report the donations.

The first order of business was to set a fundraising goal: rake in infinite dollars. Stephen called for the audience to go to ColbertSuperPAC.com, become a member, and donate.

People who donated got their names displayed on a "Heroe$ crawl" at the bottom of the screen during *Report* broadcasts for several weeks. Stephen took a moment to recognize some of the donors on the crawl, who could type in any name they wanted when they donated money, such as "Suq Madiq."

Starting a 501(c)(4)

But to take his fundraising to the next level and attract more corporate donations, Stephen would need to take a cue from Karl Rove and give his donors anonymity. So like Rove, he started a 501(c)(4) shell corporation called Colbert Super PAC SHH Institute. Because they are supposedly nonprofits, these organizations can collect money and then turn them over to Super PACs without ever disclosing the donors' names. Or, as Stephen put it, create "an unprecedented, unaccountable, untraceable, cash tsunami that will infect every corner of the next election."

The money from 501(c)(4)s could only be used for issue advertising, though. Stephen explored this boundary by making an issue ad featuring congressman

Buddy Roemer saying, "Because this is an issue ad about Super PACs not coordinating with candidates, I can be in it. As long as I don't say [bleep] for me."

South Carolina primary sponsorship

Colbert knew the Republican party needed help raising money to hold its 2012 primaries in South Carolina, and he came up with an idea: pay to have the primary renamed the Colbert Super PAC South Carolina Primary.

As Colbert later explained to a live audience at the University of Pittsburgh:

> "I went to the Republicans in South Carolina and said 'I would like to buy your primary. I would like to buy the naming rights to your primary.' And they said 'that sounds good to us. That'll be $400,000.' And I said, 'I would also like to buy some referendums on the ballot.' And they said 'that's $50,000 apiece.' Now, no one I had spoken to, even in political reporting, even knew that that was true, that you could do that."

And it almost happened. As Colbert told *The Yale Herald*, "there was actually a change in South Carolina law, at the last minute, that made the state pay for the primary instead of the party, and so they didn't need my money anymore. But it really came down to the 11th hour. I thought that was going to be the best thing we could do with the money."

As for the referendum question he wanted on the ballot (did the people of South Carolina agree that corporations are people, or only people are people?), the state's Supreme Court ruled that "nonbinding, advisory questions" could not be placed on ballots.

Transferring the Super PAC to Jon Stewart

When he was shown outpolling actual candidate Jon Huntsman in South Carolina, Stephen was forced to consider running for president (of South Carolina). But becoming a candidate meant that he could not maintain control of his Super PAC. As a candidate and the owner of a Super PAC, he would be coordinating with himself if he ran any ads, so he would have to transfer it to his "business partner" Jon Stewart. Stewart came on the show to accept the PAC, and Potter provided them with "the one document" required to make it possible. Colbert Super PAC was dead, but the Definitely Not Coordinating with Stephen Colbert Super PAC was born. The process gave Stewart "a pure cash erection."

Super PAC under Jon Stewart

The Definitely Not Coordinating with Stephen Colbert Super PAC was staffed by Stephen's own employees, working from within Stephen's building, alongside staff members who were working on his presidential exploratory committee.

And it was all completely legal, because "we are in no way coordinating," Stephen promised. He proved it by showing how the staff was split into "red team" (wearing blue shirts) and "blue team" (wearing red shirts) to prevent any confusion.

Stewart started spending the Super PAC's money on attack ads. They aired on local stations in Des Moines, IA, except on WOI-TV, which rejected the ads because they believed they would confuse voters. An ad called "Attack in B Minor for Strings" stated that if corporations are people, then Mitt Romney is a serial killer—"Mitt the Ripper."

As Stephen explained on MSNBC's *Morning Joe*:

> "My staff did not make that ad. Jon Stewart's staff made that ad. And they happen to be the same staff that used to work for me on my Super PAC, that Jon hired away from my staff. And they can work in my building with other members of my staff who are working on my exploratory committee. But we keep them separate."

Stephen asked on his show that the Super PAC not "run vicious character assassination ads that impugn and borderline slander any candidate—if in any way those ads can be traced back to me." The Super PAC then ran an attack ad against Stephen himself so they wouldn't give the appearance that Stephen and the Super PAC were coordinating.

The Super PAC also endorsed Herman Cain for president. Cain had dropped out of the race, but it was too late for him to be removed from the South Carolina ballot. And Stephen couldn't get on it because there was no provision for write-ins and he'd missed the filing deadline. So Stephen encouraged people to vote for Herman Cain to signify support for Stephen. 'Herman Cain' lost, so Stephen's exploratory presidential bid ended.

Regaining control of the Super PAC

Stephen wanted his Super PAC back, but Stewart didn't give it up easily.

As Stewart was closing out the January 30, 2012 episode of *The Daily Show*, Stephen walked onto the set to take back what was rightfully his. Stewart tried to refuse, saying that the unlimited Super PAC money was better off in his hands. Stephen threatened Stewart with a version of Liam Neeson's monologue from *Taken*, and Stewart pretended he was going to give the Super PAC back—but at the last moment, he made a run for it.

The two engaged in a cartoonish chase scene through the *Daily Show* building, through a nearby park (where they sipped tea and admired their stunt doubles doing flips and cartwheels), and onto the set of *The View* where Stewart hid among the hosts wearing a blonde wig. Stephen sniffed him out, though, so Stewart ran outside and jumped into a horse-drawn carriage. When the driver turned around, it was Stephen. Stephen finally cornered Stewart in the basement of the *Colbert Report* studio, where Stewart tried to make a desperate deal to share the money.

Stephen was having none of it. He caught Stewart in a snare trap, and while he hung upside-down, Stephen grabbed his face and sucked the money and power back into his body. A green vapor showed it flowing out of Jon's mouth and into Stephen's.

Finally, Stephen had his PAC back. And it was well worth taking back: the Super PAC reported to the FEC that as of January 30, 2012, the day it reverted to Stephen, it had collected $1,023,121.24. (Minus what Stewart had spent on attack ads.)

Spreading influence

Running a Super PAC was easy. So easy that even a college student could do it. So, Stephen suggested that college students actually do it, and got the ball rolling by selling a Colbert Super PAC Super Fun Pack starter kit that included the official FEC application, a mini-Ham Rove ("Hamlet Rove"), and tube socks. College students and other members of the Colbert Nation rose to the challenge, creating dozens of Super PACs with names that paid homage to Americans for a Better Tomorrow, Tomorrow. The kit also included an extremely complex treasure hunt that required participants to decode hidden messages and find clues spread across many states. A student from the University of Pittsburgh eventually followed the clues to Dixon, Illinois. Inside a fake log, he found an email address to contact Stephen and collect the prize: an antique silver turtle and a promise that Colbert would visit his college campus.

Stephen gets scared

When Barack Obama was re-elected, the cable news networks concluded that all of the money spent by Super PAC owners like Karl Rove had been wasted. Stephen worried that "anonymous, scary donors" would track him down and demand to know where their money went.

Stephen tried to throw Stewart under the bus, saying most of the money was spent under his watch, but Stewart immediately walked onto the set and yelled, "You sonofabitch! You're not pinning this on me!"

Still, someone had to pay, so if the donors needed "a head on a platter" they could have Ham Rove—Stephen's "trusted, salted advisor," who was literally on a platter. There was only one thing to do. Stephen viciously stabbed Ham Rove to death.

Shutting it down

Having committed murder, Stephen needed a lawyer, and Potter returned to the show. Stephen wished he could "somehow give the money to myself and thereby hide it forever from all eyes and use it in the way that I wish."

Potter said this was possible by transferring money from his Super PAC into his 501(c)(4) and then into a second, unnamed (c)(4) where it would be untraceable. He told Stephen:

> "What we want to do then is have you transfer the money from your Super PAC over to 501(c)(4).and what we'll do is what the tax lawyers call an agency letter which simply means you write a letter that tells the (c)(4) exactly what to do with the money. And if you do that, the IRS doesn't consider it to have been the (c)(4)'s money. And it doesn't end up on the tax return."

Even the IRS would know nothing—so Stephen told Trevor, "Thanks for nothing."

Epilogue

On December 12, 2012, Stephen received a letter from "an organization calling itself the Ham Rove Memorial Fund, which I was surprised to learn that I am on the board of."

The letter stated that the organization was founded to honor Ham's memory with charitable gifts, and they had just received a sizable donation from an anonymous source.

Coincidentally, the fund received an untraceable amount of $773,704.83—the exact amount of money remaining in the Super PAC when Stephen closed it. Per Ham's wishes, the money was donated to various causes: $125,000 each to the DonorsChoose.org Hurricane Sandy relief fund, Team Rubicon's Sandy outreach, Habitat for Humanity, and the Yellow Ribbon Fund. The remaining money was divided between the Center for Responsive Politics and the

Campaign Legal Center, with the caveat that they each name one of their conference rooms after Colbert Super PAC and Ham Rove respectively.

The Super PAC segments earned the Report a Peabody Award in 2012. Stephen said he shared the award with "the members of the Supreme Court, whose Citizens United ruling made it possible."

Colbert later said, "I would never have learned all the ways you could use money in a campaign if I hadn't actually tried to do it." And he wasn't alone. In 2014, an Annenberg Public Policy Center study found that people who saw the Super PAC segments were significantly better informed about campaign finance than viewers of any other news programs or news channels.

Sweetness (2008-2014)
(See also: Audience Guy Carl, Ear, Finale)

Stephen had an intimate relationship with his .38 special, Sweetness. His beloved handgun was always at his side when he addressed gun-control issues, and he lovingly caressed her, kissed her, and whispered sweet nothings into her chamber.

Sweetness would "speak" back to Stephen, yet he was the only one who could hear her. Based on Stephen's side of the conversation, Sweetness often tried to convince him to fire her, wanted reassurance that the audience was applauding for her as loudly as they were for him, and expressed concern that the outfit Stephen gave her made her butt look fat.

Stephen repeatedly accidentally shot an audience member, played by executive producer Tom Purcell, in the leg. (When this happened, propmaster Brendan Hurley could be spotted in the seat behind him, operating the mechanism that made fake blood pour out of the wound.)

T

Table of Contents (2005-2014)

Tonight! Then! Plus! Stephen kicked off the show with this high-energy series of three jokes about what was coming up on that night's episode, looking into a different camera for each one. A fourth joke (either about another news story, or simply positioning Stephen as the bringer of truth) and "THIS is *The Colbert Report*!" cued the show's theme song and opening sequence. The first episode produced during the Writers Guild of America strike in 2008 featured Stephen simply yelling "tonight . . . then . . . plus . . ." without any jokes in between. When the show ran long, the Table of Contents was the first thing to be cut. (Sometimes it was edited out, sometimes it wasn't shot at all).

Tad the Building Manager (2005-2014)
(See also: Col-Bunker, Stephen Jr.)

Stephen had a "close" relationship with his loyal building manager, Tad, played by Colbert's longtime collaborator and *Report* writer/producer Paul Dinello. Tad first appeared on the *Report* in 2005, when Stephen forced his staff to execute an emergency evacuation plan. As part of the drill, Tad followed his boss's orders to kill a wheelchair-bound employee, Toby (played by writer Tom Purcell), rather than leave him behind in the stairwell.

In subsequent appearances, the nature of Stephen and Tad's relationship revealed itself to be more complicated, (maybe) involving more than friendship, with innuendo reminiscent of the not-so-secret gay affair between Colbert and Dinello's characters in the series *Strangers with Candy*. Stephen and Tad "tumble" together, revealed when their *Strangers* costar Amy Sedaris appeared on the show and the trio performed an acrobatic routine they created while cast members at Chicago's Second City. Stephen also enlisted Tad to be his "Heterosexual

Accountability Buddy" during an interview with sex columnist Dan Savage, to keep him "on the straight and narrow."

Tad was occasionally sent outside the studio to complete tasks for Stephen, such as open the Stephen Colbert Museum and Gift Shop in Colbert County, AL; find a mate for Stephen's "son," Stephen Jr.; and attempt to hunt down politically illiterate Columbia University students to mock.

Tall Women Lifting/Carrying Heavy Things

Stephen's frequently Googled fetish. He asked Google CEO Eric Schmidt why his search engine doesn't return more results for it.

Tapings (2005-2014)

If you ever got tired of chanting "Stephen! Stephen!" in the privacy of your own home, you could do so in person. *The Colbert Report* taped Monday-Thursday at 513 W. 54th St. in New York City, and tickets were free.

Attendees went through a lengthy waiting game on taping day: a lineup outside the studio, a trip through metal detectors, up to an hour's wait in a small holding room, and some final minutes of anticipation inside the studio with a warm-up comedian to keep them occupied. In 2013, Stephen read aloud Yelp reviews of prisons mixed in with Yelp reviews of his studio, the latter describing the experience as "a dangerous, crowded, cramped situation."

When Stephen was introduced by the warm-up comedian, he typically ran onto the stage, high-fived his crew, and high-fived the first row of the audience, all while Cheap Trick's *I Want You to Want Me* blasted throughout the studio.

Audiences then had the rare opportunity to interact with Colbert out of character. He took four or five questions "to humanize me before I say these terrible things." People frequently questioned Colbert about his real-life passions, such as *Dungeons and Dragons* and *Lord of the Rings*, or his infamous White House Correspondent's Dinner speech.

Every night before the cameras start rolling, Stephen's hairstylist approached his desk and fixed his hair. And every night he returned the favor, looking deep into her eyes as he reached out to caress her locks. That simple move functioned as more than a joke: the audience's reaction indicated to Colbert how closely they were paying attention, and thus how hard he'd have to work to engage them at the top of the show.

Colbert then tossed out WristStrong bracelets to the audience from behind his desk. He developed a nightly gag where he reached under his desk for each bracelet one by one, until finally emerging with a fake dagger instead, which he threatened to throw into the clamoring audience blade-first.

Colbert applauds First Lady Michelle Obama after her 2012 appearance.

During breaks, producers gathered around Stephen's desk to review the next act's script while some of his favorite high-energy songs blare through the studio. "Fell In Love with a Girl" by the White Stripes, "Holland, 1945" by Neutral Milk Hotel, "Fuck You" by Cee-Lo Green, "Steven's Last Night In Town" by Ben Folds Five, "Rehab" by Amy Winehouse, and "Even Flow" by Pearl Jam were in regular rotation, often prompting Stephen to stand up and dance while still consulting his producers.

A taping was also a chance to see Stephen make mistakes, much to the audience's amusement (and his own). When he had to redo a scene because he stumbled on a line, he assured the audience that the jokes are funnier the second time, and that "nobody will find out about this if none of you blog." (Or write a book.)

Tek Jansen (2006-2014)

Tek Jansen is the main character of Stephen's 1,800-page self-published novel, *Stephen Colbert's Alpha-Squad 7, Lady Nocturne: A Tek Jansen Adventure*. In an effort to find a publisher for this erotic sci-fi vanity tome (in which the hero looks remarkably like a buff version of Stephen), he read passages on-air and posted sample chapters to the Colbertnation.com website. *Tek Jansen* was made into a series of animated shorts by J.J. Sedelmaier Productions, which aired on *The Colbert Report* from 2006-2009. It was also published as a five-part comic book adaptation, which were subsequently combined into a single graphic novel. In 2013, Tek Jansen made a short cameo in the infamous Daft Punk "Get Lucky" dance montage.

Thought for Food (2010-2014)

The "healthstapo" are always trying to regulate what Americans can and can't eat for lunch. Stephen shared his thoughts on all things food-related, from major nationwide problems like obesity to new menu items at Friendly's. Stephen covered the strangest—or most newsworthy—foods that restaurant franchises introduce like the Carl's Jr.'s Footlong Burger, about which he said, "in lieu of flowers, next of kin would like a side of onion rings."

ThreatDown (2005-2014)

And the #1 Threat facing America is . . . bears! One of the show's best-known segments, the ThreatDown was a countdown of the top five threats currently facing America—at least, according to Stephen. Each item on the list was inspired by a current news story, and Stephen used his own questionable logic to identify where the threat lay. The number one threat was frequently bears, or as Stephen referred to them, "Godless killing machines."

The ThreatDown debuted on the show's premiere episode, and was originally written with a different animal in mind: alligators. But by the time the show hit the air, the news story that inspired it—about an alligator eating its way out of a snake's stomach—was no longer fresh. The writers decided to replace it with a story involving a bear.

In a 2008 edition, the #1 Threat was "Happiness," which prompted a dream sequence depicting what the show would look like if Stephen was happy all the time. The ThreatDown became the JoyDown, with Stephen in a pink dress shirt and yellow sweater tied around his shoulders, listing the #5 Joy as "bears" ("they're so warm and fuzzy!").

The ThreatDown has also had a number of themed editions, including the Science and Technology Edition, Muslim Edition, and Homo-Sexy Edition.

Time-Traveling Brandy Thief (2010, 2014)

Stephen reported that a 25-year-old bottle of Mexican brandy went missing from a time capsule opened in an Arizona town. He immediately blamed the Time-Traveling Brandy Thief, who he claimed was also responsible for stealing his own brandy in the night ("I cannot tell you how many times I've gone to bed with a full bottle of brandy, only to wake up and find it empty"). The Time-Traveling Brandy Thief—a dandy, mustachioed gentleman played by writer Peter Grosz—showed up in person to taunt Stephen and steal his brandy yet again. When Grosz left the show in 2010, Colbert bid him farewell on the air, and also noted the departure of the Time-Traveling Brandy Thief. The Thief returned in 2014, and attempted to disprove Stephen's declaration that time travel does not exist.

Tip of the Hat/Wag of the Finger (2005-2014)

Also referred to by Stephen as "T-Dubs" or "Tip/Wag," Tip of the Hat/Wag of the Finger was among the longest-running recurring segments, debuting in the show's first week.

In it, Stephen either expressed his approval or disapproval of a recent news story. He figuratively either tipped his hat or wagged his finger, usually giving praise to people or organizations doing amoral or foolish things, and wagging his finger at those who do the right thing.

Stephen's flawed logic sometimes yielded confusing results, like the same person receiving a tip of the hat and a wag of the finger for the same reason. For example, he gave Australian Prime Minister John Howard a tip of his hat for making negative remarks about President Obama, and then a wag of his finger for criticizing an American citizen.

Stephen often issued his wag of the finger when he perceived that someone or something was part of the gay agenda. For example, Stephen wagged his finger at "gay wizards" after J.K. Rowling told the media that the *Harry Potter* character Albus Dumbledore was homosexual, warning that the authors of children's books are trying to turn us gay.

Like many other segments, this one occasionally had a special theme, like a Gun edition, a Quitters edition, and an All-China edition.

Toss (2005-2014)

"Before we go…." Because *The Colbert Report* was an extension of Colbert's character from *The Daily Show*, and the two programs aired back-to-back on Comedy Central, it was natural for *The Daily Show* to promote *The Colbert Report* when it launched. The chosen method—known as The Toss—was in the works months before the show's premiere.

At the end of *The Daily Show*, host Jon Stewart would "check in with our good friend Stephen Colbert." The two would appear side by side in a "double box" (split screen) as Stephen gave viewers a preview of what was coming up.

This segment was written by *Daily Show* producer David Javerbaum, and made possible by a fiber-optic cable running underground between the two studios.

The nightly bits became increasingly silly over time. The ridiculous sketch-style premises were popular among fans of both shows because of the chemistry between Stewart and Colbert, and the likelihood that they would make each other laugh. (Colbert once said that making Jon crack up mid-bit is one of his "greatest joys.")

Fan favorites included "Jon's Beard," with Stephen insulting Stewart's new goatee; "Stating the States," featuring Stephen listing off every state in 22.4 seconds and proving that his stopwatch matched the script; "Proofreader" with Stephen speaking entirely in typos because his teleprompter proofreader was out sick; and "Universal Health Care," which falls apart immediately when Stephen stumbles on his first line but surprises Stewart by trying to continue.

The two shows eventually ran into scheduling difficulties (*The Daily Show* taped while *The Colbert Report* was still in rewrites), making the tosses less viable to produce. For a brief time in early 2007, the tosses were pretaped without an audience, but this practice was abandoned after audience outcry. A toss addressing the tosses aired on the May 21, 2007 episode of *The Daily Show*, and the two promised that going forward, they'd produce two tosses per week, taped live in front of their respective studio audiences. This was sustained for a short period, but the frequency continued to dwindle. The last traditional toss aired in February of 2011. It returned three times after: for the shows' live election night specials in 2012 and 2014, and to preface *The Colbert Report's* finale.

The Colbert Report once featured a toss in reverse, where Stephen ended his show by "checking in" with Stewart over at *The Daily Show*. They cut to a post-show Stewart in his office, wearing his street clothes, unprepared for a toss. Stewart tried to reason with Stephen, but ultimately sprinted out of his office to escape Stephen's camera.

When tosses were filmed, audience members at both *The Daily Show* and *The Colbert Report* were treated to real conversation between the two as they tested the signal before shooting the toss. Colbert once said the unaired banter itself was worthy of "a DVD extra that I would pay for someone to put together."

One of these pre-toss exchanges finally did make it to air, as the closing moment of *The Colbert Report's* finale.

Truthiness (2005)
(See also: The Wørd)

The first edition of The Wørd featured the term "Truthiness," which Colbert has frequently cited as the entire thesis statement of the show. Truthiness means believing the answer that comes from your "gut" and suits your emotions, as opposed to the answer supported by facts—a concept prevalent among the pundits the show satirizes.

The word itself was originally supposed to be "truth." But as he explained to *New York Times* columnist Ben Zimmer, shortly before taping the premiere episode he decided it wasn't quite right:

> "I thought, 'Nah, it's not dumb enough,' because I wanted the first word to be a joke. I wanted everything to be a joke. And it's not even really about truth. I'm not asking people what truth is, because truth is too easily associated with fact. So I said, 'Well, it's not truth. It's like truth. It's truthish. It's truthy.' But I needed a noun. So I said, 'It's truthiness.'"

Truthiness was named 2005's Word of the Year by the American Dialect Society and 2006's Word of the Year by Merriam-Webster. *The New Oxford Dictionary* defines it as "the quality of seeming or being felt to be true, even if not necessarily true" and cites it as being "coined in the modern sense by the U.S. humorist Stephen Colbert."

Tube Socks (2005-2012)

All Stephen sleeps in. Bulk tube socks represented Stephen's economic ideology, simply due to the fact that you could get a 12-pack for $1.99. He coveted his right to low-cost tube socks so much that he believed cheap child labor should never be eliminated, lest the price increase to $2.99. A pair of tube socks was included in each of the Colbert Super PAC Super Fun Packs sent to college students hoping to start their own political action committees.

Twitter (2008-2014)

(See also: Ching-Chong Ding-Dong/#CancelColbert, Colbert Galactic Initiative)

Stephen joined Twitter in September 2008, using the handle @StephenAtHome. His first tweet? "A well-made suit gives you the illusion of a physique."

His presence on Twitter wasn't acknowledged on the *Report* right away. The account continued to post out-of-context jokes or statements at a rate of about four or five per week, but fans weren't entirely clear whether Stephen himself was really doing the tweeting. When he live-tweeted his own interview with Twitter co-founder Biz Stone in April of 2009, there was no longer any doubt.

In December of 2010, Stone was back on the *Report* to award Stephen with the first-ever Golden Tweet Award. Stephen's tweet about the BP oil spill ("In honor of oil-soaked birds, 'tweets' are now 'gurgles.'") was the most retweeted tweet of the year.

Over time, the content of the account became more refined, and included jokes that had been cut from the show as well as new tweets written by Colbert and his writers. Although the account was Colbert's, the content was a collaborative effort.

After the #CancelColbert scandal in 2014 (when Comedy Central tweeted an out-of-context quote from the @ColbertReport account, interpreted by some to be racist), Colbert took tighter control of the content originating from his @StephenAtHome account. He and his head writer began meeting every day to review the jokes that would be tweeted. To fill the void left by the @ColbertReport account, Colbert also began tweeting links to the show's latest videos, prefacing each one with "Last night's show, my best yet."

The @StephenAtHome account had 7.2 million followers when the series ended.

2011: A Rock Odyssey (2011)
(See also: Charlene, StePhest Colbchella)

In an attempt to revive his (allegedly) successful career as the frontman of the '80s new wave group Stephen and the Colberts, Stephen enlisted the help of the White Stripes' Jack White. In a three-part series aired during StePhest Colbchella '011, Stephen set out to re-brand himself and record a follow-up to "Charlene (I'm Right Behind You)."

Stephen traveled to Nashville, TN, the home of White's label, Third Man Records, so White could prepare him for his comeback and certain Grammy victory. After suffering through a trying interview (Stephen firmly believed "Seven Nation Army" should be adapted for a yogurt commercial), White reluctantly took Stephen under his wing. He assessed Stephen's marketability, and determined he'd have to join forces with "actual" musicians The Black Belles, an all-female goth-rock quartet.

But Stephen had his priorities straight, so before entering the studio, he insisted on doing his photo shoot. To revitalize his image, he obviously needed a new look. But what? Stephen emerged from a dressing room in red jeans and red t-shirt, a look made famous by White himself. (Stephen tried his hardest, but White wouldn't let him appropriate his style.) Next up: an all-black ensemble, complete with a cape and black lipstick. Much better! Cue the photo shoot montage, featuring Stephen doing over-the-top dance moves in front of the stone-faced Black Belles.

White visited the *Report* studio to help unveil the results: "Charlene II (I'm Over You)," available on vinyl, as an .mp3, and best of all: live! Stephen and The Black Belles debuted the song on the *Report*, with Stephen singing the angsty lyrics.

It did not win a Grammy.

U

Un-American News (2005-2012)

"What are those foreigners saying about us?" To Stephen's surprise, very little. Stephen gave a rundown of the top stories from foreign papers that dared to have nothing to do with America. Small inconveniences like not speaking the language didn't hold Stephen back from interpreting articles and political cartoons written in Spanish or "chicken scratches" (Arabic). Still, it wasn't always easy for Stephen to navigate the cultural nuances of the foreign presses—especially places with weird quirks like Israel (a country whose language is read right to left) consistently putting their most important news on the "back page" of their paper.

Still, looking at foreign news did have its advantages: it allowed Stephen to temporarily let go of his dislike of Obama while the President was improving America's image in "the most anti-American place in the world: the rest of the world."

United Farm Workers of America (2010)

Take our jobs—please! When he appeared on the *Report*, Arturo Rodriguez, president of the United Farm Workers of America, personally invited Stephen to participate in a challenge issued by his organization: anyone who believed that migrant workers were taking jobs away from American citizens was free to step in and do physical labor on the land. Rodriguez argued that American citizens were not willing to work under the same hard conditions that undocumented immigrants face, while receiving paltry wages that are barely enough to live on. Rodriguez pointed out that only three Americans had accepted his offer to work in the fields, proving him right. But Stephen was determined to show Rodriguez he was mistaken, and agreed to become the fourth person to take back a job from the "illegal immigrants."

In a two-part edition of Fallback Position, Stephen visited Gill Corn Farms in Hurley, NY, where he met with "Chairwoman of the House Committee on Immigration and notorious Mexican hugger" Rep. Zoe Lofgren in the farm's hayloft. Lofgren explained to Stephen that food still comes from farms and that being a migrant farm worker is different from fat camp—even though both happen to involve vegetables and exercise. She also declined to even think about making an "anchor baby" with Stephen (although she let *him* think about it).

Next, it was time for Stephen to put his beans where his mouth was and prove himself a worthy migrant farm worker. Sam, the farm's manager, got Stephen off to a good start building boxes for packing corn. But Stephen immediately got distracted and turned the boxes into forts instead, and then started a corn fight with other workers. After that, Stephen flirted with the corn packers until he realized he wasn't going to be able to keep up with the ladies, and jumped on the conveyor belt to escape Sam. Finally, Stephen learned that picking beans involved a whole lot of bending over, and, to his relief, Sam told him he was not qualified for the job.

After his experience literally in the field, Stephen went to Congress to testify about the plight of migrant workers. When Lofgren invited Colbert to speak, he warned her that he would be testifying in character—and that it might not go over well.

As he predicted, some members of Congress were hostile to the announcement that Colbert would be testifying in character. Republican Representative Steve King had never heard of *The Colbert Report* and had to ask his staff to pull clips for him to watch before the hearing; he told Fox News "there was no rational reason" for Colbert's testimony. At the start of the hearing, animosity came from the other side of the aisle too, as Democratic Rep. John Conyers asked Colbert to leave the room altogether.

But Stephen remained in his seat, and offered five minutes of prepared testimony in the House Judiciary hearing titled "Protecting America's Harvest." He acknowledged that the migrant labor market had its problems, and that his initial solution (stop eating vegetables) was not viable, as evidenced by his most recent colonoscopy. What did Stephen tell Congress he had learned from his day on the farm? "Please don't make me do this again. It is really, really hard."

Colbert ended his testimony on a serious note. Democratic Rep. Judy Chu asked Colbert why he was interested in the plight of migrant workers. With the bravado gone from his voice, Colbert said:

> "I like talking about people who don't have any power, and it seems like one of the least powerful people in the United States are migrant workers who come and do our work, but don't have any rights as a result. . . . You know, 'whatsoever you do for the least of my brothers,' and these seem like the least of my brothers right now."

As for Rep. Conyers, he later told CNN the testimony was "pretty profound," and wrote Colbert a letter thanking him for appearing.

V

Vancouver Olympics (2010)
(See also: Speedskating)

As the driving force behind the Colbert Nation's sponsorship of U.S. Speedskating, Stephen was personally invested in the 2010 Winter Olympics, and decided he would attend. But if he was going to go? He insisted on going as a member of the U.S. Olympic Team—nothing less.

To decide on which event he'd compete in to bring home the gold, Stephen visited team training facilities to try out various Olympic sports in a series called Skate Expectations.

In Lake Placid, NY, he donned a revealing red spandex number to train with skeleton world champion Zach Lund, and rode with the four-man bobsled team, Team Night Train. In both cases, Stephen's game wasn't as tight as his outfit, and he failed to make the cut. He tried again in Plainfield, NJ, home of the U.S. men's curling team. Alas, he didn't have the sweeping skills to join them either.

"But as I lay there on the ice, I asked myself, 'why am I walking away from my first love, speed skating?'"

Since he was responsible for the team's sponsorship, Stephen headed to Salt Lake City, UT to take his rightful place on the U.S. Speedskating team. All he had to do was beat reigning Olympic champion Shani Davis in a race. And learn how to skate.

Despite being coached by team member Tucker Fredericks, and having a lengthy head start on Davis (who was still en route to the arena when Stephen said "go!"), Davis won by more than 13 minutes. While he was heartbroken by the loss, Stephen was still offered a spot on the team as their assistant sports psychologist.

To Vancouver he would go! But it wasn't easy to take the *Report* there, since NBC owned the broadcast rights to the Games. Intellectual property lawyer Ed Colbert, who represented the U.S. Olympic Committee for a decade (and just happens to be Stephen's brother), guided Stephen through all the things he couldn't say on air. To get around the restrictions, Stephen dubbed his coverage Exclusive Vancouverage of the 2010 Quadrennial Cold Weather Athletic Competition: Defeat the World.

The Olympic-themed shows aired the week of February 22-25, and were an unusual combination of segments filmed in Vancouver the week prior, and segments recorded in the *Report* studio the week they aired. Stephen tied the shows together in the cozy "Colbert Report International Broadcast Centre," overlooking the Vancouver skyline. (In reality, it was Colbert's New York studio, transformed using green-screen backgrounds and two leather club chairs borrowed from Colbert's actual office.) From there, he threw to interview segments taped in front of daytime audiences in Vancouver's Creekside Park on February 17 and 18, and pretaped pieces of himself exploring the Olympic festivities and fulfilling his official duties with the U.S. Speedskating team.

The show was cleared to film inside the Richmond Olympic Oval thanks to a real agreement reached with NBC Universal Sports, as outlined by chairman Dick Ebersol in his January 20, 2010 *Report* appearance.

Vilsack Attack (2006-2010)

The Vilsack juggernaut stops here! As of November 2006, Iowa governor Tom Vilsack was the only official presidential candidate for the 2008 election, and therefore the automatic frontrunner. For that reason alone, Stephen felt he should focus all his energy on taking this Democrat down. He had a long list of one scandal to focus on: Iowa State Fairgate. Vilsack had told Charlie Rose that "There's nothing you can't do at the Iowa State Fair." Stephen quickly pointed out that that was a lie, because you definitely can't ice fish at the Iowa State Fair. Stephen promised to keep digging for more dirt.

When "Vil-No-Sack" dropped out of the race, Stephen took the credit, and asked Vilsack to run for "anything else" so he could use the graphic he made for Vilsack Attack again. Days after he withdrew from the race, Vilsack appeared on Stephen's first (only) segment of Profiles in Quitters ("You dropped out before Joe Biden?!") and Stephen tried to convince him that if his withdrawal was really all about money, he should sell his soul to evil corporate overlords for campaign cash.

By 2010, Vilsack had become the Secretary of Agriculture, and he appeared on *The Colbert Report* to talk about America's relationship with food. Vilsack brought Stephen a gift: a sculpture of Stephen's head, made out of 25 pounds of organic cheddar cheese.

W

Was It Really That Bad? (2005-2008)

Tragedy plus time equals silver linings. Stephen thought history's darkest moments didn't seem all that terrible in retrospect. If the 1906 San Francisco earthquake hadn't put Chinese and Italian people in the same refugee camps together, we never would've ended up with Rice-A-Roni. And while the Bubonic Plague wiped out a third of Europe's population, it did spark significant job growth in some sectors: "gravediggers, mass gravediggers, and diggers of graves for mass gravediggers."

Watership Down (2005-2014)

Richard Adams's novel about a society of rabbits at war, which sat on Stephen's bookshelf in the "nonfiction" category. This joke is often cited in interviews by former co-executive producer Allison Silverman as a prime example of the character's idiocy.

Wax On & Wax Off at Madame Tussauds (2012)

Stephen takes his rightful place alongside the U.S. Presidents. He's been celebrated in many ways, but to join "the largest collection of glassy-eyed fake celebrities outside of the Bravo network" was the ultimate honor.

Throughout June 2012, a team of studio artists from famed wax museum Madame Tussauds visited Stephen in New York to photograph and measure him, and immortalize his "unique style, exact eye color, build, and overall allure, including his signature raised eyebrow."

Before his wax figure was unveiled, Stephen visited the Madame Tussauds in Washington, D.C. to see its future home. As he toured the exhibits, Stephen repeatedly misidentified famous figures (in all fairness, Harriet Tubman does bear a slight resemblance to Tiger Woods), and asked to lick most of the likenesses—to general manager Dan Rogoski's great offense.

"Ladies and gentlemen, one . . . two . . . me!" Stephen was present when his other self was unveiled to the press in November. He said becoming a "Waxican American" was an honor, and called his wax doppelganger "100% accurate." Colbert also told the *Huffington Post* that the figure depicts "Stephen" the character, and that his likeness freaked him out. Stephen finally did get to lick a wax figure—himself—and said he was "delicious."

What Number Is Stephen Thinking Of? (2005-2007)

"Dear Stephen: Is it 16?" Stephen offered a huge prize to a hero who could prove he or she thought just like him, by knowing the number he was thinking of. He crossed guesses off of a board numbered 1-500, but noted that just because those were the numbers on the board, that didn't mean the number he was thinking of was within that range.

Stephen reminded viewers of the importance of the year-long contest in 2007 and said that the only way to "end this contest with dignity" would be to guess the right number together. To make the contest more exciting, Stephen upped the ante by doubling the number he was thinking of. He also revealed that after guessing the right number, the winner would have to flip over the board of numbers from 1-500 and play "What Prize Is Stephen Thinking Of?" Again, the prize Stephen was thinking of might not be one of the ones on the board.

In a separate challenge, Stephen said he was thinking of a number between 1 and 10, and the answer was Prokash Datwani. Stephen acknowledged that Prokash Datwani was more of a name than a number, but said his twist just made the contest more challenging.

Wheat Thins (2012)

Sponsorships were more than just sponsorships when placed in the *Report*'s hands. The show took on four invasive segment sponsors each year, and when Wheat Thins came on board, Stephen was only obligated to say "brought to you by Wheat Thins." But as Colbert explained at a 2013 New York Comedy Festival panel, they always went further than that:

> "We want to hug the bear, we want to hug the evil close to our chest. We were gonna do the Wheat Thins thing, and somebody in the room said, 'Oh, you've got the e-mail. Don't forget, we've got the e-mail.' I said, 'What e-mail?' And [co-executive producer Rich Dahm] said, 'Well there's an e-mail for how we can and cannot talk about Wheat Thins.'"

That e-mail contained the marketing brief for the product, an over-the-top description of how Wheat Thins fits into the life of its target demographic. The brief included such gems as: "Wheat Thins are not a crusader or rebel looking to change an individual's path or the world," are "a snack for anyone who is actively seeking experiences," and "keep you on the path to and proud of doing what you love to do, no matter what that is."

Since nothing could be more ridiculous than the e-mail itself, Colbert gleefully read out those excerpts and more on the show. Stephen also showed that you can put anything on Wheat Thins ("Cheese? Yes. Hummus? Sure. A discarded strip of truck tire? It can handle it."), and tempted fate by attempting to eat 17 crackers—one more than the e-mail allowed.

But what some called mocking, others called "integration." The ad agency that facilitated the sponsorship proved that Wheat Thins also pair well with giant brass balls. They submitted the *Report* segment for advertising industry awards, and boasted about how the piece fulfilled the objective to "ignite an edgy conversation among millennials." It earned the agency a prestigious Gold Lion at the 2012 Cannes Lions International Festival of Creativity, in the category of Best Brand or Product Integration into an Existing TV show or Series.

White House Correspondents' Dinner (2006)
(See also: Atone Phone, Toss)

Colbert's performance at the annual White House Correspondents' Association Dinner in Washington, D.C. made headlines after he delivered a scathing in-character roast of President George W. Bush—while standing just feet away from the man himself.

Some hailed it as brave, others thought he went too far. But from Stephen's perspective, it was one of the greatest weekends of his entire life. After all, he got to shake ("very soft") hands with his "main man" President Bush, and his speech was received with a "very respectful silence" from the crowd of journalists and politicians.

In a panel discussion in 2007, Colbert said his one regret about the evening was that he had a joke he didn't tell at the dinner: Stephen presenting President Bush with the highest award he could give, a Certificate of Presidency recognizing that George W. Bush was indeed the president. That bit was supposed to happen in the middle of the speech, but Colbert looked over at Bush at that moment and decided against it. He had the certificate framed on his wall as "a woulda shoulda coulda award to me."

A recording of Stephen's speech at the Dinner surpassed an audiobook of Barack Obama's memoir, *The Audacity of Hope*, on the iTunes store's Top Audiobooks list. "In your handsome, multiracial face, Obama!"

In 2012, guest Diane Keaton asked Stephen why he wasn't at the most recent Correspondents' Dinner. Stephen said he hadn't been to one "since they alerted security . . . about six years ago."

Who's Attacking Me Now? (2006-2014)
(See also: Ballz for Kids, Ching Chong Ding Dong/#CancelColbert)

When Stephen was attacked for telling the truth, he always attacked back. This segment was introduced when the Humane Society told the *Philadelphia Inquirer* that they were "livid" about a Ballz for Kids segment educating kids about bear hunting. Naturally, Stephen called the Humane Society to accept their apology.

When Anderson Cooper commented that anger and outrage are the only emotions cable news reporters can express, Stephen took this personally and dedicated a segment to firing back at him—with anger and outrage, of course. The Canadian Broadcasting Corporation (CBC) reported that Stephen called Windsor, Canada the "Earth's rectum," but Stephen pointed out that he had only *asked* whether it was. Besides, according to the CBC's own online poll, calling Windsor the Earth's rectum was considered good for Windsor's reputation by over 75% of respondents—proof that he'd given the city the Colbert Bump.

Who's Honoring Me Now? (2006-2013)
(See also: Truthiness)

Stephen is America, therefore news about people praising him was what "matters most to the average American." Stephen acknowledged all of the people who gave him the praise he was due, including Merriam-Webster for naming "truthiness" their Word of the Year and *Maxim* magazine for including him in the Hot 100 Most Beautiful Women in the World (the first man to make the list, at "the sexiest number" 69). When Stephen was nominated for a People's Choice Award in 2013, he hedged his bets with a segment called "Who Might Be Honoring Me Next?"

Who's Not Honoring Me Now? (2006-2013)
(See also: Peabody, HipHopKetBall: A Jazzebration)

Sometimes, award-givers just didn't recognize Stephen's greatness. When the Peabody Awards overlooked Colbert in 2006, he called them out for denying him the "sugar sugar" he had earned by "shilling for the award for years." The Peabody Awards were a repeat offender, but so were most other awards—including the Teen Choice Awards and the MacArthur Foundation genius grants, which go to "eggheads and hippies you've never heard of." In 2006, the MacArthur Foundation passed over Stephen yet again and honored John Zorn, an avant-garde jazz musician who Stephen believed ripped off his squeaky saxophone performance in HipHopKetBall: A Jazzebration.

Who's Riding My Coattails Now? (2006-2011)
(See also: Jimmy Fallon, Rock and Awe: Countdown to Guitarmageddon)

"There's a fine line between flattery and theft." Stephen appreciated praise, but he hated people who tried to steal his thunder. This included repeat guests the Decemberists, who copied Stephen's idea of filming a video in front of a green screen and asking fans to finish it. Vince Vaughn, too, rode Stephen's coattails by stealing his signature pose for photographs: grinning with one arm around the other person. And Jimmy Fallon had the nerve to use a picture of Stephen singing "Friday" on *Late Night* on the screener DVDs he submitted for Emmy consideration.

Wikipedia (2006, 2008, 2011-12)

Did you know that Stephen saved the African elephants? Wikipedia said so, so it must be true! Stephen called upon his audience to alter Wikipedia entries to suit his version of reality, or as he called it in a segment of The Wørd, "Wikiality" (a reality we can all agree on).

Striking a crushing blow to environmentalists, Stephen asked viewers to edit Wikipedia to state that the population of African elephants had tripled in the last decade. The page was locked to prevent further editing after the Colbert Nation heeded Stephen's call and descended on it.

In 2011 Sarah Palin erroneously claimed that Paul Revere rang bells to warn that the British were coming. Stephen suggested that the audience change history to make it align with Palin by editing the Wikipedia entry for "bells" to state they were used in Revere's midnight ride. In 2012, Stephen encouraged viewers to edit the Wikipedia entries of Mitt Romney's potential running mates, again resulting in the pages being locked.

Stephen also edited the entry for former U.S. President Warren G. Harding to make the G stand for "Gangsta," and then cited it when he argued that Harding was a "secret negro president."

Wilford Brimley Calls (2005-2006, 2009, 2012)

The world's most famous diabetic and oatmeal huckster has quite a mouth on him. At least, Colbert's rough-around-the-edges impersonation of him does. Stephen played audio recordings of "Wilford"—a longtime mentor—calling him up in the middle of the night to aggressively solicit donations for John McCain, rant about his own weight, and ask Stephen to cover a cockfighting debt in Mexico.

The Wørd (2005-2014)
(See also: Allison Silverman, Truthiness)

"Which brings us to tonight's Wørd . . ." Inspired by *The O'Reilly Factor*'s Talking Points Memo segment, The Wørd became an immediate audience favorite after it introduced the world to "Truthiness" on the *Report*'s premiere.

On the left side of the screen, Stephen delivered a lengthy discourse on an issue in the news. On the right side, bullet points reinforced (or sometimes counteracted) his statements. Stephen's argument came full circle, ending with the same word or phrase that appeared next to him at the beginning.

The verbal portion almost always followed the same construction: An explanation of the news story and the real problem at hand, the real solution (or proposed solution), and a satirical extension of that solution. Colbert's writers have cited Jonathan Swift's "A Modest Proposal" as a model for the format of the verbal essay. (Swift satirizes English attitudes towards the impoverished Irish, suggesting that Irish families could solve their poverty by selling their children to rich people as food.)

For example: in a Wørd entitled "Gateway Hug," Stephen noted that states that taught abstinence-only education had a higher rate of teen pregnancy (the problem). In response, lawmakers in Tennessee prohibited teachers from teaching "gateway sexual activity" like holding hands and kissing (the solution). Stephen believed this policy should go even further and prohibit "gateway gateway sexual activity": no being attractive allowed, no flipping your hair, no eye contact—in fact, even going through puberty should be banned. "And if our children lack the self-control to hold in their hormones, then we have no option but to spay or neuter them" (extension of the solution). He acknowledged sterilization may sound cruel, but it's necessary to protect what's near and dear to us: "our belief that abstinence-only education works."

The writers treated the bullet as a character, with its own personality. Occasionally, Stephen acknowledged its existence. For example, in a 2006 Wørd about jokes called "Kidding," it essentially played "The Dozens" with him, and Stephen angrily told the bullet it was "uncool" when it called his mother a whore. But for the most part, Stephen didn't react to what's on screen beside him.

One challenge the show's writers faced: making sure the bullet didn't hog all the laughs. The format naturally leant itself to a set/punch rhythm between Stephen and the bullet, but an ideal Wørd included plenty of jokes within the essay portion too.

Sound complicated? Head writer Opus Moreschi said it was the hardest thing for the staff to write, and took "a perfect storm" of factors for a news story to lend itself to a Wørd. Never mind managing to create a new one every night, as the writers did at the beginning of the show's run. Even Colbert struggled to make the segment come full circle, as he explained on the *A.D.D. Comedy* podcast in 2012:

> "If I cannot end it, there's something wrong with my problem. I wasn't clear about what my problem was, and it is always so. I always can go 'what was my problem I described? What was my thing I was trying to fix or celebrate?' And if I wasn't clear about that, then I can never end it and it always feels unsatisfying. But if I can identify that clearly, I can usually end it in a way that surprises the audience."

And sometimes, a surprise also came from a tweak to the format. "Sigh" was an entirely nonverbal Wørd, with the bullet relaying Stephen's thoughts as he had a meltdown over the results of the 2006 Midterms. During the *Report*'s week of shows in Philadelphia for the 2008 primaries, presidential candidate John Edwards delivered a Wørd of his own (dubbed The Ed Wørds). "Troops Out Now" sent us to an alternate universe where Stephen had long hair, wore a tweed jacket, and smoked a pipe. Stephen's Latino counterpart Esteban Colberto delivered the Wørd "El Comandante."

And that's The Wørd!

WristStrong (2007-2014)
(See also: NASA, Tapings, Yellow Ribbon Fund)

Who knew one little broken bone could generate so much comedy—and money for charity?

Colbert's preshow ritual included running around his set to Cheap Trick's "I Want You to Want Me," circling his desk, leaping off the platform where his desk sat, and high-fiving the front row of his audience.

But on June 21, 2007, Stephen didn't quite have it in him to successfully navigate the "leaping" part. He'd been putting in late nights working on *I Am America (And So Can You!)*, and the manuscript was due the next day. In his exhaustion, his feet slipped out from under him, and he landed on his left wrist. The front row didn't get their high-fives, but they did get Colbert's entire body. He lay across four people as he tried to recover.

"They were so sweet. They pet me as I moaned," he later told NPR's *Fresh Air*.

Colbert suspected he might have a broken wrist, but didn't go to the doctor until it got "puffier and puffier." He went a full month without a cast, during which time he took a trip home to South Carolina and built a boat by hand. All that time, he had a chip fracture of the triquetrum.

On the July 26, 2007 episode, he revealed his cast to the Nation, and explained how it all went down—sort of. In his character's version, he was running around the set to Beyoncé instead of Cheap Trick, and the accident took place just the night before.

He also showed actual footage of the fall. A camera happened to be running when it happened, and just barely caught Colbert as he went horizontal.

"The frame is still, and I leave the frame as though I'm on an invisible gurney," Colbert said.

If Stephen cared about it, it was news, and there was nothing he cared about more about than his own tragic injury. He used his show to milk it for all it was worth, fishing for sympathy with fake wincing, asking celebrities and politicians to sign his cast, getting addicted to painkillers, and decrying Hollywood's constant glorification of "wrist violence."

To increase awareness of this offensive movie trope, Stephen unveiled the WristStrong bracelet, a red silicone band modeled after Lance Armstrong's yellow Livestrong bracelets.

WristStrong bracelets were sold on the show's website, with proceeds going to the Yellow Ribbon Fund. Stephen's instructions to the Nation: if you meet someone famous, you must give them your WristStrong bracelet.

After selling over 30,000 bracelets, Stephen presented the Yellow Ribbon Fund with a check for $171,525. Stephen's doctor removed his celeb-signed cast on the Aug. 23 episode, amid great fanfare. The cast was auctioned off for $17,200, also for the Yellow Ribbon Fund.

Until the set was redesigned in 2010, an outline of Stephen's body was marked on the studio floor with white tape, on the spot where he fell. Colbert continued to wear a WristStrong bracelet on the air every night.

Writers Guild of America Strike (2007-2008)
(See also: Andrew Young, Table of Contents)

The members of the Writers Guild of America (WGA) went on strike in 2007, immediately shutting down all unionized scripted shows including *The Colbert Report*. The November 1, 2007 episode would be the final new *Report* for that calendar year, with reruns filling the timeslot. The strike also put an end to the planned week of shows to be taped in South Carolina in January 2008.

The Colbert Report staged a live (not broadcast) "On Strike!" edition at the 150-seat Upright Citizens Brigade Theatre on December 3, 2007. Proceeds of the $20 tickets went to the production staff, who were out of work during the strike. Colbert performed in character at a makeshift desk, and delivered material written prior to the strike and loaded onto a laptop in front of him (including two editions of The Wørd). His writers played supporting roles, holding up the Wørd's bullet-point graphics on poster board, performing a

Sonic restaurant commercial (with writer Peter Grosz reprising his role in the series of ads), and reading portions of *I Am America (And So Can You!)*.

The strike was still going strong when it was announced that the *Report* (along with *The Daily Show*) would return to the air with new—and writerless—episodes, widely believed to be the result of pressure from Comedy Central.

In a joint statement, Colbert and Stewart said, "We would like to return to work with our writers. If we cannot, we would like to express our ambivalence, but without our writers we are unable to express something as nuanced as ambivalence."

Some viewers decried the decision as anti-union, and many wondered how the show could have any content. A strict interpretation of the WGA rules could mean that Colbert couldn't perform in-character at all, even if he improvised.

When *The Colbert Report* returned on January 7, 2008, Stephen explained to his audience that he was having a bit of a technical issue.

"Jim, I got a problem here. There are no words in my prompter. What the hell is going on?" he asked, instructing the camera operators to shoot each other's cameras to prove the prompters were empty.

Jimmy explained that the writers were on strike, but Stephen didn't get how that had anything to do with the teleprompter.

"My understanding is that this little magic box right here, it reads my thoughts and lays them up on the screen," he said.

Colbert pronounced his name with a hard "T" throughout the strike, leaving some fans speculating that by using a slightly different name, he could claim he was performing an entirely different character and was therefore not violating WGA rules.

He deftly improvised (or semi-improvised) his way through six weeks of shows, dedicating more time to in-studio interviews, and using clips of past shows to prop up his points. Colbert even performed scripts that were written for (and cut from) pre-strike episodes. A January 8, 2008 segment about meteorites was accompanied by a graphic reading "script completed October 29, 2007." The January 9, 2008 good night, depicting Stephen's studio on fire, was captioned "originally scheduled to air October 3, 2007."

But the most memorable time-filler was a late-night battle conceived by Colbert, Stewart, and Conan O'Brien (whose *Late Night* was also back on the air with no writers).

It started with Conan and Stephen each attempting to take credit for presidential hopeful Mike Huckabee's strong showing in the Republican primaries. Stephen said it was entirely due to Huckabee getting the Colbert Bump from his show. Conan believed it was because Huckabee has the endorsement of Chuck Norris, the subject of Conan's recurring "Walker, Texas Ranger Lever" bit.

As the two argued over who "made Huckabee," Stewart entered and made his own claim of making Huckabee via making Conan; Conan then claimed he made Colbert. The trash talk escalated (and the logic de-escalated) until it finally came to a head with a three-show crossover on the night of February 4, 2008. The trio repeatedly confronted each other mid-broadcast—moving from *The Daily Show*, to *The Colbert Report*, and finally to *Late Night With Conan O'Brien*—as they sought a mutually convenient time to hold their brawl. *Late Night* viewers were treated to an over-the-top fight sequence filmed in the hallways outside O'Brien's studio, which he described to the Associated Press as "three people with a box full of props playing for about an hour."

The WGA strike was settled on February 12, 2008, and Colbert's writers returned to work the next day. On their first show back, the writers approached Stephen's desk one by one to accept new pencils. The team had presumably gone through some changes, as pencils were allotted to a few new faces, including Kevin Bacon and Mr. Met.

Y

Yacht race (2011)

Ahoy, Stephen! Colbert was the honorary skipper of the Spirit of Juno, Team Audi's boat, in an annual race from Charleston, SC to Bermuda. Colbert told the Associated Press that when he first participated in the race in 2005 it was "the most pleasant disaster I have ever been a part of." Stephen returned to *The Colbert Report* after the 2011 race with a beard, a captain's hat, and a pipe, and announced that he "won the race . . . the race to come in second place."

Yahweh or No Way (2009-2012)

"Someone has got to speak for God, and God told me it should be me." Stephen examined cases where someone tried to invoke God to win an argument, and decided whether God really endorsed their argument or not. Could Jesus defeat Thor in a fight? *The Passion of the Christ* made more money in its opening weekend than *Thor*, so Yahweh! Should God factor into online dating? No Way. After all, when God thought Adam seemed lonely, he created a bunch of animals to keep him company before it ever occurred to him to create Eve, which means "God is a horrible matchmaker."

Yellow Ribbon Fund (2008-2014)

Discussing his support for members of the armed forces, Colbert told the Associated Press "Sometimes, my character and I agree." The Yellow Ribbon Fund, which aids injured veterans and their families, is a favorite charity of both Stephen and the real Colbert. Proceeds from the sale of WristStrong bracelets, the auctions of both the autographed cast Stephen wore on his broken wrist and Bill O'Reilly's stolen microwave, and a portion of Super PAC donations were all donated to the Yellow Ribbon Fund.

Yet Another Day (2005)

Just because you stayed up late to watch the *Report* doesn't mean you couldn't get up early for *Yet Another Day*! Stephen would throw to the perky Christina (played by improviser Christina Gausas) and her always-new cohost sitting on their morning show set, to tell folks what they had coming up. ("Ever wondered if you should pet your cat? We'll fill ya in on some of the hidden dangers.") The segment aired just three times, during the *Report*'s first few weeks.

Z

Z96 Morning Asylum with Stevie C and Dr. Dave (2009)

Stephen's 1980s Chicago morning radio program. Cohosted by a bleached-blonde Stephen and "Dr. Dave" (portrayed in the visual mock-up by writer Peter Gwinn), the show also featured "news on the nines with the farting gerbil."

In the End…

"Stephen Colbert to replace David Letterman on *Late Show*"

The headline that dominated the Internet on April 10, 2014 brought with it the logical consequence: *The Colbert Report* would come to an end eight months later.

How would the character of "Stephen Colbert" deal with the transition? He wouldn't. Since it was the man, not the character, who landed the gig at CBS, all "Stephen" knew was that Letterman was retiring.

"I do not envy whoever they try to put in that chair," he remarked the night of the announcement.

While oblivious to his alter-ego's pending move, Stephen did make a conscious decision to end his show. When he dropped by *The Daily Show* a few weeks later, he told Jon Stewart that he had "won television." There was simply no point in continuing his show.

It was, and remained, as simple as that.

The lengthy countdown to the end wasn't accompanied by any of the big "games" the show had become known for, but there was plenty of closure in the final weeks. Stephen and a bear—his arch nemesis—became friends (with benefits). He finally interviewed President Obama during an episode filmed in Washington, D.C. He sold off nine years' worth of props and gifts in a *Colbert Report* yard sale, filmed in October and aired in the penultimate episode.

The final *Colbert Report* aired December 18, 2014. It was the highest-rated episode in the show's history, with 2.5 million viewers tuning in to watch Stephen say goodbye.

Works Cited

To get this list with clickable links to all web sources, visit
www.colbertfanguide.com/citations

"A Conversation With Comedian Stephen Colbert." *Charlie Rose*. PBS. New York, NY, 08 December 2006. Television.

"A personal message from Stephen Colbert to the reddit community." *reddit*. reddit Inc., 14 September 2010. Web.

ABC7 WJLA. "Stephen Colbert Wax Figure Unveiled at Madame Tussauds." YouTube. YouTube LLC, 16 November 2012. Web.

Adalian, Josef. *NBC hits 'Daily' double*. Variety Media, LLC, 08 December 2002. Web. "Allison Silverman." *IMDB*. Amazon.com. Web.

"Amazing Spider-Man Vol 1 573." Marvel Database. Web.

Americans for a Better Tomorrow, Tomorrow. "REPORT OF RECEIPTS AND DISBURSEMENTS For Other Than An Authorized Committee." 31 January. 2011. Web.

"Americone Dream." *Ben and Jerry's*. Ben and Jerry's. Web.

"An Evening with Stephen Colbert." Interview by Ken Burns. 92Y. New York, 19 October 2012.

Associated Press. "Aptostichus stephencolberti: Stephen Colbert Gets A Spider Named After Him." *The Huffington Post*. 09 August 2008. Web.

Associated Press. "Colbert: I Am a Super PAC!" *YouTube*. YouTube LLC, 30 June 2011. Web.

Associated Press. "Colbert, Stewart, Obrien 'fight' over Huckabee." *CTV News*. 06 February 2008. Web.

Associated Press. "Raw Video: Colbert Approved to Form Super PAC." *YouTube*. YouTube LLC, 30 June 2011. Web.

Associated Press. "Stephen Colbert Gears up for Olympics." CBCnews. CBC/Radio Canada, 11 February 2010. Web.

Associated Press. "Stephen Colbert Gets A Falcon Namesake." The Huffington Post. 24 March 2009. Web.

Atkinson, Nancy. "COLBERT on the ISS." COLBERT on the ISS. Universe Today, 14 April 2009. Web.

"AUCTION FOR THE MICROWAVE I STOLE FROM BILL O'REILLY." *EBay*. Web. 14 October 2014.

Aybara-max. "The Colber Report: Taping Report." A Place to Squeek. Live Journal, 15 December 2009. Web.

Badvideos78. "Esteban Colbert, Peregrin Falcon, Eating Lunch." YouTube. YouTube LLC, 24 December 2011. Web.

Bash, Dana. "Conyers: Colbert 'pretty Profound'" CNN Political Ticker RSS. 24 September 2010. Web.

Berkes, Howard. "U.S. Speedskating Finds Savior In Stephen Colbert." NPR, 19 January 2010. Web.

"Bluster and Satire: Stephen Colbert's 'Report'." *Fresh Air*, NPR, 7 December 2005. Radio.

branchness. "(no subject)." *Colbert Nation*. LiveJournal Inc., 04 December 2007. Web.

Callaway, Ewen. "Is Stephen Colbert's spider a unique species?." *Short Sharp Science*. 06 August 2008. Web.

Carlos, Jordan. "My Shtick? Being Black." *Washington Post*. The Washington Post, 07 January 2007. Web.

"Clara And Esteban Colbert Hatch A Fourth Falcon." *KTVU.com*. KTVU, 22 April 2009. Web.

Coates, Ta-Nehisi. "Why 'Accidental Racist' Is Actually Just Racist." *The Atlantic*. The Atlantic Monthly Group, 09 April 2013. Web.

Colbertguy. "Regarding What Happened Tonight on Colbert..." RedditLog Snapshots, 07 August 2013. Web.

"Colbert Builds 'Report' with Viewers, Readers." *Fresh Air*. NPR. 09 October 2007. Radio.

"Colbert in South Carolina." *Public Policy Polling*. Public Policy Polling, 10 January 2012. Web.

"Colbert Show' Back From Iraq." *Fresh Air*. NPR. 22 June 2009. Radio.

"Colbert Portrait on Display at Eatery." *The Washington Post*. The Associated Press, 30 November 2006. Web.

'Colbert: 'Re-Becoming' The Nation We Always Were." *Fresh Air*. NPR. 04 October 2012. Radio.

"Colbert's spirited support." *The Windsor Star*. Canada.com, 27 January 2007. Web.

Colbert, Stephen. *America Again: Re-becoming the Greatness We Never Weren't*. Grand Central Publishing – Hachette Book Group, Inc., 2012.

Colbert, Stephen. *I Am a Pole (and So Can You!)*. Grand Central Publishing – Hachette Book Group, 2012.

Colbert, Stephen. *I Am America (And So Can You!)*. Grand Central Publishing – Hachette Book Group, 2007.

Colbert, Stephen. "The Ham Rove Memorial Fund. *Colbert Super PAC*. Web.

"Comedy Central The Colbert Report HD Broadcast Environment" Jack Morton. Web.

"Complete List of 2007 Peabody Award Winners." *The Peabody Awards*. Peabody Awards, 02 April 2008. Web. *Internet Archive*.

Cook, Jia-Rui. "Voyager Project Scientist Honored by NASA--Via Stephen Colbert." NASA, 04 December 2013. Web.

Copenhagen TVFestival. "All About The Colbert Report, CPH TV Festival 2013." *YouTube*. YouTube LLC, 11 October 2011. Web.

Cote, David. "Joyce Words." *Time Out New York*. Web. *Internet Archive*.

Courtney Beth. "The Colbert Report - Nutz Soda, Ben Karlin, and Overly Done Alcoholic Beverages." *Colbertsheroes.org*. 02 May 2006. Web. *Internet Archive*.

Coyle, Jake. "Colbert, House's odd relationship." *TODAY.com*. 02 May 2010. Web.

Coyle, Jake. "NASA: Colbert Name on Treadmill, Not Room." *Msnbc.com*. Associated Press, 14 April 2009. Web.

Crook, John. "'Daily Show' Correspondent Anchors 'Colbert Report'." *Zap2It*. Tribune Media Services, 15 October 2005. Web. *Internet Archive*.

Crouse, Karen. "Davis, Colbert Can Laugh Together Now." The New York Times. The New York Times Company, 11 February 2010. Web.

Czajkowski, Elise. "Behind the Scenes of 'The Colbert Report' with Colbert and His Writers." *Splitsider*. The Awl, 08 November 2013. Web.

Dague, Sean. "The Daily Show with David Javerbaum at Bard." *Sean's Mental Walkabout*, 18 November 2006. Web.

Daly, Steven. "Stephen Colbert: the second most powerful idiot in America." *The Telegraph*. Telegraph Media Group, 18 May 2008. Web.

Day, Patrick Kevin. "Stephen Colbert Walked the Floor at Comic-Con as 'Prince Hawkcat'" *Los Angeles Times*. Los Angeles Times, 18 September 2014. Web.

Davis, Caris. "Jon Stewart and Stephen Colbert Head Back to Work." *PEOPLE.com*. 21 December 2007. Web.

de Moraes, Lisa. "Historic 2.5 Million Watch Colbert Immortalized On Series Finale." *Deadline Hollywood*. Penske Business Media LLC, 19 December 2014. Web.

Dominick, Pete. "Pete's Big Mouth." *Indie Talk*. Sirius Radio. 13 March 2008. Radio.

Dominick, Pete. "Stand Up! with Pete Dominick." *P.O.T.U.S.* Sirius XM Radio. 20 August 2009. Radio.

Dunbar, Brian. "NASA To Air Stephen Colbert Message On Eve Of Shuttle Launch." NASA. NASA, 21 August 2009. Web.

Elliot, Stuart. "Again, It's (Dorito) Colbert Nation." Media Decoder Blog. The New York Times Company, 20 March 2008. Web.

"Eric Drysdale." *Wikipedia, The Free Encyclopedia*. Wikimedia Foundation, Inc. 22 June 2014. Web.

Fama, Jilian. "Colbert Causes Wikipedia to Lock Down Potential VP Pages." *ABC News*. ABC News Network, 09 August 2012. Web.

feattie. "Stephen Colbert Interview at Harvard: 4 of 7." *YouTube*. YouTube LLC, 12 January 2009. Web.

Feld, Rob. "Not the Nightly News - The Colbert Report's Jim Hoskinson." *DGA Quarterly*, Fall 2012. Web.

Fountain, Henry. "A Smelly Puzzle, Solved." The New York Times. The New York Times Company, 16 January, 2007. Web.

Fowler, James H. "The Colbert Bump in Campaign Donations: More Truthful than Truthy." PS: Political Science & Politics 41.03 (2008): 533-39. Apsanet.org. PS Online, July 28. Web.

Fox, Jesse D. "Daft Punk, Maurice Sendak, and 6 Other Topics Covered in The Colbert Report's NYCF Panel." *Vulture*. 08 November 2013. Web.

Fox Pocket. "Stephen Colbert America Again Book Signing Question and Answer Session." YouTube. YouTube LLC, 02 October 2012. Web.

Gallagher, Kona. "TV Review: The Colbert Report - On Strike (Live)." *Cinema Blend*. Cinema Blend LLC, 04 December 2007. Web.

Godless_Heretic_. "A peek under Stephen Colbert's desk…" *reddit*, reddit Inc., 20 February 2013. Web.

Gray, Ellen. "A conversation with the real Stephen Colbert." *Philadelphia Daily News*. 13 April 2008. Web. *Internet Archive*.

Havlan, J.R. "Opus Moreschi." *Writers Bloc Podcast*. 04 December 2013. Web.

Heller, Emily, and Lisa Hanawalt. "Episode 50: Rob Dubbin/Jim VanBlaricum." *Baby Geniuses*. 25 September 2013. Web.

Hermida, Alfred. "ANATOMY OF THE STEPHEN COLBERT TWITTER STORM." *Reportr.net*. 28 March 2014. Web.

Herzog, Brad. "Observe and Report." *Cornell Alumni Magazine*. September-October 2011. Web.

Hughs, Carol. "Scientists name 'diving beetle' for Colbert." *asu news [now]*. 06 May 2009. Web.

"I Am America (and So Can You!)." *Fresh Air*. NPR. 09 October 2007. Radio. "I am Trevor Potter, Stephen Colbert's personal lawyer for the Colbert Super PAC, former Chairman of the Federal Election Commission (FEC), member of #waywire, Inc. Advisory Committee -- AMA" *reddit*, reddit Inc. Web.

"Immigrant Farm Workers." *C-SPAN*. National Cable Satellite Corporation, 24 September 2010. Web.

"Institute for Wildlife Studies." Interactive Track an Eagle. Web.

Italie, Hillel. "Philip Roth to appear on Stephen Colbert's show." The Associated Press. 21 May 2014. Web.

Jennie. "SPOILER: Surprise guest on 'The Colbert Report', and interview shocker!" *No Fact Zone*. 10 August 2007. Web.

Johnson, Sharilyn. "Stephen Colbert at the New Yorker Festival." Third Beat Magazine. 05 October 2008. Web.

Johnson, Sharilyn. "10 Moments with Stephen Colbert at the 92nd St. Y." Third Beat Magazine. 20 October 2012. Web.

Joyner, James. "Wikipedia Handles Colbert Elephant Prank." *Outside the Beltway*. Outside the Beltway, 09 August 2006. Web.

Kearns, Taylor. "Ft. Jackson drill sergeant attempts to 'train' Stephen Colbert." *WISTV*. Worldnow and WISTV, 17 June 2009. Web.

"Ken Burns in Conversation with Stephen Colbert." *iTunes*. Apple Inc, 14 February 2014. Web.

Kienzle, Claudia. "Colbert Goes Commando in Iraq." *TV Technology*. New Bay Media, 12 August 2009. Web.

Kingkade, Tyler. "Stephen Colbert's Super PAC Inspires College Students To Create Campus Chapters." *The Huffington Post*. 09 May 2012. Web.

Korngold, Alice. "Charity And Service: Giving Like The Stars." *Fast Company*. 20 December 2011. Web.

"Kraft Wheat Thins and Stephen Colbert Integration." *MediaVest*. 08 December 2011. Web.

Kronfeld, Melissa Jane. "Petition to Keep Stewart Off Air." *New York Post*. 02 January 2008. Web.

"Late Night with Seth Myers: Stephen Colbert is Captain America's Biggest Fan." *Hulu*. 20 September 2014. Web.

Laura. "JJ Sedelmaier." *Animation Insider*. 30 October 2013. Web.

Levine, Stuart. "Stewart's Passion Impresses Colbert." *Variety*. 20 January 2009. Web.

Lipke, David. "Stephen Colbert's American Grandstand." *WWD*. Women's Wear Daily, 11 October 2012. Web.

Liepmann, Erica. "Colbert To Honor Troops Returning From Iraq." *The Huffington Post*. 20 August 2010. Web.

lockhart43. "Richard Branson." *Colbert News Hub*. Colbert News Hub, Web. 02 December 2011, 3:15 p.m. Comment.

"Lost: 4 turtles in sea race They were among 11 wearing tracking equipment." *Philly.com*. 19 September 2007. Web.

Ly, P. "Truth? Not on the Colbert Report." *Asian Media Watch*. 16 December 2005. Web. *Internet Archive*.

Mak, Tim. "Stephen Colbert: Newt Gingrich a 'Southern Gentleman.'" *Politico*. 20 January 2012. Web.

"Mark Waid on Teaming Colbert and Spider-Man." *Newsarama*. Web.

Marketwire. *Stephen Colbert Joins DonorsChoose.org Board of Directors*. New York: Marketwire, 12 January 2009. Web.

Marshall, Rick. "Election Upset! Stephen Colbert Loses To Barack Obama, Won't Be US President In Marvel Universe." *Splash Page*. MTV Networks, 05 November 2008. Web.

Mathis, Sommer. "Jon Stewart rally: Huge turnout forces early retreat to nearby bars." *TBD Neighborhoods*. ABC7 Allbritton Communications Company, 30 October 2010. Web.

McGlynn, Katla. "15 Things You Might Not Know About 'The Colbert Report'" *The Huffington Post*, 08 November 2013. Web.

Meckler, Laura. "Colbert Hosts 'Shutdown Wedding'." *Washington Wire*. Dow Jones & Company, Inc, 04 October 2013. Web.

Mecurio, Paul. "#26: Stephen Colbert" *The Paul Mecurio Show*, 11 August 2012. Web.

Merrill, Cristina. "Stephen Colbert Book I Am A Pole (And So Can You!) Is NOT For Children." *International Business Times*. IBT Media Inc., 08 May 2012. Web.

"Megyeri Bridge." Bridges of Budapest. Web.

Molnar, Matt. "Virgin America Airbus A320 N621VA Air Colbert." Photograph. *NYC Aviation*. Web.

Montopoli, Brian. "Jon Stewart Rally Attracts Estimated 215,000." *CBS News*. CBS Interactive Inc., 31 October 2010. Web.

Moore, Lori. "Rep. Todd Akin: The Statement and the Reaction." *The New York Times*. The New York Times Company, 20 August 2012. Web.

Njus, Elliot. "With Stephen Colbert's Help, Powell's Ships 9,000 Copies of Edan Lepucki's 'California'" *OregonLive.com*. The Oregonian, 08 July 2014. Web.

"Norton to Colbert: Is It All Over Between Us?" Congresswoman Eleanor Holmes Norton. 10 April 2004. Web.

Notdagreatbrain. "Stephen Colbert Incognito at Comic-Con 2014."*reddit*. reddit Inc., 01 August 2014. Web.

Oxenford, David. "Colbert Super PAC Ad Rejected by Iowa TV Station - Can They Do That?" *Broadcast Law Blog*, 15 August 2011. Web.

Pergament, Alan. "Stephen Colbert Girds for His Sold-out Appearance at UB." *The Buffalo News*. 04 March 2008. Web. *Internet Archive*.

Peyser, Marc. "The Truthiness Teller." *Newsweek*. Newsweek LLC, 13 February 2006. Web.

Plotz, David. "Stephen Colbert." *Working*. Slate. 16 October 2014. Web.

Plys, Cate. "The Real Stephen Colbert." *Northwestern*. Northwestern University. Web.

"President Obama with Stephen Colbert." Online video clip. YouTube. *YouTube LLC*, 17 June 2009. Web.

Public Policy Polling. *Obama leads Romney by five points nationally*. Raleigh: Public Policy Polling, 17 January 2011. Web.

Puzzanghera, Jim. "Running for Office? Better Run from Colbert." *Los Angeles Times*. Los Angeles Times, 22 October 2006. Web.

Rabin, Nathan. "Stephen Colbert." *A.V. Club*. Onion Inc., 25 January 2006. Web.

Rayfield, Jillian . "Karl Rove addresses Colbert's "Ham Rove"." *Salon*. 24 March 2013. Web.

Razowsky, Dave. "Stephen Colbert." *A.D.D Comedy*. 20 November 2012. Web.

"Redskins Launch Washington Redskins Original Americans Foundation." *Redskins*.com. 25 March 2014. Web. Remnick, David. "Reporter Guy" *The New Yorker*. Condé Nast, 15 July 2005. Web.

Restoring Truthiness. "Stephen Colbert Testifies Before FEC - Super Pac Is Formed (Part 1 of 2)." *YouTube*. YouTube LLC, 30 June 2011. Web.

"Return Of Late Night, Or Train-Wreck TV?" *CBSNews*. CBS Interactive, 27 December 2007. Web.

Richardson, Jake. "Stephen Colbert Has New Species Named After Him." *Ecolocalizer*. Web.

Robertson, Campbell. "In Iraq, Colbert Does His Shtick for the Troops." *The New York Times, Television*. The New York Times Company, Web. 07 June 2009.

Rochelle, Robert (TheRobRochelle). "@StephenAtHome Was Awesome! Got to See a Musical Act for next Week but Can't Say What It Was. #RobinThicke." 30 July 2013, 8:43 p.m. Tweet.

Rodgers, Patrick. "Comparative Literature 101." *Rosen-blog*. The Free Library of Philadelphia. Web.

Romano, Andrea. "Stephen Colbert Denied Job as New Captain America." *Mashable*. 17 July 2014. Web.

Rose, Bonnie. "Green Screen Challenge Win." *YouTube*. YouTube LLC, 07 April 2007. Web.

Rose, Lisa. "Stephen Colbert interview: Speaking several decibels lower than expected." *NJ News*. New Jersey On-Line LLC, Web. 26 October 2009.

"Rosenbach Acquires Objects from Stephen Colbert's I Am a Pole (And So Can You!)." *Rosenbach Museum and Library*. The Free Library of Philadelphia, July 2012. Web.

Sacks, Mike. "How I Made It in Comedy: Allison Silverman." Reader. 02 July 2009. Web.

"Santa Cruz Ship Endorses Stephanie Colburtle the Turtle." YouTube. YouTube LLC, 22 April 2007. Web.

Sayers, Robin. "The Prop Masters Series: Brendan Hurley of The Colbert Report." *Martha Stewart Living*. Martha Stewart Living. Omnimedia, Inc., 21 June 2012. Web. *Internet Archive*.

Schiller, Gail. "Doritos still the word for Colbert." *The Hollywood Reporter*. Associated Press, 07 November 2007. Web.

Schiraldi, Mike. "Update on the Colbert-Stewart march / rally." *Reddit Blog*, reddit Inc., 01 October 2010. Web.

Schurke, Eric. "VoiceNation is Called on Again to Provide Stephen Colbert's Atone Phone." *PRWeb*. 16 September 2010. Web. "Season 21, Episode 127." *The Late Show with David Letterman*. CBS. 22 April 2014. Television.

Scott, E.J. "Episode #055: Opus Moreschi." *Scratch the Surface*. 24 September 2013. Web.

Shakir, Faiz. "Fox Apoplectic Over Colbert Testimony: Megyn Kelly Demands Apology, Rep. Steve King Calls Him A Liar." *ThinkProgress*. 24 September 2010. Web.

Shah, Beejoli. "*The Colbert Report's* New Twitter Feed Praising Fox News Is Brilliant." *Defamer*. Gawker Media, 05 November 2013. Web.

"Shepard Smith Tours the Revolutionary Fox News Deck." Fox Nation. Fox News Network, LLC. Web. Silverleib, Alan. "Colbert Storms Capitol

Hill for Migrant Workers." CNN. Turner Broadcasting System Inc., 24 September 2010. Web.

"Sitting down with Stephen Colbert." *The Yale Herald*, 22 October 2013. Web.

Sixpack, Joe. "Colbert Puts Bud Light Lime in the Limelight on TV and at Rosenbach." *Philly.com*. 27 July 2012. Web.

Snierson, Dan. "Stephen Is King!" *Entertainment Weekly*. Time Inc., 11 January 2007. Web. "Sponsor US Speedskating." *YouTube*. YouTube, LLC. Web.

stationminute. "Colbert Talks to Space Station (part 1)." *Youtube*. Youtube, LLC, 08 July 2008. Web.

stationminute. "Colbert Talks to Space Station (part 2)." *Youtube*. Youtube, LLC, 08 July 2008. Web.

Steinberg, Jacques. "'Daily Show' Personality Gets His Own Platform." *The New York Times*. The New York Times Company, 03 May 2005. Web.

stellastellaish. "Colbert Dinello – Stella." *Youtube*. Youtube, LLC, July 2010. Web. "Stephanie Colburtle the turtle." Seattle PI. Hearst Seattle Media, LLC, 12 April 2007. Web.

"Stephen Colbert at Madame Tussauds Washington, D.C." Madame Tussauds. Web.

"Stephen Colbert denied South Carolina primary run." *Reuters*. Reuters, 01 November 2007. Web. "Stephen Colbert has answered your questions." *reddit*, reddit Inc., 30 November 2010. Web.

"Stephen Colbert, Jr., World's Most Famous Bald Eagle, Debuts on Free Endangered Species Ringtone Site." Free Endangered Species Ringtone Site. Web.

"Stephen Colbert: Meet the Author." Interview. Audio blog post. iTunes. 26 October 2007. Web.

"Stephen Colbert, Noel Gallagher, Viggo Mortensen." *New York Times*. The New York Times Company. 09 September 2008. Web.

"Stephen Colbert to Help Fund $800,000 in Grants for South Carolina Teachers." NBCNews.com, 7 May 2015. Web.

"Stephen Colbert, Wonderful Pistachios Unite In Super Bowl Commercial (VIDEO)." *Huffpost Sports*. The Huffington Post, 03 February 2014. Web.

"Stephen Colbert's New Latin Motto." *Talk Show News*. 07 January 2010. Web.

"Stephen Colbert on "Colbert's Super Pac"." The Peabody Awards. Web.

"Stephen Colbert's Bald Eagle." Narr. Michael Stein. *BirdNote*. Nature.org. June 2014. Web.

"Stephen Colbert's Premature Clipping." Online video clip. YouTube. *YouTube*, LLC. 11 June 2009. Web

"Stephen Colbert's Tek Jansen - Oni Press." *Stephen Colbert's Tek Jansen - Oni Press*. Web. Strauss, Neil. "Stephen Colbert on Deconstructing the Colbert Nation." Rolling Stone. 02 September 2009. Web.

Strauss, Neil. "The Subversive Joy of Stephen Colbert." Rolling Stone. 17 September 2009. Web.

Stubbzilla. "Colbert Report Show Open 2005 – 2009." *Vimeo*. Vimeo, LLC. Web. Subramanian, Courtney. "Stephen Colbert's Super PAC Satire Lands Him a Peabody." *Time*. Time Inc., 05 April 2012. Web. Talks at Google. "Stephen Colbert, 'America Again: Re-Becoming the Greatness We Never Weren't.'" *Youtube*. Youtube LLC, 14 December 2012. Web.

teridon. "Stephen Colbert Interviews Neil deGrasse Tyson at Montclair Kimberley Academy - 2010-Jan-29." *Youtube*. Youtube, LLC. Web. "The Colbert Report." Application Story. Christie Digital Systems USA, Inc. Web.

"The Colbert Report." The Emmys. Academy Of Television Arts & Sciences. Web.

"The Colbert Report: Show Open and Package." Mr. Wonderful. Web.

"The Jimmy Fallon / Stephen Colbert Project." DonorsChoose.org. Web.

"The NUTZ." Wildfruitz Beverages Inc. Advertisement. Web. *Internet Archive*.

"'The Rally to Restore Sanity and/or Fear' Honored With Four Daytime Emmy® Nominations." *PR Newswire*. PR Newswire Association LLC, 11 May 2011. Web.

"THE TICKER: Comedy Central gives pub to Spirit." *Detroit Free Press*. 18 August 2006. Web.

The Tonight Show Starring Jimmy Fallon. "Stephen Colbert Sings Friday with Jimmy Fallon and The Roots (Late Night with Jimmy Fallon)." *Youtube*, YouTube LLC. Web.

theGoose_aPrisoner. "So I went to the Colbert Report tonight…" *reddit*. reddit Inc., 18 August 2011. Web.

Thompson, Andrea. "Science Confirms 'The Colbert Bump'" NBCNews.com, 18 April 2008. Web.

Thorn, Jesse. "Let's Put On A Show!" *The Sound of Young America*. 21 Feb. 2007. Web.

Truitt, Brian. "New Captain America announced on 'Colbert Report'." *USA Today*. 17 July 2014. Web.

"Truthiness." *Oxford Dictionaries*. Web.

"Truthiness: The Silly Word that Feels Wrong in Your Mouth." Word Routes : Thinkmap Visual Thesaurus. Web.

"Truthiness Voted 2005 Word of the Year." *American Dialect Society*. Web.

"What We Do." *Yellow Ribbon Fund*. Web.

Weigel, David. "In Which Stephen Colbert Dedicates a Campaign Finance Group's Conference Room With Secret Cash." *Slate*. 22 March 2013. Web.

Weigel, David. "Stephen Colbert vs. the Hashtag Activists." *Slate*. 28 March 2014. Web.

Wetherbee, Brandon. "Stephen Colbert Wax Figure Unveiling At Madame Tussauds D.C. Wax Museum: 'It Freaks Me Out' (PHOTOS)." *The Huffington Post*. 16 November 2012. Web.

Wilke, Christina. "Colbert Appearance Causes Mixed Feelings." *TheHill*. 24 September 10. Web.

Williams, John. "On E-Books and Stephen Colbert: A Few Words With Maurice Sendak." *The New York Times*. The New York Times Company, 08 May 2012. Web.

Wilson, Nick. "Stephen Colbert at PITT Q and A." *Youtube*. Youtube, LLC, 19 April 2013. Web.

Wood, Sam. "Penn study: Colbert's civics lesson 'not just a proliferation of jokes'." *Philly.com*. Interstate General Media, LLC, 02 June 2014. Web.

Woodyard, Chris. "Stephen Colbert Sets Sail for Bermuda with Team Audi." *Drive On*. USA Today, 22 May 2011. Web. "Word of the Year 2006." *Merriam-Webster*. Merriam-Webster. Web.

xitiomet. "Anyone else catch this? just now?" *reddit*, reddit Inc., 02 November 2010. Web.

Yazchattiest. "Fox News Deck vs. Colbert's 'Info News Veranda'" YouTube. YouTube, 11 October 2013. Web.

Zakarin, Jordan. *Ian McKellen: 'Silly' Stephen Colbert Cracked Under 'Hobbit' Excitement*. The Hollywood Reporter, 07 December 2012.

"3 Peregrine Falcon Chicks Hatch Atop San Jose City Hall." *CBS San Francisco*. CBS, 08 April 2014. Web.

5 Questions for Felicity Huffman." *USATODAY.com*. USA Today, 24 January 2007. Web.

Works Cited – The Colbert Report & The Daily Show with Jon Stewart

The following segments originally aired on Comedy Central, and titles are listed as they appeared on Comedy Central's web properties. All segments are from *The Colbert Report*, unless noted as *The Daily Show*.

To get this list with clickable links to videos on the official *Colbert Report* and *Daily Show* websites, visit www.colbertfanguide.com/citations

A Colbert Christmas
"Peter J. Gomes." 15 September 2008.

Air Colbert
"Richard Branson." 22 August 2007.

All You Need To Know
"All You Need to Know - Proper Condom Use." 15 October 2006.

Allison Silverman
"The Word – Allison!" 17 September 2009.
"NPR Correction" 1 May 2007.

Alpha Dog of the Week
"Alpha Dog of the Week - Cecilia Gimenez." 20 September 2012.
"Alpha Dog of the Week - David Beckham" 18 July 2007.

Americone Dream
"Ben and Jerry - Introducing Americone Dream." 5 March 2007.
"Willie Nelson." 20 March 2007.
"Ice Cream Fight with Jimmy Fallon." 3 March 2011.

Andrew Young
"It's All About Stephen" 22 January 2008.
"Andrew Young." 22 January 2008.
"Let My People Go." 22 January 2008.

Aptostichus Stephencolberti
"Spida of Love - Jason Bond." 6 August 2008.

Art Stephen Up Challenge
"Steve Martin Pt. 2." 8 December 2010.

Atone Phone
"1-888-MOPS-KEY" 12 September 2007.
"Atone Phone - Emmy Awards." 22 September 2009.

Audience Guy Carl
"30 Days with The Colbert Report." 24 August 2006.
"Stephen's Moral Dimension." 23 February 2009.

Balls for Kidz
"Balls for Kidz - Bear Hunting." 10 January 2006.

Basketcase: Stephie's Knicks Hoop-de-Doo
"Basketcase - Stephie's Knicks Hoop-De-Doo Pt. 1." 29 June 2010.

Bats**t Serious
"Stephen Colbert's Bats**t Serious - Bullet Conspiracy Theory." 06 May 2013.
"Stephen Colbert's Bats**t Serious - Hillary Clinton Shoe-spiracy Theory." 21 April 2014.

Bears & Balls
"Bears & Balls – Gas." 15 January 2007.

Better Know A District
"Better Know a District - Utah's 3rd - Jason Chaffetz." 6 January 2009.
"Better Know a District - California's 27th - Brad Sherman." 22 March 2006.
"Better Know a District - New York's 17th - Eliot Engel." 19 January 2006.
"Better Know a District - Florida's 19th - Robert Wexler." 20 July 2006.

"Better Know a District - Georgia's 8th - Lynn Westmoreland." 14 June 2006.
"Better Know a District - California's 50th - Randy "Duke" Cunningham." 29 November 2005.
"Better Know a District - Georgia's 1st - Reuniting with Rep. Jack Kingston." 9 December 2014.

BKA Beatle
"Better Know a Beatle – Paul McCartney." 28 January 2009.

BKA Challenger
"Better Know a Challenger - Florida's 3rd - Jake Rush." 8 May 2014.
"Better Know a Challenger - New York's 19th - John Hall." 19 October 2006.

BKA Cradle of Civilization
"Better Know a Cradle of Civilization - Barham Saleh." 10 June 2009.

BKA Enemy
"Better Know an Enemy – Yemen." 5 January 2010.

BKA Founder
"Better Know a Founder - Benjamin Franklin." 1 March 2006.
"Better Know a Founder - Thomas Jefferson." 15 November 2006.

BKA Governor
"Better Know a Governor - Mark Sanford." 21 January 2008.
"Governor Alert - The Search for Mark Sanford." 23 June 2009.

BKA Lobby
"Better Know a Lobby - Human Rights Campaign Pt. 1." 6 February 2008.
"Better Know a Lobby - Drug Policy Alliance." 12 March 2008.

BKA President
"Better Know a President - Theodore Roosevelt." 17 May 2006.

BKA Riding
"Better Know a Riding - Vancouver's South." 22 February 2010.

BKA Stephen
"Better Know a Stephen - Stephen King." 16 December 2009.

Big Gay Roundup
"Stephen Colbert's Big Gay Roundup - Military Bestiality & Homosexual Penguins." 14 December 2011.
"Stephen Colbert's Big Gay Roundup." 27 June 2013.
"The Midterm Round-Up." 4 September 2014.

Big White Chocolate
"ThreatDown - Science and Technology Edition." 4 October 2007.

Bill O'Reilly
"Bill O'Reilly." 18 January 2007.

Black Friend Alan
"The Word – Overrated." 25 October 2005.
"Alan Town." 3 May 2006.
"Search for a New Black Friend - First Submissions." 7 June 2006.
"America Again: Re-Becoming the Greatness We Never Weren't." 27 September 2012.

Bleep Blorp
"Droid Rage." 30 September 2010.

Blitzkrieg on Grinchitude
"The Blitzkrieg on Grinchitude - Hallmark & Krampus." 9 December 2009.
"Blitzkrieg on Grinchitude - Festivus Pole in the Florida Capitol." 11 December 2013.

Bobby the Stage Manager
"Apology." 05 December 2005.
"Farewell to Bobby." 21 April 2008.
"The Ghost of Stage Manager Bobby." 11 December 2008.
"Big Bang Theory." 28 October 2009.

Bring 'em Back or Leave 'em Dead
"Bring 'Em Back or Leave 'Em Dead - Asian History." 15 November 2005.
"Bring 'Em Back or Leave 'Em Dead - Teacher's Edition." 18 January 2006.

Brooks Brothers
"My Fair Colbert - Hugo Vickers Pt. 3." 7 April 2011.

Buckley T Ratchford
"Found Goldman Sachs MasterCard." 13 December 2010.
"Goldman Sachs Lawyers Want Buckley T. Ratchford's Card Back." 14 December 2010.

Bud Light Lime
"Belgians Buy Budweiser" 14 July 2008.
"The Word – Ownership Society" 28 July 2010.

California
"Amazon vs. Hachette - Sherman Alexie." 4 June 2014.
"Amazon's Scorched-Earth Tactics and Edan Lepucki's "California"." 12 June 2014.

Called Out Board
"On Notice - How the On Notice Board Is Made." 2 August 2006.
"Jon's Apology." 14 August 2006.

Cameos
"Obama's ISIS Strategy - Frank Underwood." 3 September 2014.
"Jimmy Fallon & Stephen Reminisce." 15 September 2011.
"John Lithgow Performs Gingrich Press Release." 19 May 2011.
"Stephen's Grammy Nomination - Billy Crystal." 16 December 2013.
"Been There, Won That - Joe Biden & Yogi Berra." 8 September 2010.

Captain America
"The Word - Comic Justice." 8 March 2007.
"Sign Off - Captain America Shield." 12 March 2007.
"Joe Quesada." 29 January 2008.
"Stephen & Friends - We'll Meet Again." 18 December 2014.

Carell Corral
"The Carell Corral." 7 July 2010.

Catholicism
"Pope Coming to NYC." 8 April 2008.
"Popewatch Indeschism 2013 - One Pope over the Line." 26 February 2013.
"Philip Zimbardo." 11 February 2008.

Character breaks
"Prince Charles Scandal." *The Daily Show*. 10 November 2013.
"Stephen's Laws of Love." 9 February 2006.
"The Word - We Shall Overcome." 1 February 2007.
"ThreatDown - Record Breaking Gays, Koalas & Purell." 29 September 2010.
"All You Need to Know - Proper Condom Use." 15 October 2006.
"Colbert Super PAC - The Heroes Respond." 4 August 2011.
"Pap Smears at Walgreens." 11 April 2011.
"The Word - Love Handles." 20 October 2005.

Charlene
"Charlene (I'm Right Behind You)." 9 February 2006.
"Better Know a District - Ohio's 11th - Marcia Fudge Pt. 1." 26 August 2014.

Cheating Death
"Cheating Death – Vaxadrin." 7 May 2007.
"Cheating Death - Placebo Effect, Immortality & Wild Lynx." 6 January 2011.
"Cheating Death - Snus & Placebo Effect." 29 September 2009.
"Cheating Death - Sensor-Enabled Pills & Facelift Bungee Cords." 8 August 2012.

Ching Chong Ding Dong / #cancelcolbert
"Intercepted Satellite Feed." 8 Novermber 2005.
"Sport Report - Professional Soccer Toddler, Golf Innovations & Washington Redskins Charm Offensive." 26 March 2014.
"Intro - 3/31/14." 31 March 2014.
"Who's Attacking Me Now? - #CancelColbert." 31 March 2014.
"Biz Stone Pt. 1.".31 March 2014.

C.O.L.B.E.R.T. treadmill

"Space Module: Colbert - Name NASA's Node 3 After Stephen." 3 March 2009.
"Space Module: Colbert - Sunita Williams." 14 April 2009.

cOlbert Book Club

"cOlbert's Book Club." 25 April 2013.
"cOlbert's Book Club - "The Great Gatsby"." 6 May 2013.
"cOlbert's Book Club - Learning "The Great Gatsby." 9 May 2013.
"cOlbert's Book Club - Jennifer Egan & "The Great Gatsby"." 9 May 2013.
"cOlbert's Book Club - Tobias Wolff & "The Catcher in the Rye"." 10 September 2013.
"cOlbert's Book Club - Shane Salerno on J.D. Salinger." 10 September 2013.
"cOlbert's Book Club - Michael Chabon & "A Farewell to Arms"." 21 January 2014.

Colbert Bump

"Ron Paul's Colbert Bump." 21 June 2007.
"5 x Five - Colbert Moments: The Colbert Bump." 14 October 2013.
"Better Know a District - New York's 19th - John Hall." 8 November 2006.
"Ron Paul's Colbert Bump." Vincent Bugliosi.
"The 2012 People's Party Congress of Charlotte - Colbert Bump." 7 Septermber 2012.
"Colbert Bump Cocktail - David Wondrich." 4 August 2009.

Colbert Cruise

"Colbert Cruise - Write Off." 26 January 2006.
"Fun in the Sun." 25 September 2006.
"Jihadis of the High Seas." 1 December 2014.

Colbert Galactic Initiative

"Colbert Galactic Initiative." 8 April 2013.

Colbert Info News Veranda

"Because Shep - Fox News Deck." 10 October 2013.
"Because Shep - Fox News Deck - Colbert Info News Veranda." 10 October 2013.

Colbert on the Ert
"Ethnic Slurs." 9 April 2007.
"The Word - Medium Matters." 8 October 2007.
"Glenn Beck Attacks Social Justice - James Martin." 18 March 2010.
"Don't Shoot the Schlessinger." 18 August 2010.

Colbert Platinum (& Colbert Aluminum)
"Colbert Platinum - Butler Shortage." 12 June 2007.
"Colbert Platinum - $1,000 Dishes." 13 May 2009.
"Colbert Aluminum – Paris." 20 October 2008.
"Colbert Platinum - Urbane Nomads, Gigayacht & Michael Jackson Diamond." 19 August 2009.

Colbert Report Special ReporT
"Tony Hawk." 11 July 2006.
"Coddling Our Kids." 11 July 2006.
"The American Worker: A Hero's Salute to the Besieged Heroes of the American Jobscape." 1 February 2005.
"A Salute to the American Lady." 10 October 2006.
"American Pop Culture: It's Crumbelievable! – Intro." 21 August 2003.
"A Nation Betrayed - A Fond Look Back: '74." 4 August 2014.

Col-bunker
"Emergency Evacuation Plan." 1 November 2005.

Cold War Update
"Cold War Update." 28 February 2008.
"Cold War Update - Normalized Relations with Cuba." 17 December 2014.

Cooking with Feminists
"Jane Fonda and Gloria Steinem." 10 October 2006.

Craziest Fucking Thing I've Ever Heard / Most Poetic Fucking Thing
"Craziest F#?king Thing I've Ever Heard - Snake and Hamster." 31 January 2006.
"Craziest F#?King Thing I've Ever Heard – TomTatoes." 24 October 2013.
"Craziest F#?ing Thing I've Ever Heard - Gored Bullfighter." 2 June 2010.

Credits
"The 2013 Government Shutdown Wedding of the Century Pt. 1." 3 October 2013.
"Queen Noor." 7 April 2009.
"Honorary Doctor." 8 June 2006.
"Talib Kweli & Yasiin Bey (A.K.A. Mos Def)." 5 October 2011.
"Interview No-Show, Mike Tyson." 23 July 2012.
"White House State Dinner." 12 February 2014.

DaColbert Code
"The DaColbert Code - The Election." 30 October 2008.

Daft Punk
"StePhest Colbchella '013 - Special Guest Stephen Colbert!." 6 August 2013.

Dartmouth
"Seth Meyers." 8 November 2011.

Das Booty
"Das Booty - Hitler's Gold Pt. 1." 3 March 2008.
"Das Booty - Hitler's Gold Pt. 2." 18 March 2008.

Dead to Me
"On Notice/Dead to Me - Word of the Year." 9 January 2006.
"On Notice/Dead to Me - Juan Gabriel." 16 November 2005.

Delawert Report
"The Delawert Report" 27 September 2010.

Democralypse Now
"Democralypse Now – Ferraro." 13 March 2008.
"Democralypse Now - Hillary Concedes." 9 June 2008.

Difference Makers
"Difference Makers - Tim Donnelly." 18 May 2006.
"Difference Makers - Johnna Mink." 16 July 2007.

Doom Bunker
"Doom Bunker - Glenn Beck's "War Room"." 4 March 2009.
"Doom Bunker - Jack Jacobs and Stephen Moore." 4 March 2009.

Doris Kearns Goodwin
"Doris Kearns Goodwin." 4 September 2014.
"Cheating Death - Vaxa International, Lap-Band Surgery & Restless Leg Syndrome." 25 April 2011.

Doritos
"Morgan Spurlock." 13 April 2011.
"Sign Off - Doritos Suit." 13 April 2011.
"Thought for Food - Fruit Pouch, Doritos Ad & Super Big Gulp." 13 January 2011.
"Hail to the Cheese - Filing Papers." 17 October 2007.
"Hail to the Cheese - Campaign Coverage Finance." 18 October 2007.

Dressage
"Mitt Romney's Blue-Collar Equestrian Pastime." 12 June 2012.
"Mitt Romney's Disinterest in Dressage." 30 July 2012.
"Stephen's Dressage Training Pt. 1." 30 July 2012.
"Stephen's Dressage Training Pt. 2." 31 July 2012.

Duets
"Manilow – 'I Write the Songs' Duet." 30 October 2007.
"Tony Bennet – Who's Got the Last Laugh Now?" 26 September 2007.
"Alicia Keys." 15 December 2009.
"Elvis Costello." 19 November 2009.
"Pete Seeger." 29 January 2014.
"Placido Domingo & Stephen Colbert – 'La Donna E Mobile.'" 23 February 2012.
"Audra McDonald – 'Summertime.'" 5 March 2012.
"Sign Off -- Audra McDonald – 'Baby, It's Cold Outside.'" 11 December 2012.
"Dolly Parton – 'Love Is Like a Butterfly.'" 27 November 2012.
"Neil Young – 'Who's Gonna Stand Up? (and Save the Earth)'" 14 October 2014

Dungeons and Dragons
"Sign Off – End of an Era.'" 2 March 2006.

Ear
"Ian McKellen." 3 December 2012.
"Big Momma's Snub." 3 December 2012.

Edit Challenge
"For Your Editing Pleasure." 26 March 2007.

Eleanor Holmes Norton
"Better Know a District - District of Columbia - Eleanor Holmes Norton." 27 July 2006.
"Robert Wexler and Eleanor Holmes Norton." 7 November 2006.
"Eleanor Holmes Norton." 22 March 2007.

Emmys
"Stephen's Emmy Awards." 24 September 2013.
"Intro - 8/26/14." 26 August 2014.

Enemy Within
"The Enemy Within – Hedgehogs." 9 April 2009.
"The Enemy Within – Unicyclists." 13 April 2011.

Esteban Colberto
"Formidable Opponent – Immigration." 5 April 2006.
"Mitt Romney's Hispanic Outreach - Esteban Colberto." 20 September 2012.
"Obama's Immigration Plan - Esteban Colberto." 18 November 2014.

Fallback Position
"Fallback Position - Astronaut Pt. 1." 21 June 2010.
"Fallback Position - Championship NFL Quarterback." 28 January 2014.
"Fallback Position - Peter Earnest Pt. 1." 6 November 2008.
"Fallback Position - James Blake." 12 October 2009.
"Operation Iraqi Stephen - Fallback Position - Air Force Thunderbirds." 11 June 2009.

Fantasies Board
"On Notice - Jane Fonda Fantasies." 31 January 2007.

Filliam H. Muffman
"Stephen's Laws of Love." 9 February 2006.
"Scrabble Allows Proper Names." 6 April 2010.

Finale
"Texan's Truck in Syria." 18 December 2014.
"Results of The Colbert Report Raffle." 18 December 2014.
"The Word - Same to You, Pal." 18 December 2014.
"Cheating Death - Grimmy's Goodbye." 18 December 2014.
"Stephen & Friends - "We'll Meet Again"." 18 December 2014.
"Sign Off - From Eternity." 18 December 2014.

Flameside
"Leap Day." 3 March 2008.
"Norway's "National Firewood Night"." 20 February 2013.

Formidable Opponent
"Formidable Opponent - Don't Ask, Don't Tell." 9 June 2009.
"Formidable Opponent - Offshore Drilling." 13 August 2008.
"Formidable Opponent - Torture Report." 15 December 2014.

Formula 401
"Sperm Donor." 15 March 2006.
"Mitt Romney's Hispanic Outreach." 20 September 2012.
"Australian Sperm Shortage." 11 May 2010.
"Formula 401: A Star Is Born." 6 October 2009.
"Sign Off - Formula 401 Rumors." 4 October 2011.

Four Horsemen of the A-Pop-Calypse
"Four Horsemen of the A-Pop-Calypse - Justin Timberlake." 26 September 2006.
"Four Horsemen of the A-Pop-Calypse – Shaq." 27 June 2007.
"Four Horsemen of the A-Pop-Calypse – 300." 13 March 2007.

Fract
"Fract – Americana." 21 February 2006.
"Fract - Civil War." 2 November 2005.
"Fract - Frnap: The Freedom Snap." 7 November 2005.
"Fract - Commemorative Spoons." 28 March 2006.

Frank the Roommate
"Frank the Roommate." 29 July 2009.
"Intro - 07/30/09." 30 July 2009.

Franklin F. Flagworth
"Sign Off - Historic Hoax." 16 August 2006.
"Difference Makers - Donald Trump." 10 May 2011.
"Flagworth 2012." 13 July 2011.

Future Stephen
"Willie Nelson's Cobbler." 13 March 2007.
"Sign Off - Future Stephen." 28 October 2009.
"One Hour in the Future." 8 November 2010.
"Waiting Forever for Immigration Reform." 8 September 2014.

Gipper
"The Word – Cat." 2 November 2005.

Glenn
"Corporate Twitter Hacks." 21 February 2013.
"Tim Pawlenty Appeals to Youth Vote." 5 April 2011.

God Machine (June 5/07)
"The God Machine?." 5 June 2007.

Gorlock
"Dow Hits 11,000." 13 April 2010.

Government Shutdown Wedding of the Century
"The 2013 Government Shutdown Wedding of the Century Pt. 1." 3 October 2013.

Grammys
"Al Gore Steals Stephen's Grammy." 9 February 2009.
"Stephen Apologizes for Feeding His Grammy Baby Food." 9 February 2010.
"Stephen's Grammy Nomination - Carol Burnett." 16 January 2014.

Green Screen Challenge
"Better Know a District - California's 6th - Lynn Woolsey." 10 August 2006.
"Green Screen Challenge - The Finalists." 11 October 2006.
"Green Screen - George Lucas." 11 October 2006.
"Green Screen Challenge - The Winner." 11 October 2006.

Ham Rove
"Karl Rove's New Book" 3 November 2010.
"Colbert Super PAC - The Ham Rove Memorial Fund." 13 December 2012.

Hans Bienholtz
"Kermit the Frog's German TV Offense - Hans Beinholtz." 2 May 2012.
"Sport Report - Team USA vs. the Group of Death & Hans Beinholtz on the World Cup." 12 June 2014.

HD
"Intro - Goodbye, Old Set." 4 January 2010.
"High-Definition Upgrade." 4 January 2010.

High Five
"Anthony Weiner's Comeback." 4 October 2013.

HipHopKetball: A Jazzebration
"Tip/Wag - Addicted to Cute." 9 January 2006.
"HipHopKetball II: The ReJazzebration Remix '06." 14 March 2006.

Hobby Hovel
"Intro - 11/1/10." 1 November 2010.

Hoo-Ha Lady Zone 5000
"Todd Akin's Abortion Gaffe." 28 August 2012.

House
"House Returns the Favor." 10 May 2010.
"On Notice - Jane Fonda Fantasies." 31 January 2007.

Hungarian Bridge
"Tip/Wag - Hungarian Bridge." 9 August 2006.
"Hungarian Bridge - Andras Simonyi." 14 September 2006.

"I Called It"
"Elephant Vasectomies." 18 October 2006.
"Math Is Hard." 7 February 2006.
"Nevada Caucus." 21 January 2008.

I Am A Pole
"I Am a Pole (And So Can You!)." 24 April 2012.

I Am America (And So Can You!)
"The Stephen Colbert Interview." 9 October 2007.

The In-Box
"The In-Box – Terry." 8 February 2006.
"The In-Box - Flight vs. Invisibility." 5 December 2013.

Indecision 2008
"Indecision 2008: Barack Obama Wins." *The Daily Show*. 4 November 2008.

Jay the Intern
"USA Board of Ophthalmological Freedom." 22 June 2010.
"Unpaid Internship Crackdown." 12 April 2010.

Jane Fonda
"Jane Fonda." 9 May 2007.

Jimmy
"Employee Performance Reviews." 21 March 2006.

Jimmy Fallon
"Ice Cream Fight with Jimmy Fallon." 3 March 2011.
"Ice Cream Hallucination With Jimmy Fallon." 3 March 2011.
"Jimmy Fallon Promises a Performance by Stephen." 29 March 2011.
"Jimmy Fallon & Stephen Reminisce." 15 September 2011.

Jon Stewart
"TiVo Cleaning." 27 November 2006.
"Daily/Colbert - High-Definition Ski Mask." *The Daily Show*. 10 February 2010.
"The Rumble in the Air-Conditioned Auditorium Debate Prep." *The Daily Show*. 3 October 2012.
"Stephen's Emmy Awards." 24 September 2013.
"The Daily Show Blackout." *The Daily Show*. 16 July 2013.
"Jon Stewart Returns." *The Daily Show*. 3 September 2013.
"Jon Stewart Pt. 2." 20 November 2014.

Judge Jury and Executioner
"Judge, Jury & Executioner - Copyright Law." 26 November 2012.
"Judge, Jury & Executioner – Adultery." 30 January 2007.
"Judge, Jury & Executioner – Adultery." 30 January 2007.

Ken Burns
"Ken Burns." 1 November 2005.

Killer
"Rescue Stephen Jr." 26 July 2006.
"Controlled Burn of a Natural Gas." 12 May 2010.
"Was It Really That Bad? - Cold War." 16 August 2006.
"Employee Performance Reviews." 21 March 2006.
"DIY Cold Medicine." 18 December 2006.

Knut the Polar Bear
"ThreatDown - Polar Bear Cub." 20 March 2007.
"The Word - Modest Porpoisal." 24 July 2007.

Lady Heroes
"Stephen Colbert's Lady Heroes - Glen Grothman." 10 April 2012.

Laser Klan
"Laser Klan." 27 February 2014.

Le Colbert Report (with Stephane Colbert)
"Olympics Wrap-Up - Michael Buble." 1 March 2010.

Leg wrestling
"Better Know a District - Utah's 3rd - Jason Chaffetz." 6 January 2009.

Lord of the Rings
"Elijah Wood." 15 November 2011.
"The Republican Ring of Power." 28 July 2011.
"Ian McKellen." 3 December 2012.
"Smaug." 11 December 2014.

Lorna Colbert
"Remembering Lorna Colbert." 19 June 2013.
"Sign Off - Stage Fall." 19 June 2013.

Lorraine
"Steve Carell." 7 July 2010.

March on Washington
"Martin Luther King Jr. Memorial Paraphrase." 7 September 2011.

Meg the Intern
"Sexy Voice Study." 6 May 2008.
"Nightgown Novel Model." 29 March 2007.

Meta-Free-Phor-All
"Sean Penn Unleashes on President Bush." 27 March 2007.
"Meta-Free-Phor-All: Shall I Nail Thee to a Summer's Day?" 19 April 2007

meTunes
"MeTunes - Chinese Democracy." 20 November 2008.
"MeTunes - Grammy Vote - Dan Auerbach, Patrick Carney & Ezra Koenig." 11 January 2011.

Michael Stipe
"Stephen Colbert's meReporters." 28m November 2011.
"StePhest Colbchella '012 – Rocktaugustfest." 23 July 2012.
"Stephen's Yard Sale." 17 December 2014.

Microwave
"O'Reilly's Microwave." 18 January 2007.

Monkey on the Lam
"Monkey on the Lam – Oliver." 15 August 2007.
"Monkey on the Lam – Florida." 11 March 2010.
"Monkey on the Lam – Alabama." 14 March 2012.
"Monkey on the Lam – Missouri." 3 October 2007.

Movies That Are Destroying America
"Movies That Are Destroying America – Transamerica." 16 January 2006.
"Movies That Are Destroying America: Chuck and Larry." 24 July 2007.
"Movies That Are Destroying America - A Scanner Darkly." 27 June 2006.

My Fair Colbert
"My Fair Colbert - Hugo Vickers Pt. 1." 6 April 2011.
"My Fair Colbert - Hugo Vickers Pt. 2." 7 April 2011.

Mysteries of the Ancient Unknown
"Pharaoh's Phallus Pt. 1." 6 December 2010.
"Mysteries of the Ancient Unknown - Yo Mama Jokes." 1 March 2012.

Nailed 'Em
"Nailed 'Em - Richard Eggers." 14 February 2013.
"Nailed 'Em - Mormon Church Trespassing." 3 November 2009.
"Nailed 'Em - Library Crime." 27 July 2009.

NASA
"Garrett Reisman." 8 May 2008.

Neil deGrasse Tyson
"Neil deGrasse Tyson." 26 October 2005.

Nutz
"Tax Form." *The Daily Show*. 12 April 2001.
"Nutz Election Center." *The Daily Show*. 7 October 2003.
"Stephen's Sound Advice – Taxes." 3 April 2006.

On Notice
"On Notice - Caramel Apples." 19 October 2005.
"On Notice/Dead to Me - Juan Gabriel." 16 November 2005.
"On Notice - Pope Francis." 24 September 2013.

Oopsie Daisy Homophobe
"Accidental Racist Song." 17 April 2013.

Operation Iraqi Stephen
"Shout Out - The Colbert Report Overseas." 17 March 2009.
"Where and When Is Stephen Going to the Persian Gulf? – Qatar." 22 April 2009.
"The Word - Why Are You Here?." 8 June 2009.

P.K. Winsome
"Rising Calls for Obama's Impeachment - P.K. Winsome." 22 July 2014.
"P.K. Winsome - Black Republican." 2 November 2006.
"P.K. Winsome - Anti-Obama Collectibles." 20 August 2009.
"P.K. Winsome - Obama Collectibles." 14 August 2009.

Patterson Springs, NC
"Bill O'Reilly Inside Edition." 13 May 2008.

Peabody Awards
"Stephen's Missing Peabody." 19 June 2008.

People Who Are Destroying America
"People Who Are Destroying America - Johnny Cummings." 14 August 2013.
"People Who Are Destroying America – Teachers." 1 March 2012.
"People Who Are Destroying America - Landscaping Goats." 14 October 2010.

Portrait

"Sign Off - Eighth Anniversary Portrait." 2 December 2013.
"National Treasure Pt. 1." 10 January 2008.
"Steve Martin Pt. 2." 8 December 2010.

Presidential Run (2007)

"Stephen for President - Answering the Call." 13 September 2007.
"Indecision 2008: Don't F%#k This Up America - Presidential Bid." 16 October 2007.

Presidential Run (2012)

"Stephen's Approval Rating." 18 January 2012.
"Colbert Super PAC - Coordination Resolution with Jon Stewart." 12 January 2012.

Prince Hawkcat

"Undercover at Comic-Con - Prince Hawkcat." 17 September 2014.
"Undercover at Comic-Con - Stephen's Movie Pitches." 17 September 2014.

Pumpkin Patch

"I Tried to Sign Up for Obamacare - Health Care Navigators." 23 October 2013.
"Fallback Position - Championship NFL Quarterback." 28 January 2014.
"Fallback Position - Astronaut Pt. 2." 22 June 2010.
"Regina Spektor." 7 June 2012.
"Sean Hannity's Defense of Adrian Peterson." 18 September 2014.

@RealHumanPraise

"@RealHumanPraise for Fox News." 4 November 2013.

Rain

"He's Singing in Korean." 10 May 2007.
"Rain Dance-Off." 5 May 2008.

Rally

"Rally to Restore Sanity Announcement." *The Daily Show*. 16 September 2010.

Reddit
""Friends of Hamas" Rumor." 21 February 2013.
"Alexis Ohanian." 14 November 2013.
"Nicholas Carr." 30 June 2010.

Remix Challenge
"Lawrence Lessig." 8 January 2009.
"Stephen's Remix Challenge." 21 January 2009.

Richard Branson
"Colbert-Branson Trainwreck." 16 August 2007.
"Richard Branson-Shaped Ice Cubes." 2 May 2012.

Rock & Awe: Countdown To Guitarmageddon
"Who's Riding My Coattails Now? – Jeopardy." 29 November 2006.
"Green Screen Challenge - Counter Challenge." 7 December 2006.

Russ Lieber
"Lieber - Minimum Wage." 1 February 2006.

Saginaw Spirit
"Hungarian Bridge Progress Report." 15 October 2006.
"Steagle Colbeagle the Eagle – Mascot." 3 October 2006.
"Sport Report - More With Coach Mancini." 25 January 2007.
"Stephen Colbert Day." 29 January 2007.

Shofar
"Heritage." 25 September 2006.
"1-888-MOPS-KEY." 12 September 2007.
"Tip/Wag - German Campaign, Russian Dogs & Flying Rabbis." 18 August 2009.

Shout Out
"Shout Out! - USS Rhode Island." 8 May 2007.
"Shout Out! - From Baghdad to The Report." 11 October 2006.
"Shout Out - Kids Edition." 27 April 2009.

Smile File
"Smile File - Kim Jong-un at the Lube Factory." 6 August 2014.

South Pole Minute
"Shout Out! - Michael Rehm." 9 November 2007.

Speed Skating
"Sport Report - NYC Marathon & Olympic Speedskating." 2 November 2009.
"Sign Off - Donate to U.S. Speedskating." 5 November 2009.
"Stephen Challenges Shani Davis." 14 December 2009.
"Stephen Challenges Shani Davis - Katherine Reutter." 14 December 2009.
"Blade in the USA - Dutch Coach's Anti-America Rant." 24 February 2014.

Spiderman
"Tip/Wag - Marvel Comics." 13 November 2008.

Sport Report
"Sport Report - Steroids, Commonwealth Games & Brett Favre's Sexting." 13 October 2010.
"Sport Report - Swimming Pools for Football Fans & Governors' Hockey Wager." 10 June 2014.
"Sport Report - Vasectomies, Chess Boxing & Golf." 17 March 2010.
"Sport Report - Miami Heat, FIFA & Freestyle Canoe Dancing." 13 June 2011.

Starbucks
"Thought for Food - Caffeine Edition - Funeral Home Starbucks & Car Coffee Makers." 16 June 2012.
"Tip/Wag - American Academy of Pediatrics & Starbucks." 3 March 2010.
"Growing Intelligence Community - Richard Clarke." 16 August 2010.
"Starbucks Price Hike." 5 October 2006.
"Threatdown - Starbucks." 27 February 2008.

Stelephant Colbert
"Stelephant Colbert the Elephant Seal." 5 February 2009.

Stephanie Colburtle
"The Great Turtle Race." 11 April 2007.

Stephen & Melinda Gates Foundation
"One American Dollar." 17 July 2006.
"Stephen & Melinda Gates Foundation - DonorsChoose.org." 27 September 2011.
"Melinda Gates." 27 September 2011.

Stephen Jr.
"Baby Eagle." 28 March 2006.
"Crying." 5 April 2006.
"Stephen Jr. Hatches!." 18 April 2006.
"Stephen Jr. Update." 13 June 2006.
"Rescue Stephen Jr." 26 July 2006.
"The Colmandos." 13 September 2006.
"Stephen Jr.'s Christmas Miracle." 13 December 2006.
"Save Stephen Jr." 5 February 2007.
"A Girl for Stephen Jr." 12 April 2007.
"Stephen Jr. Campaigns for McCain." 21 October 2008.
"Stephen Jr. on Christmas Eve." 12 January 2009.

Stephen Settles The Debate
"Stephen Settles the Debate - Whales/Cod vs. Polar Bears/Seal Hunters." 19 October 2005.
"Stephen Settles the Debate - Ramadan or Halloween?" 31 October 2005.
"Stephen Settles the Debate - Science vs. Faith." 28 November 2005.
"Stephen Settles the Debate - FDR vs. TR." 25 September 2009.

Stephen's Sound Advice
"Stephen's Sound Advice - Civil War Do's & Don'ts." 8 March 2006.
"Stephen's Sound Advice – Taxes." 3 April 2006.

StePhest Colbchella
"StePhest Colbchella '011 - Rock You Like a Thirst-Icane" 20 June 2011.
"StePhest Colbchella '012 - Welcome to Rocktaugustfest." 13 August 2012.
"StePhest Colbchella '013 - The Song of the Summer of the Century." 6 August 2013.

Steve ColberT
"Gorillaz." 22 April 2010.
"Sign Off - This Is a Fun Job." 22 April 2010.

Studio
"First Show." 17 October 2005.
"Own a Piece of Histor-Me - Original C-Shaped Anchor Desk." 26 January 2010.
"Sign Off - Original Interview Table Auction." 20 January 2010.

SuperPAC
"Colbert PAC Ad." 10 March 2011.
"Colbert PAC." 30 March 2011.
"Colbert PAC - Trevor Potter." 30 March 2011.
"Viacom Ruins Stephen's PAC Dream." 14 April 2011.
"Colbert Super PAC - Trevor Potter." 14 April 2011.
"Corp Constituency - Trevor Potter." 11 May 2011.
"Sign Off - Stephen's Super PAC Needs Support." 12 May 2011.
"Stephen Files Super PAC Request." 16 May 2011.
"Colbert Super PAC - Pushing the Limits." 11 July 2011.
"Colbert Super PAC Ad - Undaunted Non-Coordination." 7 November 2011.
"Colbert Super PAC - Stephen's South Carolina Referendum." 7 December 2011.
"Colbert Super PAC - Coordination Resolution with Jon Stewart." 12 January 2012.
"Colbert Super PAC - Mitt Romney Attack Ad." 16 January 2012.
"Colbert Super PAC - Mitt Romney Attack Ad." 16 January 2012.
"Colbert Super PAC Ad - Attack in B Minor for Strings." 15 January 2012.
"Colbert Super PAC Ad - Modern Stage Combat." 19 January 2012.
"The Word - Raise Cain." 16 January 2012.
"Exclusive – Colbert Super PAC – The Great Chase." *The Daily Show*. 30 January 2012.
"Colbert Super PAC - Return of the PAC." 30 January 2012.
"Stephen Offers Colbert Super PAC Super Fun Pack." 29 March 2012.
"Colbert Super PAC - Super Fun Pack Treasure Finder." 28 June 2012.
"Colbert Super PAC SHH! - Karl Rove & Jon Stewart." 12 November 2012.
"Colbert Super PAC SHH! - Secret Second 501c4 - Trevor Potter." 12 November 2012.
"Peabody Award for Colbert Super PAC." 4 April 2012.

Sweetness
"Better Know a Challenger - Florida's 3rd - Jake Rush." 8 May 2014.
"Guns in National Parks." 1 June 2009.
"Concealing Weapons in Style." 30 April 2012.
"Stephen's Moral Dimension." 23 February 2009.

Table of Contents
"Intro - 1/7/08." 7 January 2008.

Tad the Building Manager
"Emergency Evacuation Plan." 1 November 2005.
"Heterosexual Accountability Buddy." 12 June 2011.
"Alabama Miracle - Helen Keller Museum." 28 November 2006.
"A Girl for Stephen Jr.." 12 April 2007.
"'Watters' World" - Tad's Turf." 1 May 2014.

Tall Women Carrying/Lifting Heavy Things
"Eric Schmidt." 21 September 2010.

Tapings
"Yelp Prison Reviews." 29 April 2013.

Tek Jansen
"Big Brass Balls Award." 9 February 2006.
"Tek Jansen - Operation: Heart of the Phoenix - Dead or Alive." 8 August 2006.
"StePhest Colbchella '013 - Daft Punk'd." 6 August 2013.

Thought for Food
"Thought for Food - Domino's Smart Slice & Doritos Jacked." 19 June 2014.
"Thought for Food - Kentucky Tuna & Grilled Cheese Burger Melt." 7 July 2010.
"Thought For Food - Cereal, Foot-Long Cheeseburger & Ecobot III." 29 July 2010.

Threatdown
"ThreatDown – Bears." 23 February 2006.
"ThreatDown – Happiness." 10 December 2008.

"ThreatDown - Science and Technology Edition." 4 October 2007.
"ThreatDown - Muslim Edition." 11 October 2010.
"ThreatDown - The Homo-Sexy Edition." 19 June 2006.
"ThreatDown - Fox, the Obamas & Time-Traveling Brandy Thieves." 5 April 2010.

Time-Traveling Brandy Thief
"ThreatDown - Fox, the Obamas & Time-Traveling Brandy Thieves." 5 April 2010.
"Sign Off - Time-Traveling Brandy Thief." 13 March 2010.
"Time Travel Research in Cyberspace." 7 January 2014.

Tip of the Hat, Wag of the Finger
"Tip/Wag - John Howard." 12 February 2007.
"Tip/Wag - Sleep Deprivation." 29 October 2007.
"Tip/Wag - Gun Edition - United Nations, Senate Republicans & Video Games." 10 April 2013.
"Tip/Wag - Quitters Edition." 13 November 2006.
"Tip/Wag - All-China Edition." 17 December 2013.

Toss
"Daily/Colbert – Jon's Beard." *The Daily Show*. 29 July 2010.
"Daily/Colbert – Stating the States." *The Daily Show*. 6 December 2006.
"Daily/Colbert – Proofreader." *The Daily Show*. 25 April 2006.
"Daily/Colbert – Universal Health Care." *The Daily Show*. 23 July 2009.
"Comrades." *The Daily Show*. 21 May 2007.
"Sign Off - Toss to Jon." 8 August 2006.
"Daily/Colbert - The Colbert Report Finale." *The Daily Show*. 18 December 2014.
"Sign Off - From Eternity." 18 December 2014.

Truthiness
"The Word – Truthiness." 17 October 2005.
"On Notice/Dead to Me - Word of the Year." 9 January 2006.

Tube Socks
"Burritos Happy Holidays." 7 December 2005.
"Kid Gloves - Marc Kielburger" 17 November 2009.
"Stephen Offers Colbert Super PAC Super Fun Pack." 29 March 2012.

Twitter
"Biz Stone." 2 April 2009.
"Stephen Wins Twitter - Biz Stone." 14 December 2010.

2011: A Rock Odyssey
"2011: A Rock Odyssey Featuring Jack White Pt. 1." 21 June 2011.
"2011: A Rock Odyssey Featuring Jack White Pt. 2." 22 June 2011.
"2011: A Rock Odyssey Featuring Jack White Pt. 3." 23 June 2011.

Un-American News
"Un-American News - Financial Edition." 6 October 2008.
"Un-American News – Spain." 28 September 2006.
"Un-American News - North Korea." 20 October 2005.
"Un-American News - Rest of the World." 6 April 2009.

United Farm Workers
"Arturo Rodriguez." 8 July 2010.
"Fallback Position - Migrant Worker Pt. 1." 22 September 2010.
"Fallback Position - Migrant Worker Pt. 2." 23 September 2010.

Vancouver Olympics
"Skate Expectations - Skeleton Team Tryouts." 3 December 2009.
"Skate Expectations - Skeleton Team Tryouts - Zach Lund." 3 December 2009.
"Skate Expectations - Bobsled Team Tryouts - Team Night Train." 10 December 2009.
"Skate Expectations - Curling Team Tryouts." 4 January 2010.
"Skate Expectations - Speedskating Team Training." 19 January 2010.
"Skate Expectations - Speedskating Team Training - Colbert vs. Davis." 20 January 2010.
"Vancouverage 2010 - Ed Colbert." 22 February 2010.
"Stephen Distracts Bob Costas." 25 February 2010.

Vilsack attack
"Vilsack Attack.". 30 November 2006.
"Stephen's Sound Advice - Avoiding Humiliation on the Campaign Trail." 26 February 2007.
"Profiles in Quitters - Tom Vilsack." 28 February 2007.
"Tom Vilsack." 30 November 2010.

Was it Really That Bad
"Was It Really That Bad? - Black Death." 29 November 2005.
"Was It Really That Bad? - San Francisco Earthquake." 17 April 2006.

Watership Down
"Oprah's Book Club." 23 January 2006.

Wax On & Wax Off at Madame Tussauds
"Stephen Colbert: Wax On & Wax Off at Madame Tussauds Pt. 1." 6 December 2012.
"Stephen Colbert: Wax On & Wax Off at Madame Tussauds Pt. 2." 6 December 2012.

What Number Is Stephen Thinking Of?
"The In-Box - Kicking Ass." 3 November 2005.
"What Number Is Stephen Thinking Of? - Doubled Up." 11 January 2007.
"What Number Is Stephen Thinking Of? - Between One and Ten." 2 October 2007.

Wheat Thins
"Wheat Thins Sponsortunity." 23 February 2012.

White House Correspondents Dinner
"White House Correspondents' Dinner." 1 May 2006.
"Emmy Panel: Woulda shoulda coulda…" 5 February 2007.
"Obama vs. Colbert." 28 February 2007.
"Diane Keaton." 30 April 2012.

Who's Attacking Me Now?
"Who's Attacking Me Now? - Humane Society." 19 January 2006.
"Who's Attacking Me Now? - Anderson Cooper." 28 February 2006.
"Who's Attacking Me Now? - Canadian Broadcasting Corporation." 14 November 2012.

Who's Honoring Me Now?
"Who's Honoring Me Now? - Peabody Awards & Maxim's Hot 100." 29 May 2012.

"Who's Honoring Me Now? - Merriam-Webster's Word of the Year." 12 December 2006.
"Who's Honoring Me Now? - Peabody Awards & Maxim's Hot 100." 29 May 2012.
"Who Might Be Honoring Me Next? - People's Choice Awards." 7 November 2013.

Who's Not Honoring Me Now?
"Who's Not Honoring Me Now? - Peabody Awards." 31 March 2010.
"Who's Not Honoring Me Now? - Obama, NRA & Teen Choice Awards 12 August 2009.
"Who's Not Honoring Me Now? - The MacArthur Foundation." 20 September 2006.

Who's Riding My Coattails Now?
"Who's Riding My Coattails Now? – Jeopardy." 29 November 2006.
"Who's Riding My Coattails Now? - Vince Vaughn." 15 January 2008.
"Who's Riding My Coattails Now? - Jimmy Fallon." 1 June 2011.

Wikipedia
"Paul Revere's Famous Ride." 6 June 2011.
"Mitt Romney's Protective Press Pool & Running Mate Clues." 7 August 2012.
"ThreatDown - Secret Negro Presidents." 9 June 2008.

Wilford Brimley Calls
"Wilford Brimley Calls – Donation." 8 April 2008.
"Wilford Brimley Calls - Quaker Oats Makeover." 4 April 2012.
"Wilford Brimley Calls – Mexico." 10 July 2006.

The Wørd
"The Word - Gateway Hug." 18 April 2012.
"The Word – Kidding." 7 February 2006.
"The Word – Sigh." 8 November 2006.
"The Word - Troops Out Now." 2 October 2007.
"The Word - El Comandante." 16 August 2006.

WristStrong
"Dr. Jerry Vizzone." 1 August 2007.

"Wrist Watch - Fighting Back." 8 August 2007.
"WristStrong Bracelets." 20 August 2007.
"Big Check." 23 January 2008.
"Free at Last." 23 August 2007.

Writers Guild of America Strike
"Nothing in the Prompters." 7 January 2008.
"Meteorite Market." 8 January 2008.
"Studio on Fire." 9 January 2008.
"The Writers Return!" 13 February 2008.
"Conan and Jon." 4 February 2008.

Yacht race
"Charleston to Bermuda Yacht Race." 31 May 2011.

Yahweh or No Way
"Yahweh or No Way - Roland Burris." 8 January 2009.
"Yahweh or No Way - Thor & Apocalypse Billboard." 10 May 2011.
"Yahweh or No Way - Online Christian Dating & Seven Days of Sex." 17 January 2012.

Yellow Ribbon Fund
"Big Check." 23 January 2008.
"Cast Auction." 10 September 2007.
"Auction for Bill O'Reilly's Stolen Microwave." 20 February 2014.

Yet another day
"Yet Another Day - Soup and Pets." 25 October 2005.

Z96 Morning Asylum with Stevie C and Dr. Dave
"Exclusive - The Morning Asylum." 2 October 2009.

In the End…
"David Letterman's Retirement." 10 April 2014.
"Stephen Colbert Says Goodbye." 23 April 2014.
"Survival Tips From Good Morning America." 17 November 2014.
"Stephen's Yard Sale." 17 December 2014.
"President Barack Obama Pt. 1." 8 December 2014.

Acknowledgements

The authors thank:

Our editor, Karen Backstein, for being the one-in-a-million combination of expert word surgeon and Colbert nerd. Katt Downey and our beta readers for keeping us sharp. Kurt Firla, who went above and beyond with our cover art. And thank you to every cog in the joy machine: even if we never saw you, we felt you.

Sharilyn would like to thank:

Remy for joining me in the trenches. All my improv teachers for instilling the reflex to say "yes," even to my own dumb ideas. Victoria for tolerating my constant "do you remember which…" Facebook messages. Mark for making those early tapings so special. Barry, Tom, Eric, Allison, and Stephen for being kinder than I would've been to me. The sane people of the Colboards (we were the 1%). Andrew Clark for being my gold standard. And Bonnie R., for the wonderful talks (we'll meet again).

Remy would like to thank:

Sharilyn for the opportunity to collaborate on this book. She would also like to thank all of her friends who tolerated her speaking about nothing else for several months. Thanks also to Rafalca, the Romney family dressage horse, for inspiring her favorite *Colbert Report* moment ever.

About the Authors

Sharilyn Johnson is a Toronto-based entertainment journalist specializing in comedy. She's written for the *Toronto Star*, *NOW Magazine*, *Uptown Magazine*, *Winnipeg Free Press*, and *the Huffington Post*; has appeared on CBC Radio's *LOL* and NPR's *Radio Time*s; and runs the comedy news site *Third Beat Magazine*. Sharilyn has trained in improv and comedy writing in Toronto, New York, and Chicago. Her solo show *Fake News Fangirl*, about the world of *Daily Show* and *Colbert Report* fandom, was staged at theatre festivals across Canada.

Remy Maisel is the co-author of "Is Satire Saving Our Nation? Mockery and American Politics," which she wrote with Dr. Sophia A. McClennen while she was an undergraduate at Penn State University. She has contributed to *Politico*, *Salon*, and other outlets, and has appeared on MSNBC as a commentator on satire. She graduated early from PSU with a BA in Media Studies with high distinction, and is pursuing her MA in Creative Writing at City University in London, England.